Intimate Strangers

THE SCOTTISH ARTS COUNCIL

*The publisher acknowledges subsidy
from the Scottish Arts Council towards
publication of this volume.*

Intimate Strangers

*Political and Cultural Interaction
Between Scotland and Ulster
in Modern Times*

GRAHAM WALKER

JOHN DONALD PUBLISHERS LTD
EDINBURGH

For Elda

ISBN 0 85976 417 6

A catalogue record for this book is available from the British Library.

Typeset by Pioneer Associates Perthshire
Printed and bound in Great Britain by Bell & Bain Ltd., Glasgow

Preface

This is a study of aspects of a relationship with striking historical depths and an ambiguous contemporary character. Scotland and Northern Ireland are culturally interwoven: political graffiti in contemporary Scotland is as likely to refer to the Northern Ireland conflict as any issue which bears more directly on Scotland. This reflects the durability of essentially Irish cultural influences in Scotland, particularly in the west of the country. In strict political terms, on the other hand, the two places stand in contrast: Scotland participates in the British political system in a way Northern Ireland does not; Scotland remains politically stable notwithstanding emotions aroused by the Northern Ireland situation and an increasingly fraught relationship with the British State. For all the historical and cultural links, Scotland most of the time contrives to behave like the rest of Britain in relation to Northern Ireland: it keeps it at a safe distance. The Scottish contribution to the Northern Ireland debate in the course of twenty five years of troubles has been neither distinctive nor distinguished.

This book is intended both to highlight historical common ground and to stimulate debate about Northern Ireland in Scotland and vice-versa, and the wider context of constitutional concerns to which both places relate. It is written in the belief that both places could more positively interact with one another, perhaps to the end of mutually beneficial political and constitutional change; and that their shared history in many ways obliges them to do so. The more the Scottish dimension to Irish history and culture is appreciated, the more questions of identity might be defined in less polarised and sterile terms; the more the Northern Ireland situation is appreciated in Scotland the more Scots might learn of the influences which have shaped so much of their modern social and cultural makeup.

The book is essentially concerned with political and cultural interactions, connections, parallels and comparisons since the advent of Irish Home Rule as a political issue of seismic significance in the 1880s. An opening chapter provides a brief overview of the relationship from the time of the Scottish (and English) plantations in Ulster (the nine county province) in the early seventeenth century to the emergence of Home Rule in the late nineteenth. Chapter Two then looks in detail at the 'Home Rule era' from 1886 until the establishment of the Northern Ireland State (comprising six of the Ulster counties) in 1921: a period encompassing the high tide of British Imperial identity and a wide-ranging constitutional debate relating to the whole United Kingdom. The following three chapters consider political and cultural themes of significance to both places during the period of Northern Ireland's existence as a devolved unit within the UK: Popular Unionism; varieties of Nationalism; Labourism; Protestant and Catholic 'ethnic' identities. Finally, Chapter Six explores the impact of the Northern Ireland troubles on Scotland, looks at the persistence of religious sectarianism as a dynamic cultural force, and discusses the two places within the broad context of the contemporary constitutional debate in the UK.

The mixture of the book is predominantly political and social history and contemporary history/political analysis. There are passages of kite-flying, speculation and polemic, and it is hoped that the discussion will provoke future debate as well as illuminate some hitherto obscured aspects of a shared past.

Any book about Northern Ireland encounters problems of disputed terminology. Some readers will be unhappy with my occasional loose employment of the word 'Ulster' in relation to what is known officially as 'Northern Ireland'. This derives from the word's association from the time of the Home Rule controversies with the theme of Unionist politics — a central one in the book.

Contents

Preface   v

1. The Scottish-Ulster Relationship: an Overview
   c. 1600–1880   1

2. Religion, Nationality and Empire in the Home Rule Era
   c. 1880–1920   17

3. Popular Unionist and Protestant Politics in Scotland and
   Northern Ireland c. 1920–70   61

4. Nationalisms, the Politics of Identity, and the Catholic
   Experience in Scotland and Northern Ireland
   c. 1920–70   99

5. A Study in Contrasts: Labour Politics in Scotland and
   Northern Ireland c. 1920–70   126

6. The Northern Ireland Troubles, Scottish Reactions and
   Echoes, and the Contemporary Constitutional Debate
   in the UK c. 1970–95   149

Index   196

Acknowledgements

I benefited from the critical reflections and encouragement offered by my colleagues in Belfast, in particular Bob Eccleshall on whom draft chapters were inflicted, and my co-grafters in Irish political history Paul Bew, Richard English and Margaret O'Callaghan. Much stimulation was provided by discussions on the general theme of Scottish-Ulster relations with David Officer and Ian McBride. My thanks also to friends in Scotland, Richard Finlay, Elaine McFarland, Ian Wood, and Iain Patterson, for advice and help regarding source materials. I am grateful to James Mitchell for permission to cite certain of his political survey findings, and to Lorna Goldstrom who prepared the manuscript to a tight deadline with, in the circumstances, remarkable good humour. Part of the research for this book was carried out with the assistance of a grant from the Nuffield Foundation.

This book was largely written after the death of my friend Kieran Hickey. Throughout the process he was in my thoughts. A Dubliner, Kieran taught me more about Ireland, north and south, than anyone else, and his love of Scotland stimulated me to learn more about my own country. I am proud to have known him and, along with his legion of friends, I miss him.

My partner Elda's trenchant Greek perspectives on both Scotland and Northern Ireland alleviated much of the agony of the book's production. For putting up with a Glaswegian football fanatic obsessed with the past, and for so much else she alone knows, I dedicate the book to her with love.

1

The Scottish-Ulster Relationship: an Overview c. 1600–1880

I

'At the core of the Ulster problem is the problem of the Scots . . .' wrote A. T. Q. Stewart in his illuminating study, *The Narrow Ground.*[1] He was referring to the pattern of Scottish settlement in Ulster in the 17th century and the many precedents in earlier centuries for population movement between the two places; and also to the development of an Ulster-Scottish Protestant culture which would define itself to a great extent against the gaelic and Catholic culture of the vast majority of indigenous Irish in the era of the plantations.

'The problem of the Scots' is indeed central to any analysis of Ulster or Irish history. Much of a folksy, mythical and often historically inaccurate nature is made of the Ulster-Scottish connection, but its significance in the popular imagination persists. Even after centuries of intermarriage and racial and ethnic mixing, people still evince a tendency to reduce the historical lines of conflict in Ulster to 'Irish Gaels and Scottish settlers'.[2] Such a conceptualisation of the historical development of the Ulster imbroglio has the effect of obscuring, for example, the significance of the humbler portion of the English settlement of Ulster, of the Church of Ireland as the church largely of the Protestant poorest as well as the wealthiest; similarly, it passes over the anomalous contribution to the cultural mosaic of the Scottish gaelic, and Catholic, settlers of the 15th and 16th centuries.

Yet scholarly objections, while valid and substantial, cannot detract from the popular influence still wielded by such a typology. Ulster Loyalist symbolism in contemporary Northern Ireland often

1

proclaims identification with Scotland, not least on paramilitary wall murals in working class areas.[3] Less politically, local Ulster communities regularly celebrate their Scottish roots with pageants and festivals.[4] Ulster Presbyterians, through Church organisation and worship and historiography, maintain a pronounced Scottish pedigree.[5] Even popular history-writing of recent years, such as the work of Ian Adamson, while stressing the complexities of Ulster's cultural and political history, has arguably had the effect of reinforcing binary perceptions of the Irish Catholic/Ulster-Scottish Protestant kind.[6]

At different points in history the stirring and heroic sagas of the 'Ulster Scots' or 'Scotch-Irish' have been deployed in a perceived propaganda war. In the late 19th and early 20th centuries as Irish Home Rule controversies ebbed and flowed, such accounts were regularly produced.[7] One such, published in 1888, paid the standard tribute to the Ulster Scots as a resilient and resourceful people and observed:

> They have had a hard fight for existence during the centuries they have been in Ireland; and now when they have begun to enjoy the full fruits of the Union of 1801, we need not wonder if they protest, not loudly but deeply, against any attempts to impair the arrangement which has brought to them good government and prosperity. Time will, we trust, help to bridge over the deep chasm which separates the Scot and the Irish in Ireland; but the cleavage is more likely to be closed if they both continue to live in the full communion of that great empire in which both may well glory.[8]

In the 1960s the Northern Ireland Unionist government sponsored the Ulster-Scot Historical Society to foster an historical identity for the state which took on the epic quality of the 'Scotch-Irish' passion play, in particular the 'log cabin to White House' representation of their North American experience.[9] This perceived propaganda task has been taken up in more recent times by the Ulster Society with its publications placing a similar stress on the 'Scotch-Irish' Presbyterian contribution to American history, and also the role of the Province in the Allied War effort in the Second World War.[10] Unionists, like Nationalists in Ireland, have amply demonstrated the uses of history, if in a select and partisan fashion; the Scottish connection in this regard has been fashioned and re-fashioned to suit the purposes of the Irish political moment.

The intention in this opening chapter is not to mount a scholarly counter-offensive against over-simplistic history; nor is it to investigate in any depth the major themes of the Ulster-Scottish relationship from the Plantation to the Home Rule era. Rather, it is simply to sketch by way of background the salience of that relationship before the onset of the political controversies occasioned by Irish Home Rule, and the subsequent political interactions between the two places as they experienced the 20th century.

II

The 17th-century plantations have been the subject of several distinguished scholarly studies.[11] It has been demonstrated how patchy and halting the plantations in the reign of James VI and I, widely assumed to have been the critical years of settlement, actually were. Such also was the traumatic effect of the rising by the native Catholics in 1641 that the future vitality of the Protestant settler communities, of both Scottish and English origin, looked to be precarious. However, in the second half of the 17th century there occurred decisively voluminous influxes particularly from Scotland, often on account of the Covenanting troubles of the period there. Many people from a Covenanting background, from the south-west of Scotland, fled government persecution to the milder conditions of Ulster. Macafee calculates that the Scottish population in the Province rose from around 20,000 in 1630 to nearly 70,000 by the late 1660s, and Scottish Protestants continued to settle in significant numbers during the remaining decades of the seventeenth century.[12] Their place of settlement, moreover, confirmed the earlier trend of Scottish Protestants to put down roots in the northern and eastern part of Ulster.

The covenanting identity brought by those migrants was of an uncompromising, often fanatical Calvinism; it was a mentality of persecuted righteousness in which the idea of the Scots in Ulster as a tribe chosen to do the work of God in conditions of constant danger and threat, could be nurtured. It was the ethos of 'God's Frontiersmen' which would be transported to America in the 18th century with all its legendary results. In the 17th century in Ulster it was a community identity fortified through periodic rituals and revivals.[13] For better or worse it was also an identity which facilitated permanent and entrenched settlement.

If Ulster thus could appear in part a Scottish 'colony' by the end of the 17th century, it should nonetheless be remembered that movements of population between the two places had regularly occurred long before the national identities of Scotland and Ireland had crystallised — indeed, the west of Scotland in pre-Roman times had been part of the Ulster kingdom of Dalriada. In 1977 A. T. Q. Stewart made the point that some of the planters may well have been descendants of earlier Ulster migrants to Scotland, a notion explored by Ian Adamson in his influential work, *The Cruthin*. Adamson's thesis is that the earliest inhabitants of Ireland were not the Gaels but the Cruthin, a people closely related to the Scottish Picts. The Cruthin, he argues, took refuge in Scotland from the aggressively expansionist Irish Gaels, so that it is likely that some of those returning to Ulster much later were descendants of the original inhabitants of the Province. Adamson thus offers a qualification to the view that all ancient Irish culture is gaelic, an attractive notion to some Protestants in recent times who have been concerned to cultivate a distinctive Ulster identity in contradistinction to Irish nationalism and its identification with gaelic culture.[14]

III

In the penal era of the 18th century Presbyterianism in Ulster, in its endurance of civil and religious disabilities and degradations at the hands of the Anglican ascendancy, experienced contrasting fortunes to the established 'mother church' in Scotland.[15] Presbyterians, constituting the vast majority of 'Dissenters', were burdened along with Roman Catholics by the payment of tithes to the established Anglican Church of Ireland; moreover, marriages performed by Presbyterian ministers were denied official recognition, an indignity which even the beleaguered Catholic Church did not have to bear. On the other hand the Presbyterian Church did receive a measure of official status in the form of a bounty from the monarch (not parliament) called the 'regium donum'. This grant from the Crown was first bestowed in the reign of Charles II, and was endorsed by King William III after the 'Glorious Revolution' settlement. It was withdrawn during the last years of the reign of Queen Anne, but restored at the accession of the Hanoverians. Subsequently it was occasionally used, notably after the United Irishmen rebellion of 1798, as a means of exerting pressure on the Presbyterians to be loyal to the crown and constitution; in 1869, along with the disestablishment of the Church of Ireland, it was discontinued.

Another penalty, that of Presbyterians being denied access to study at Trinity College Dublin, effectively ensured that for a large part of the 18th century the sons of Ulster Presbyterian ministers, merchants and tenant farmers were mostly educated at the Universities of Glasgow and Edinburgh. This was a source of intellectual interaction between Ireland and Scotland which was to have far-reaching effects for both countries and beyond.

The Irish Presbyterian students accounted for almost one third of the student body at the University of Glasgow in the middle decades of the 18th century.[16] At Glasgow many came into contact with their fellow Ulster Presbyterian, Frances Hutcheson, who was Professor of Moral Philosophy during the 1730s, and many more were influenced by the intellectual currents which Hutcheson inspired. Historians have recently begun to appreciate the contribution made by Hutcheson to the shaping of the Scottish Enlightenment of David Hume, Adam Smith, Adam Ferguson, Dugald Stewart, and John Millar among others; and to the political and philosophical ideas which underpinned the American Revolution and subsequent constitution.

Ian McBride, for example, has argued that the civic humanist ideas of the Scottish Enlightenment are traceable to 'the didactic moralism' of Hutcheson's teaching and cites the Scottish moral philosopher Dugald Stewart's opinion that Hutcheson's arrival in Glasgow began a 'cultural awakening'.[17] A. T. Q. Stewart has recently made a similar case for the recognition of the Ulster intellectual contribution to the Scottish Enlightenment in his study of the United Irishmen movement.[18] Hutcheson's influence on Francis Allison, a Scot who was to contribute substantially to the political thought of the American Revolution, has also been well highlighted.[19]

This was indeed an era of distinguished intellectual activity which derived to a great extent from the so-called 'New Light' tendency in Irish and Scottish Presbyterianism, itself a result of the rationalism of the European Enlightenment. 'New Light' represented a movement away from the rigid Calvinism of the Westminster Confession of Faith, and the elevation of individual conscience and rational judgement. It was a creed which stressed religious toleration, upheld citizenship rights, and linked the exercise of political authority firmly to the consent of the people.

Hutcheson, indeed, has been viewed as a key figure in the development in the 18th century of the 'contractarian' political doctrine, that is a compact between rulers and ruled.[20]

He has also been seen as a 'catalytic agent' for the development of the political ideology of the United Irishmen, a revolutionary movement largely led by Northern Presbyterians and inspired by developments in France which emerged in Ireland in the 1790s. As Elaine McFarland has put it:

> In Hutcheson's thought, the intellectual themes of Covenanting, Real Whiggery and New Light were powerfully united. In him we find the most pivotal link between Enlightenment thought at the Scottish universities and the tradition of Presbyterian Libertarianism which was to flourish in the Society of United Irishmen.[21]

One of the founding members of the United Irishmen, William Drennan, was a close friend of Hutcheson's acolyte Dugald Stewart, while Drennan's father, Thomas, had been a friend of Hutcheson's and a leading 'New Light' Presbyterian.[22] The Scottish flavour of the 'scriptural politics' of the United Irishman and Presbyterian minister William Steel Dickson, was substantial;[23] Dickson had indeed been educated at Glasgow University by Hutcheson's successors.

It was thus hardly surprising that there should have been significant interaction between the United Irishmen and like-minded radical societies in Scotland in the 'Age of Revolution'. This is the theme of Elaine McFarland's recent path-breaking work[24] in which she demonstrates the common characteristics of Presbyterian moral righteousness and elitism, shared doctrines of protest and resistance, a preoccupation with Lockean/Covenanting contractarian thought, and the organisational cement of freemasonry.[25] Overall, however, the United Irishmen were more advanced in their revolutionary motivations than the Scots, and there was no Scottish equivalent of Ireland's 1798 Rebellion. Neither was there the Scottish counterpart of the Irish sectarian divisions which cut across the Rebellion and assured it a violent and bloody fate; in the final analysis Protestant-Catholic antagonisms prevailed and the Presbyterian radicals only spoke for a part of their own community. Popular loyalism in this era of French revolutionary warfare and terror took a strong grip on the different constituent nations of the United Kingdom; in Lowland Scotland and Ulster, as in England, it became identified with the defence of Protestantism. In Linda

Colley's seminal thesis, this was a crucial stage in the forging of a 'British' national identity.[26] Scottish participation in the 1798 Irish Rebellion was overwhelmingly on the side of the government in the armed forces:[27] in some ways this was indicative of the channelling of the cult of Scottish military prowess to the service of the 'British' and 'Loyalist' cause.

Refugees from strife-torn Ulster poured into Scotland at the turn of the century: both rebels and loyalists fled the violence. Economic factors also acted to make permanent migrants of groups such as weavers whose trade had fallen on hard times in Ulster, but for whom a rising cotton-spinning industry in Scotland presented opportunities.[28] McFarland speculates that some of the refugees would have brought their radicalism with them, and the radical disposition of the largely Presbyterian weavers as an occupational group had never been in doubt. The late 18th century is an era characterised by a literary flowering among such people to whom Robert Burns was a towering influence.[29] *The Northern Star*, the newspaper of the United Irishmen, featured Burns's verse regularly, and also carried much written in Scots dialect, a reflection of the prominence of Scottish linguistic practice in many parts of Ulster.[30] The areas of settlement of the Ulster migrants in the early 19th century were overwhelmingly weaver centres such as Girvan and Maybole in Ayrshire, Paisley, Neilston, Thornliebank and Pollokshaws in Renfrewshire, the east end of the city of Glasgow, and various parts of Wigtownshire and Galloway.

However, as McFarland points out, the impact of refugee radicalism in Scotland was considerably muted in the context of the repressive atmosphere of the time and the authorities' energies in combating anything tainted with France. Furthermore, many Presbyterians, even in Ireland at the time of the Rebellion, were losing faith in the radical utopias and defining their interests diametrically against the perceived Catholic threat; this was particularly so in rural areas where agrarian sectarian conflict had long been rife. This rural sectarianism and the waves of popular loyalism which were a response to the radical activity produced the Orange Order — founded in Armagh in 1795 — and it was the spread of Orangeism in Scotland in the early 19th century which was the most visible sign of the Protestant Irish immigrant presence. This is not to say, however, that many Scots appreciated the distinction between Protestant and Catholic Irish — the latter arrived in even larger numbers; rather, they tended to be lumped together and regarded balefully as 'troublemakers' and a threat to their society's stability.[31] From the early years of the 19th century it became clear that Irish divisions, and tensions between Irish and Scots, were to be a signal feature of the social and cultural dimension to Scottish industrialisation.

IV

The Irish were by far the largest immigrant group in 19th and indeed early 20th century Scotland. Over this stretch of time the Catholic Irish made up some two-thirds to three-quarters of the total, and unsurprisingly it has been their experience which has received most scholarly investigation, from the pioneering works of Handley to the recent major re-assessments of historians such as Gallagher.[32] Much new information is coming to light and fresh insights are constantly being fashioned, but at the core of all the analyses of the Catholic community there is an acknowledgement of the strength of religious affiliation in the promotion of a distinctive ethnic identity, an identity often the more proudly and defiantly proclaimed in the light of Scottish Protestant antagonism and discrimination.[33] There is little doubt that the Catholic Church functioned as the fulcrum of this immigrant community and exercised great influence in the social, educational, and political spheres of life; in the latter Irish nationalist concerns predominated from the middle of the 19th century to the partition settlement of 1921–22. The Catholic Irish in Scotland were characterised by a political cohesiveness which represented a valuable yet ambiguous source of potential and actual support in this era, first for the Liberal Party, then for the emerging Labour movement.[34]

The story of the Protestant Irish in Scotland is much less well known. Owing to the dearth of work done in Scotland regarding the Scottish migrations to Ulster, as commented upon by John Oliver,[35] it is extremely difficult to calculate the extent to which those Protestants who migrated to Scotland in the 19th century were the descendants of families who left Scotland in earlier times. In addition, census records do not distinguish Irish immigrants by religion, and the Protestant Irish have not left the same volume of community evidence as their Catholic counterparts.

However, enough material exists to provide us with a reasonable picture of the Protestant Irish as a distinct group in Scottish society

until well into the 20th century.[36] As noted, their areas of settlement were overwhelmingly in the west of Scotland, a result as
much of economic opportunities in the textile industry and, from
mid-century, mining, engineering, steel, iron, and shipbuilding, as
of cultural and historical affinities. In the realm of heavy industry,
the possession of skills often learned back in Ireland served the
Protestant migrant workers well in the job market; in the case of
certain Scottish firms such as Bairds of Gartsherrie there was a
positive effort made to recruit Protestant workers from Ulster, and
it is likely that an Orange Order network operated for the purpose.[37]
Orange-Green friction of Ulster vintage was endemic in industries
such as mining from the mid-19th century, and there is evidence
that parts of Lanarkshire in particular became religiously 'ghet-
toised'.[38] The Protestant Irish in general did not suffer the extremes
of poverty of the Catholic Irish, but there nonetheless exists significant evidence of Protestant Irish poverty in Glasgow in the 1860s
and 70s, and many more of the earlier Protestant migrants had
been seasonal labourers and unemployed weavers than is usually
suggested.[39] The Orange Order, moreover, could in certain areas
be the 'friendly society' refuge of the poor and unskilled, just as in
others it took on a 'labour aristocrat' character and helped forge
strong paternalistic links between workers and bosses.[40] In Scotland
the Order was generally a more proletarian organisation than in
Ireland where it received significant landlord patronage, and it was
nothing like as strong or influential as freemasonry.[41]

The Protestant Irish made their mark economically and, largely
through the Conservative and Liberal Unionist parties in the later
years of the century, politically.[42] Religiously, however, their identity seems not to have been subsumed into the native Scottish
Protestant culture. Partly, this was because an unknown but
undoubtedly substantial number of the Protestant migrants were
non-Presbyterian;[43] but there was also the coolness of the Scottish
Presbyterian establishment towards the Irish presence in general.
In addition, while there was still a significant dialogue between
Presbyterianism in Scotland and Ulster,[44] the 19th century was an
era for both of upheaval and internal conflict, the roots and results
of which were quite distinctive.

In Scotland the pivotal event of the 19th century for the nation
as well as the Church was 'The Great Disruption' of 1843.[45] This
episode split the established Presbyterian Church. The issue was

that of patronage, a grievance of those who rejected the right of a patron, usually a landowner, to appoint parish ministers and who stood for the principle of 'non-intrusion' on the part of the State in the affairs of the Church. The 'non-intrusionists' pushed this issue to the point of secession, adding to the already sizeable body of Presbyterian dissenters in the country, and formed themselves into the Free Church of Scotland, a body heavily influenced by the new evangelicalism of the period. Evangelicalism also took firm root in Irish Presbyterianism,[46] but its influence here ensured the marginalisation of the theological liberalism of the late 18th century and a corresponding strengthening of the conservative and orthodox wing around the formidable Henry Cooke. In 1830 'New Light' non-subscribing Presbyterians withdrew from the Synod of Ulster.

Presbyterianism in the north of Ireland also increasingly relegated its dissenting quarrel with Anglicanism to a poor second place behind the perceived need to be vigilant against the Roman Catholic threat. Daniel O'Connell's Catholic Association of the 1820s and his Repeal movement of the 1830s and 40s, and the increasingly ultramontanist character of the Catholic Church in Ireland from around the 1830s, did much to pull Protestants of different denominations together. Cooke, indeed, attained his populist Protestant credentials in public opposition to 'the Great Liberator' (O'Connell), and to a great extent identified Ulster Protestantism with the Conservative political interest. On the other hand, Presbyterian Liberalism remained politically significant — its mouthpiece became the *Northern Whig* newspaper — but it was overwhelmingly Unionist and divorced from the separatist Irish republican nationalism which had been a hallmark of the United Irishmen.[47] The disestablishment of the Church of Ireland in 1869 removed the major symbolic dissenting grievance, although Presbyterian radical sentiment continued to be expressed around land reform issues, as was the case in Scotland, and around allegations of discrimination in the matter of public appointments.[48]

V

Ulster politics in the mid-Victorian era reflected the Conservative-Liberal polarisation of the rest of the U.K.[49] Gladstone's democratic appeal to the 'enlightened' bourgeoisie and self-improving workers brought a significant response, particularly among Ulster Presbyterians, although the levels of Liberal support paled beside

Scotland where the powerful Presbyterian dissenting community, so notably fortified after 1843, constituted the backbone of anti-Conservatism. On the eve of the 1885 general election the Liberals held nine seats in Ulster against the Conservatives' seventeen, but the issue of Home Rule for Ireland had by this time engulfed the rest of the island and led to the hegemony of the Irish Parliamentary Party headed after 1880 by Charles Stewart Parnell.

The 1885 election saw the Conservatives in Ulster benefit from the franchise extension of the previous year; their advanced organisational skills and adroit use of the socially heterodox Orange Order saw the enlistment of much of the labouring class around a populist patriotic anti-Home Rule platform. This, and a measure of Catholic tactical voting for the Conservatives, resulted in the defeat of all the Ulster Liberals. Voting behaviour was overwhelmingly polarised between Catholic support for Home Rule and Protestants for the Union.[50] The 1886 election, following Gladstone's adoption of Irish Home Rule as Liberal policy, saw the division entrenched, with the majority Liberal defectors becoming Liberal Unionists and forming with the Conservatives and their Orange Order allies a broad-based Unionist movement pledged to fight Home Rule. In Scotland too Gladstone's actions were met by a Liberal Unionist defection and the similar creation of a more populist and urban Unionist movement in alliance with the Conservatives. On the other hand, Liberalism remained dominant in Scotland, and the Orange Order's political role far less influential.[51]

Home Rule thus drew together Protestants in Ireland, of all denominations, classes, and erstwhile political allegiances, in a defensive stand against what was perceived to be a threat to their way of life. Central to this threat was the perception of the Catholic Church as bent on absolute political power in Ireland; much was made of the Catholic clergy's involvement in the Nationalist party. Protestants could, and would, not accept the idea of Home Rule as a measure balancing Irish nationalist and Unionist sentiment, as something which would be a final constitutional arrangement of Ireland's affairs within the Union. They could see in it only the threat of unbridled Catholic power and an intensified Nationalism leading inexorably to the republican goal of separation. The predominant Protestant view of the Catholic Church has been well described as 'all pervasive in influence, monolithic in scope, imperialist in intention, persecuting in its essential nature and impoverishing in its social effects.'[52]

In such a mood of impending catastrophe, the Protestant Unionists, and especially the Presbyterians of Ulster,[53] solicited support from co-religionists in Britain, and especially Scottish Presbyterians. While grateful for such support as was received, it was nevertheless a major disillusioning shock to Presbyterians in Ireland that many of their Scottish brethren were not prepared to transcend deeply-rooted political loyalties on the Irish Home Rule issue. Typical of the Ulster reaction, which will be explored in more depth in the next chapter, was that of the Reverend Hugh Hanna in a published letter to a Liberal-voting Scottish Presbyterian:

> Is it in reality so that when half a million Irish Presbyterians declare their solemn conviction that Mr. Gladstone's policy would imperil Irish Protestantism, would be fatal to the best interests of Ireland, that any section of Scotch Presbyterians should support that policy, and array itself in antagonism to their kinsmen in Ireland? Is it possible that political partisanship can dominate all the considerations of a common lineage and a common faith, and that any part of Scotland would forsake its own flesh and blood to promote the policy and restore the power of a fallen leader, proposing the most dangerous projects to recruit his political fortunes?[54]

Between the Irish and the Liberal Scottish Presbyterians there was a mutual inability to appreciate the depth of respective convictions, the first on the Home Rule issue, the latter on matters such as land reform, education and religious principles which had brought about traumatic severances on a national scale. In Scotland, many of the Presbyterian immigrants from Ireland found their sister church, the Free Church after 1843, politically uncongenial, and formed their own independent churches.[55]

Against the background of Home Rule from the 1880s, identities were re-shaped. The concentration of Unionist resistance in the north-east of the country fostered the gradual emergence of an 'Ulster' identity which proclaimed its 'Britishness' in terms of political loyalty and dire intent in the face of perceived attempts to weaken it, and accommodated an 'Irishness' which could fit with fidelity to an undiluted Union and which took little notice of the outlook of the Catholic majority.

In the next chapter these concepts of identity will be further discussed. At this point, however, it should be emphasised that the Ulster Presbyterians were perhaps the most influential architects of this emerging 'Ulster' identity. As arguably the most cohesive and socially and intellectually purposeful segment of the Protestant community of the north, the Presbyterians were able to perform something of a 'hi-jacking' job in stamping that community identity with the cultural distinctiveness of the historic Scottish bonds and the peculiar nature of the Presbyterian language and tactics of resistance and defiance.[56] Ulster's fight against Home Rule thus took on the covenanting character of Presbyterian struggles of old; the covenant came to represent that between the Protestant and Unionist population of Ulster and the British crown, rather than relating to the Presbyterian community on its own.

Even Presbyterians who remained loyal to Gladstonian Liberalism and were enthusiastic about gaelic culture in Ireland, could make a contribution to Ulster distinctiveness which exalted the Scottish connection. Thus the Reverend T. M. Johnstone, a future Moderator of the Presbyterian Church in Ireland, wrote as follows:

> Scotland gave to our rich Irish Ulster nature just that percentage of Gaelic carbon which was sufficient to transform the more pliable and easily wrought iron of Ulster resistance into one of steel-like firmness and endurance. The radical pedigree of Ulstermen is one, therefore, that is well-defined, and that marks them off clearly from the inhabitants of the other three provinces.[57]

This theme of Ulster's 'apartness' was to be pushed to new boundaries. In the political struggles of the Home Rule era, ethnic particularities, whether oriented towards racial or religious factors, would rub along, often problematically, with a wider identification with Britain and the Empire.

NOTES

1. A. T. Q. Stewart, *The Narrow Ground: Aspects of Ulster 1609–1969* (London, 1977) p. 34.
2. It might be said that even the consensus-seeking 'Cultural Traditions' organisation in contemporary Northern Ireland bases its 'two traditions' typology essentially on this polarisation.
3. See examples in B. Loftus, *Mirrors: Orange and Green* (Dundrum, 1994).
4. See *Ulster Newsletter* 6 September 1993 for report of one such pageant at Ballycarry, East Antrim.
5. See for example Finlay Holmes, *Our Irish Presbyterian Heritage* (1985), and *Irish Presbyterianism* (Presbyterian Historical Society, 1992).

6. Ian Adamson, *The Cruthin* (Belfast, 1974); *The Identity of Ulster* (Belfast, 1982); *The Ulster People* (Belfast, 1991). For a critique of Adamson's works and their use by paramilitary groups such as the Ulster Defence Association (UDA) see H. J. Morgan, 'Deceptions of demons', *Fortnight* No. 320 (September 1993). See also A. Buckley, 'Uses of history among Ulster Protestants', in G. Dawe and J. W. Foster (eds.), *The Poet's Place* (Belfast, 1991). See discussion in chpt. 4 of this book.

7. For example, John Harrison, *The Scot in Ulster* (Edinburgh, 1888); J. Heron, *The Ulster Scot* (London, 1900); Charles A. Hanna, *The Scotch-Irish* (London, 1902); J. B. Woodburn, *The Ulster Scot: His History and Religion* (London, 1914).

8. Harrison op. cit. p. 114.

9. See, for example, *The Scotch-Irish and Ulster* (1965); and comment by O. D. Edwards in his 'Scotland, Ulster and You', in Ian S. Wood (ed.), *Scotland and Ulster* (Edinburgh, 1994).

10. Examples include R. Hanna, *Land of the Free: Ulster and the American Revolution*; R. Hanna, *The Highest Call: Ulster and the American Presidency*; D. Gibson-Harries, *Lifeline to Freedom: Ulster in the Second World War*. All publications of the Ulster Society established in 1986.

11. See in particular M. Perceval-Maxwell, *The Scottish Migration to Ulster in the Reign of James I* (London, 1973); R. J. Gillespie, *Colonial Ulster* (Cork, 1985); P. S. Robinson, *The Plantation of Ulster* (Dublin, 1984). There is also much interesting comment in M. W. Heslinga, *The Irish Border as a Cultural Divide* (The Netherlands, 1979).

12. W. A. Macafee, 'The Movement of British Settlers into Ulster During the Seventeenth Century', *Familia* Vol. 2, no. 8 (1992) pp. 94–111. See also R. J. Gillespie, 'Plantations in Early Modern Ireland', *History Ireland* Vol. 1, no. 4 (Winter 1993) pp. 43–47.

13. See Stewart J. Brown, 'Presbyterian Communities, Transatlantic Visions and the Ulster Revival of 1859', in J. P. Mackey (ed.), *The Cultures of Europe: The Irish Contribution* (Belfast, 1994); also D. W. Miller, *Queen's Rebels* (Dublin, 1978) chpt. 1.

14. See Buckley op. cit.

15. See Holmes op. cit. chpt. 3; and I. McBride, 'Presbyterians in the Penal Era', *Bullan* Vol. 1, no. 2 (Autumn 1994) pp. 73–86.

16. I. McBride, 'The School of Virtue: Francis Hutcheson, Irish Presbyterians and the Scottish Enlightenment', in G. Boyce, R. Eccleshall and V. Geoghegan (eds.), *Political thought in Ireland since the seventeenth century* (London, 1993).

17. Ibid. However, see D. Allan, *Virtue, Learning and the Scottish Enlightenment* (Edinburgh, 1993) for a different view of the roots of the Enlightenment.

18. A. T. Q. Stewart, *A Deeper Silence* (London, 1993).

19. W. R. Brock, *Scotus Americanus* (Edinburgh, 1982) chpt. 5.
20. See M. Elliott, *Watchmen in Sion: The Protestant Idea of Liberty* (Field Day Pamphlet, 1985) pp. 11–13.
21. E. McFarland, *Ireland and Scotland in the Age of Revolution* (Edinburgh, 1994) p. 13.
22. For Drennan see I. McBride, 'William Drennan and the Dissenting Tradition', in D. Dickson, D. Keogh and K. Whelan (eds.), *The United Irishmen* (Dublin, 1993).
23. McFarland, *Ireland and Scotland* p. 23.
24. Ibid.
25. For freemasonry and the United Irishmen, see also A. T. Q. Stewart, *A Deeper Silence.*
26. L. Colley, *Britons: Forging the Nation 1707–1837* (New Haven, 1992).
27. McFarland, *Ireland and Scotland* p. 194.
28. See comments in Parliamentary Papers, *Report from the Select Committee Enquiring into the Condition of the Poorer Classes in Ireland. Appendix G Report on the State of the Irish Poor in Great Britain 1836 (40)*, XXXIV, 427, p. v.
29. On the 'rhyming weavers' and Scottish literacy and linguistic influences in Ulster see I. Herbison, 'Oor ain native tung', in *Talking Scots*, a supplement to *Fortnight* No. 318 (June 1993); and L. Lunney 'Ulster Attitudes to Scottishness: The Eighteenth Century and After', in Ian S. Wood (ed.), *Scotland and Ulster.*
30. Lunney op. cit.; also Billy Kay, 'The Scots Ower the Sheuch', in Wood (ed.), *Scotland and Ulster.*
31. See McFarland, *Ireland and Scotland*, chpt. 8; and G. Walker, 'The Protestant Irish in Scotland', in T. M. Devine (ed.), *Irish Immigrants and Scottish Society in the 19th and 20th Centuries* (Edinburgh, 1991).
32. J. E. Handley, *The Irish in Scotland* (Cork, 1943) and *The Irish in Modern Scotland* (Cork, 1947); T. Gallagher, *Glasgow: The Uneasy Peace* (Manchester, 1987); various articles in Devine (ed.) op. cit.
33. See W. Sloan, 'Religious Affiliation and the Immigrant Experience: Catholic Irish and Protestant Highlanders in Glasgow, 1830–50', in Devine (ed.) op. cit.
34. See Gallagher, *Uneasy Peace* chpts. 2 and 3.
35. J. Oliver, 'On Some Ulster-Scots and their origins in Scotland', in his *Aspects of Ulster* (Antrim, 1994).
36. See Walker, 'Protestant Irish' in Devine (ed.) op. cit.; also E. McFarland, *Protestants First! Orangeism in 19th century Scotland* (Edinburgh, 1991), passim.
37. McFarland, *Protestants First*, chpt. 5; also A. Campbell, *The Lanarkshire Miners* (Edinburgh, 1979) p. 223.
38. Campbell op. cit. p. 191.
39. Walker, 'Protestant Irish'.

40. McFarland, *Protestants First*, chpt. 5.
41. See E. McFarland, 'A mere Irish Faction': The Orange Institution in Nineteenth Century Scotland', in I. S. Wood (ed.), *Scotland and Ulster.*
42. See next chapter.
43. See Walker, 'Protestant Irish'.
44. See, for example, R. F. G. Holmes, *Thomas Chalmers and Ireland* (Presbyterian Historical Society, 1980). The Presbyterian Church in Ireland allied with the Free Church of Scotland after 'The Great Disruption' of 1843.
45. See Stewart J. Brown and M. Fry (eds.), *Scotland in the Age of Disruption* (Edinburgh, 1993) for fresh perspectives on this episode.
46. The 1859 Revival in Ulster was a key development — see Stewart J. Brown 'Presbyterian Communities'. The Revival had a significant impact in Scotland, especially in Free Church circles. For a wider discussion of evangelicalism's impact in Ulster see D. Hempton and M. Hill, *Evangelicalism and Ulster Society* (London, 1992).
47. J. L. McCracken, *New Light at the Cape of Good Hope* (Belfast, 1993) pp. 26–30.
48. R. McMinn, 'Presbyterianism and Politics in Ulster, 1871–1906', *Studia Hibernica* (1981) pp. 127–146.
49. B. M. Walker, *Ulster Politics: The Formative Years 1868–1886* (Belfast, 1989).
50. See B. M. Walker, 'The 1885 and 1886 General Elections: A Milestone in Irish History', in P. Collins (ed.), *Nationalism and Unionism: Conflict in Ireland* (Belfast, 1994).
51. See I. C. G. Hutchinson, *A Political History of Scotland 1832–1924* (Edinburgh, 1986) chpts. 6 and 7; McFarland, *Protestants First*, chpts. 9 and 10.
52. Hempton and Hill op. cit. p. 183.
53. Excepting a small minority who welcomed Home Rule — see next chapter.
54. Rev. H. Hanna, *Scotland, Ulster and Home Rule for Ireland: A Letter addressed to a Friend in Scotland* (Belfast, 1888) pp. 10–11.
55. McFarland, '"A Mere Irish Faction"'.
56. But note that the character of the Irish Unionist Parliamentary Party was overwhelmingly landlord-Anglican c. 1880s and 1890s. See A. Jackson, *The Ulster Party* (Oxford, 1989).
57. T. M. Johnstone, *Ulstermen: Their Fight for Fortune, Faith and Freedom* (Belfast, 1914), p. 49.

2

Religion, Nationality and Empire in the Home Rule Era c. 1880–1920

I

In 1886 Gladstone took up the gauntlet of Irish Home Rule; in 1920 the Government of Ireland Act brought the Northern Ireland State into being. Between these milestones there occurred an important constitutional debate to which Scotland and Ulster were central. This is a period rich also in evidence pertaining to questions of national and ethnic identity throughout the UK: this chapter will focus in particular on the extent to which a British imperial or British national identity was shared by Scotland and Ulster. Related to this is the wider theme of the interplay between the two places of ideas, values and assumptions which produced an interesting, yet ambiguous and tense, relationship in a crucial era of political turmoil.

II

Whether Scotland, by the late nineteenth century, was 'a nation within a nation', or 'a nation within a state', her relationship with the idea of 'Britishness' had a lot to do with the Empire. Linda Colley's recent work argues that a British nationality was forged in the eighteenth century and superimposed on older allegiances.[1] Colley points to the Empire as an attractive outlet for Scottish talents and energies, and it is implied that the Scots' imperial role, along with other factors, helped shape this overarching and politically dominant British identity. The question of whether a British *nation*, as opposed to a *state*, was in fact formed in the eighteenth century and has existed since, is a highly contentious one. Bernard Crick, to take but one sceptic, has suggested that what Colley views

17

as nationalism was simply patriotism, and that the cultural homogeneity necessary for a truly British nationalism never existed.[2] Crick's critique may be questioned in turn, but at this juncture the focus will be on the meaning of Britishness as expressed through participation in, and perception of, the Empire.

In this sense it is important to appreciate the extent to which *Scottishness* was promoted and enhanced within the Empire. Far from being eclipsed by her larger neighbour Scotland used the opportunity structure offered by the Empire to demonstrate what Scots quite immodestly considered the superiority of their nation's cultural and moral distinctiveness. The Empire, it has been argued by John McKenzie among others,[3] was used by Scots to enhance Scottish institutions and to assert their differences with England. In the late nineteenth and early twentieth century period, and arguably for a long time before, Scottish self-belief and national pride were all but unassailable. The Nationalist fringe aside, Scots did not entertain any sense of themselves as a 'failed nation'; as J. H. Grainger has written:

> Edwardian Scots were a well-tempered people, quietly assured of certain moral superiorities, well instructed in fundamentals and quite unpersuaded that they were oppressed. Scotland had no linguistic grievances. The Empire provided ample opportunities for her soldiers, entrepreneurs and administrators.[4]

The same could also be said of Victorian Scotland; there was no conflict of economic interests,[5] the Scots played a crucial political role most notably through the Liberal Party of Gladstone, and the British state and Empire provided scope for the full expression of *Scottish* qualities and talents.

The Scots saw no need to struggle to assert a distinct national identity; it was assured, it was securely in place, and it was a living, dynamic international influence.[6] As Adam Naylor, in an important unpublished thesis has put it: '. . . no Scot need look to the nature of how he was governed to establish his national identity.'[7] Indeed, most Scots who did look favourably on the idea of Scottish Home Rule, took the position of Lord Rosebery (one of three Scottish Prime Ministers in the period 1895–1905) that it would *strengthen* the UK state and Empire, leading to ultimate Imperial Federation. Rosebery wrote in 1885:

> I cannot understand people preferring separation to Home Rule. I detest separation and feel that nothing could make me agree to it.

Home Rule, however, is a necessity for both us and the Irish. They will have it within two years at the latest. Scotland will follow, then England. When that is accomplished, Imperial Federation will cease to be a dream. To many of us, it is not a dream now but to no-one will it be a dream then.[8]

Rosebery was to be disappointed in not seeing his dream fulfilled, but the Federalist idea, both in terms of the British State and the wider Empire, gained momentum among Liberals, and even some Conservatives like the Scotsman Frederick Scott Oliver, and it was an idea trumpeted in the pre-World War One period by Glasgow Liberal MP Alexander McCallum Scott whose outlook typified the proud and idealistic 'Scot with a mission'.[9] The expansive visions of the Liberal Imperialists struck deep chords in Scotland, although the Conservatives (known as 'Unionists'), as will be shown, could also turn the issue to their advantage.

Perhaps the main reason why Scotland was fertile territory for imperialistic appeals was the importance of religion in relation both to Scottish national identity and to perceptions of Empire. For Linda Colley, Protestantism was central to the British experience in the 18th century and was one of the cornerstones of the British nationality she sees as having been created. Divisions between Protestants, she argues, should not obscure the way a Protestant sense of solidarity against the Catholic 'Other', in the shape of France abroad and the threatening spectre of Jacobitism at home, helped 'Britons' to define themselves as such: 'Britons were encouraged to look through the Catholic glass darkly so as to see themselves more clearly and more complacently.'[10]

There is much in this, as indeed there is also in Colley's suggestion that the experience of governing and administering an Empire (Britain's 'second' Empire in the East) so diverse in cultures and creeds and races, helped to further cement a common 'Britishness' among the Imperialists; it is salutary, too, to be made aware of the extent to which this Empire experience was popularly disseminated throughout the United Kingdom. However, Colley's disinclination to make much of divisions among Protestants rather leads her away from consideration of how Scots might have differed from the English in their perception of, and active role in, Empire, and through this, to the issue of the differences in the nature of 'Britishness' or British 'patriotism' (following Crick) or even the British 'Nationalism' of Colley herself from the 18th century onwards. Crick justly criticises Colley for implying that the feelings

'Britishness' stirred were essentially the same in every part of the UK.[11]

For, it can be argued that the Scottish Protestant imperial impulse was part of the attempt to infuse arenas of Empire, as McKenzie has suggested,[12] with Scottish ethics and aspects of Scottish civil society. In fairness to Colley, this may be more obvious for the 19th and 20th century than for the 'long eighteenth century' period of her study. But her conclusions beg to be developed for later periods.

Scottish Presbyterianism, in its missionary character, stalked almost every colony at the Victorian high tide period of Empire. It combined ethnocentricity and paternalism with a drive in many cases for social justice and improvement, and a radical egalitarian spirit. A Scottish view of Empire which repudiated self-interest and celebrated the missionary heroics of David Livingstone and Mary Slessor, was deeply and widely felt if self-indulgent and self-congratulatory. The Scots felt that they took the task of spreading Christianity more seriously than the English, and that Scottish Presbyterianism in general was more morally serious and less corruptible.

When John Buchan took up a post under Milner in South Africa, an elder of his father's church, the John Knox Free Church in Glasgow, wrote to him as follows:

> I feared for the future of South Africa where there has been so much corruption, where Christian principles have been stifled by the craze for gold, and where there is the ever-present opportunity of the white oppressing the black. But if I knew that a man like you was helping to hold the helm, I should have confidence in its future. Rhodes and others are great men, possessed with large ideas, but they are hardly to be trusted in their treatment of the blacks and other questions. They see things from a utilitarian point of view, and from the angle of their own advantage, consequently they do not like the missionaries and their impractical notions. The ignorant sentimentality of Christian people (so they put it) is a thorn in their flesh, which they would fain be rid of, but which thank God is still of some power. If these empire-builders require to use the black races as stepping-stones to further their plans, many people will say they are justified, but I cannot, and if I can do anything to hinder them I will do it willingly. It may do for the moment, but it is sure to end in disaster.
>
> I believe, however, that Lord Milner will do what is right to the dark race, but he will need someone to help him, someone with the fear of God before his eyes.

The writer then ended by urging Buchan to remember Livingstone.[13] Buchan, moreover, made a clear distinction (as did Scottish Labour MPs in the 1920s) between the Scots' conception of themselves as, literally, the builders of Empire — the engineers, the road, bridge and railway builders, as opposed to that of the English which suggested 'public school men administering subject races'.[14]

Another Scot who epitomised a more enlightened attitude to Empire was William McGregor Ross, a civil engineer who rose to become Director of Public Works in Kenya by 1905. Ross, as his memoirs reveal, was a tireless social protester against the exploitation and degradation of the native people; he worked closely with the Church of Scotland mission to highlight social injustice and colonial government malpractice. At all times, however, Ross clung to the overall view that Empire could be 'a motive-power on the side of world progress'; racist attitudes and exploitation simply damaged the prospects of this.[15]

In certain parts of the Empire Scots established landholding systems of benefit to tenants, and struggled to break the power of the large landowners. There were other cases of Scottish social protesters in the van of struggles for press freedom and black rights.[16]

The Scots in general saw themselves as realising the constructive potential which the Empire offered,[17] and in this they might be said to have been expressing their sense of Scottish nationalist identity while not repudiating the umbrella term of 'British'. However, their interpretation of English values and behaviour could often be critical and there was a pronounced sense of competitiveness about the Scots vis-à-vis the English in relation to their role in the Empire. In this connection a distinctive religious identity was arguably the most important factor, especially since the dynamic of the Presbyterian democratic ethos was seen to lie behind the more egalitarian and anti-privilege orientation of the educational and legal systems.

Less idealistically the British and Empire connection has also been viewed as attractive to Protestant Scotland on account of being added security against the encroachment of Roman Catholicism.[18] In this respect Colley's work helps to illuminate the way many Scots came to balance out balefully dour perceptions of episcopalianism (itself a small native tradition in Scotland) with increasingly wary and fearful evaluations of Catholicism. If this was true of the eighteenth century, largely on account of external Catholic threats, then it was far more so in the nineteenth as the Catholic church in Britain, largely through its congregations of Irish immigrants, built up a stronger profile. Anxiety over Irish Catholic immigration into Scotland certainly exercised many Protestant minds, although it is not clear that, outside the ranks of demagogues (often immigrant Ulster preachers) it produced any doubts about Protestantism's cultural dominance in Scotland.

In general, up until the first World War, Scottish national and religious sentiment flow together and exude confidence. Indeed, as Bernard Aspinwall has argued, Scottish national identity was expressed significantly through a 'civic gospel' which the Scottish Protestant Churches exported, not only to the Empire, but also very tellingly to the USA. This 'civic gospel' was oriented to social problems and to the quest for Christian ethical values in modern urban life.[19] There is no sense, in this period, of any lack of purpose or any doubt about identity and role in the world, on the part of Church and Nation.

That this should have been so was arguably due in part to the wider context afforded to Scotland by 'Britishness' and the Empire, and it was in this spirit of recognition of the benefits of this wider allegiance that a British patriotism was subscribed to. However, notions of a British nationalism, especially if they appeared to threaten to absorb Scottish identity or reduce 'British' to 'English' with all the dubious values and characteristics which were deemed to be suggested by *that*, ran the risk of alienating probably the great majority of Scots. To take one example, an article in *The People's Journal* in 1890 (the biggest selling popular newspaper in Scotland in this period) in praise of the Covenanters (an impeccable and militant Protestant theme) ended by calling for more Scottish history to be taught in Scottish schools and warned that if not, they would be 'swallowed up in John Bull.'[20]

That this whole question entailed great political sensitivities was attested to by a shrewdly argued confidential memorandum on the subject of Scottish Home Rule issued by the Unionist Party in Scotland early in 1914 to its prospective candidates for a general election they believed to be imminent.[21] The Unionists opposed Home Rule for Scotland, but recognised that the issue had to be handled carefully; at the outset of the memo it was admitted that 'Scottish National sentiment is a strong force in all ranks of Scottish life'. However, the Unionists, as is clear from this document, felt that they could trump the Home Rulers by appealing to what they called 'the wider Imperial patriotism', and the need to harness Scottish National patriotism to the Empire ideal rather than the ideal of Scottish self-government. The memo stated that 'a parochial, parish-pump type' of Scottish nationalism, 'based more largely on jealousy of others than on pride in national achievements and capacities', had to be confronted by an appeal to Imperial patriotism which 'when it is properly made, Scotsmen invariably show themselves ready to respond'. In addition it was urged on the candidates to stress that Scottish Home Rule would mean English Home Rule and that that would bring to an end something which had long been a source of Scottish pride, namely the success of individual Scots in reaching the top posts in London in politics, business, religion, the press, the police and other walks of life. If the unitary state system of government was broken up, the memo argues, English posts would be kept for Englishmen, and the sense of satisfaction in Scotland regarding this brand of Scottish conquest would be extinguished.

The points made in this memorandum can be said to have reflected quite accurately the nature of most Scots' national outlook on the eve of an Imperial conflagration in Europe in which the Scots, in proportionate terms, sacrificed more lives than any other country in the British Empire.[22] At the outbreak of the First World War 90 per cent of all 'sons of the manse' volunteered for active service in His Majesty's Forces, and John Buchan's propaganda contribution in the war was to be an exceptional one.[23] The Scots responded enthusiastically in 1914, echoing, to a large extent, previous episodes such as the Boer War which the Unionist memorandum was doubtless referring to when it cited the Scottish propensity to respond to imperial appeals.[24] There was not, at this time, any real sense of Scottish destiny, whether economic, cultural or political, not being bound up firmly with Britain and the Empire; on the other hand, Scotland's secure sense of its own national identity had rendered the term 'North Britain' an historical curiosity.[25]

III

The question of Ulster's national identity in this Home Rule era has been the subject of much scholarly debate. Among the most important contributions have been those of the historians Peter Gibbon, David Miller, James Loughlin and Alvin Jackson.[26]

Gibbon's analysis, the earliest of the four, has been rejected by the others in its assertion that an Ulster nationalism emerged in the face of the Home Rule crisis and was shaped and led by the Belfast bourgeoisie which had displaced the landlord interest as the spokesmen of the Protestant Unionist community. Miller, in a seminal work published three years later, argued that Ulster nationalism did not develop but that the Ulster Protestants' sense of British loyalty was strictly conditional: that is, that the Ulster Protestants were in a 'contractarian' type of relationship with the British State and that they would be entitled to withdraw their loyalty to the State if they perceived it to be breaking the 'contract' and acting against their interests. Miller holds that the Ulster Unionists preferred to make the focus of their loyalty the Crown and the Empire; the latter he sees as providing a convenient 'way out' for the Ulstermen in that it offered a focus for their loyalty which suggested that they were more than 'merely' British. Miller sees the Ulster Protestants as a 'special case' in the British context and argues that they themselves saw it that way, that they were deeply suspicious of British governments' intentions and so insecure as to always be ready to rely on their own resources and fight for their own community.

James Loughlin, in a challenging book, has taken issue with Miller's concept of an imperial identity as a substitute for a secure sense of British national identity on the part of Ulster. He has argued that their imperial identification followed naturally from what *was* a strong and committed British identity. He disputes that Ulster felt less 'completely' British than any other part of the U.K. and cites the example of Scotland as being the exception in this sense; that is, that Scotland, in retaining separate institutions, subscribed in a far more limited degree to a 'complete' sense of U.K. nationality and sovereignty than the Ulster loyalists did. In dismissing Ulster nationalism, Loughlin says that it has often been confused with the existence of an 'Ulsterman' type or character which had developed without any nationalist pretensions and with the purpose of sharpening ethnic divisions between the Loyalists and nationalist (Catholic) Ireland.

Following Loughlin, Alvin Jackson has entered the debate to object to Loughlin's relegation, as he sees it, of Ulster to the status of a British regional identity; Jackson believes that an Ulster nation could be said to have existed in theory (although Ulster nationalism did not develop in practice), and that it should be accorded similar conceptual status as other nations in the U.K. Moreover, Jackson is concerned to show that Ulster politicians in the Home

Rule era were preoccupied with local Ulster issues rather than British or Empire ones, and he is critical of Loughlin's concept of British nationalism which he finds so 'flaccid' that even some Irish nationalists might be able to accept it. Jackson concludes that, in relation to national identity, the impression received is too ambiguous to call: 'For, if there were two or even three nations in late nineteenth century Ireland, it would appear that each of these (and every combination) was represented within Loyalism'.[27] The Irish Unionist movement (North and South), in order to preserve unity, had to accept the ambiguities and instead gear itself to the negative end of defeating Home Rule. Class and religious denominational divisions within Unionism also demanded such a course.

More recently, another historian, George Boyce, in a work of synthesis, has tried to clarify the issue as follows:

> Ulster Protestants did not develop a 'nationalism' of their own, simply because they did not need to do so: the whole basis of their creed was a denial that nationalism was a genuine or tenable political belief. It was a sham and a fraud, since there had never been a united Irish nation in the first place. And from the 1880s until the 1912 Home Rule crisis it was possible for both northern and southern Unionists to maintain that loyalty was perfectly compatible with a wider British patriotism. Their claim was that Ireland was divided into 'loyal' and 'disloyal' Ireland.[28]

Elsewhere, Boyce has also written, pace Miller, that the Ulster Protestants' belief in a British nationality was tempered by the awareness that they might have to fight for the survival of their community and that they therefore had to assert themselves as a special breed, defenders of a British heritage in Ireland under threat from a nationalist majority who were antagonistic to that heritage.[29]

This debate is eminently germane to that stimulated by Linda Colley and her argument about the forging of a British nation. Ironically, in view of Colley's decision not to consider Ireland in her study, it is Ulster which perhaps constitutes the most interesting illustration of her thesis. One scholar of the Ulster Unionist national identity has indeed taken up her arguments and related Ulster Unionists to them, arguing that Unionists defined themselves as part of a British *national* community, sharing a specifically British historical heritage. To this definition of British nation and heritage, Protestantism was indeed considered central.[30]

Many of the predominant themes of this whole debate invite comment about the respective mentalities and perceptions held in

Ulster and Scotland. For example, Loughlin's criticism of Miller is
persuasive; certainly, he is right to say that the 'contractarian' concept has at least as much relevance to Scotland. The popular understanding of the Union in Scotland in this era was very much like
that of a contract: the Union was not seen, except by a few, as a bar-
tering away of Scottish nationhood; rather it was a means by which
Scotland could prosper.[31] If Scotland, by this period, had not done
well out of the Union and the Empire, then it might be hypothesised that she would have sought to terminate the arrangement or
at least adjust it. The Union at this time was widely viewed as a
partnership, notwithstanding annoyance on the part of most Scots
at some time or other over the English habit of seeing their country
as synonymous with the concept of Britain. The Scots could accept
the arrangement all the more for the retention of their national
institutions and of a secure sense of Scottish nationhood. They,
more than the Ulster Loyalists, were concerned not to be regarded
as 'merely' British, and in this sense the Ulster Loyalists' combination of a proclaimed British loyalty and a deep sense of Ulster
independence cannot be viewed as aberrant or peculiar.

This sense of 'independence' was arguably related to the concept
of an Ulster 'type' which Loughlin refers to: the cultivation of an
image of the Ulsterman as resourceful, honest, determined and
independently-minded in contrast to the feckless, untrustworthy,
spineless and priest-ridden nationalist Celt. It was undoubtedly
true that the Ulster Protestant felt himself to be in a less secure
position, in terms of the perceived nationalist and Catholic threat,
than anyone else in the U.K., but while this situation called for the
display of the personal qualities adduced above, it did not mean
that the goal of British and Imperial protection could not be pursued with the utmost vigour. For this, it might be said, was the
main reason for Ulster's commitment to Union and Empire: for
the sense of security which would prevent them being at the mercy
of an Irish Catholic regime intent on curtailing their civil and
religious liberties and oppressing their culture and ruining their
economic and social welfare.

Leave aside the argument that these were unreasonable fears: the
point was, as will be illustrated below, that the Ulster Protestants
believed that Catholic sectarian rule in a Home Rule Ireland,
through the medium of the Ancient Order of Hibernians (AOH),
would be their fate. Folk memories and cultural traditions revolved
around episodes like the 1641 massacres, the 1688–89 Siege of

Derry, and the 1798 Wexford massacre. The other side of this coin — the Orangeist triumphalism of the Boyne — was the defiant expression of this profoundly defensive mentality. Even if the Union and the Imperial connection had not resulted in economic prosperity for Ulster — and much, of course, was made of this prosperity by Unionists — it might be hypothesized, in contrast to the Scottish case, that Ulster would not have repudiated the British link. In their case religious and cultural factors counted for more. Their sense of national identity, in a positive sense as opposed to their determination to resist Irish nationalism in a negative sense, was not clearly defined: it was multi-layered, there were, as Jackson argues, overlapping loyalties: Irish,[32] British, Ulster or Ulster-Scottish. Where Scots could regard the wider British and imperial contexts as opportunities to express their Scottishness and display the Scottish qualities about which they were immodest, the Ulster view of Britain and the Empire was overwhelmingly conceived in terms of achieving solidarity and security.

This security theme is also at the heart of Colley's invention of Britishness in the 18th century: the continental Catholic threat to British liberties and the spectre of Jacobitism inducing Protestant Scots, English and Welsh to identify with a composite national formation for the purposes of their own security and stability throughout the Kingdom. However, it might be suggested that the security factor which spawned the greatest enthusiasm for British national identity was that felt by Irish (predominantly Ulster) Protestants in the 19th century in the face of the much more credible and immediate threat of the Catholic 'other' in their own country. And it was the Protestants in Ireland, much more than anywhere else, who had the most urgent need to see Protestant ranks closed across denominational, class, national and regional barriers.

To defeat Home rule, the Unionists needed to appeal, as a minority in Ireland, to the majority in the U.K. as a whole. As one of their spokesmen speaking in Scotland in 1895 put it: 'The only majority to which you in Glasgow and we in Ireland owe allegiance is the majority of the electorate of the whole realm of the United Kingdom.'[33] Moreover, the most ringing declarations of belief in the 'higher wisdom' of a British nation were to be found in Ulster Unionist anti-Home Rule propaganda. A 1911 pamphlet referred to 'the great British Nation, in which the English, Scottish, Welsh and Irish peoples are merged', and stated that it was a prouder thing to be attached to this than 'to cling to insular nationality'.[34] It is unlikely that most Scots, English or Welsh, not to mention the Irish 'other', would have commented on the question of their national identity and allegiances in such a way.

So, the kind of feelings kindled by Britishness were arguably very different in Ulster than they were, for example, in Scotland, at least in this period. This, it might be said, was particularly true of respective attitudes to Empire. In Ulster the view of an imperial role lacked the sense of keen rivalry with which the Scots invested it in relation to England. In Ulster the Empire was frequently linked to the Protestant 'settler' past; the argument was that their role in building up Ulster as an imperial province should be rewarded with a share in the glories and benefits of the contemporary Empire.[35]

Thus while the following declaration of Arthur Balfour's in 1914 equating Scottish and 'Ulster Scot' attitudes to Empire may ring superficially true, there was no way the Ulster Loyalists could divorce the Empire from the desperate plight they considered themselves to be in, in order to hold the expansive vision described here of the Empire as a globally progressive phenomenon in its own right:

> Again, the Ulster Scot, like the Scot at home and throughout the Empire, has been true to his race and his tradition; but he has also opened his eyes to the larger vision of Empire, he has been loyal to the flag of the Union, and he has carried the British name with honour to every corner of the globe. Is it any wonder that the Ulster Scot refuses to barter away his share in the heritage of Empire.[36]

Imperial champions like Lord Milner and Andrew Bonar Law (Unionist leader from 1911) liked to portray Ulster as 'holding the pass for the Empire', but, again, this was in the negative sense of Ulster's cause being crucial to the prevention of imperial disintegration.[37] The Ulster view of Empire was more passive than that of Scotland; the Empire was something fixed as part of Ulster's *inheritance*.[38] The Scottish view was more active and crusading and suggested that Empire was something through which *new* achievements could be fashioned.

Neither did Ulster Unionists evince much interest in, nor contribute significantly to, the debates on Imperial federation which were such a feature of British politics in this era.[39] The Ulster Unionists either viewed federal or 'Home Rule All Round' schemes as too vague and a diversion from the immediate reality of the Irish threat, or held that Dublin rule would still be unacceptable in a federal-type framework, or shared the constitutional conservatism of such anti-Home Rulers as A. V. Dicey who took the view that any devolution scheme would have the effect of weakening the integrity of the U.K. and the Empire.[40] A prominent Unionist advocate, A. W. Samuels, argued that in practice in a federal system, the Imperial Parliament which was supposed to be supreme, would be subordinate to all the other assemblies, and would only be able to enforce its will in the Dominions with the assent and active co-operation of the assemblies. Samuels considered a federal scheme to be no different from an Irish Home Rule scheme in that it would inevitably lead to *separation*, as an Irish assembly increased its practical independence.[41]

Ulster, in the Home Rule era, craved strong backing from both Scotland and England; the religious and political aspects of this will be discussed below. British solidarity, not more evidence of its diversity, was asked for. The Empire thus tended to be viewed as a triumph of this kind of British unity and solidarity, and, indeed, as a kind of 'Protestant front' encompassing all denominations. The Ulster Protestants covered up the divisions within their own community which made a coherent Ulster nationalism so problematic, and encouraged the other parts of the U.K. (excepting, of course, Nationalist Ireland) to forget theirs in lending them full-blooded support. The Ulster Loyalists, indeed, may have been the only ones to believe in a truly British nation as well as a British state. Certainly, in the circumstances of their conflict with Irish nationalism, they found it easier to make do with an Ulster 'Loyalism' which stressed British and Imperial patriotism and solidarity than to construct a distinctive Ulster nationalism. Moreover, Naylor's observation about the Scots quoted earlier might be inverted in the case of Ulster: they *did* have to look to the nature of how they were governed to establish their national identity. Equally, it might be just as fair to conclude that there were several Ulster Protestant identities,[42] most of which managed to find a shared purpose in opposing Home Rule but not all, for it should not be forgotten that there was also a minority who supported Home Rule.[43]

IV

Of the different Ulster Protestant identities that of the 'Ulster Scot', identified with the Ulster Presbyterians, has carried most historiographical and folkloric weight. In this era of the three Irish Home Rule Bills and the Ulster Unionist depiction of them as a threat to their prosperity and liberties, the Ulster-Scottish relationship was put to the test in the cause of Unionist and Protestant solidarity. The ways in which the Unionists shaped their appeal with Scotland in mind, and the pattern of the Scottish response, were revealing.

The Ulster Unionists felt, from the outset of the Home Rule period, that the kinship and religious ties with Scotland, being so close and numerous, would bring them such committed support from that country that the Irish question would swing decisively in their favour. In 1886, in the midst of the first Home Rule Bill controversy, the proprietor of the Unionist *Belfast Newsletter*, James Henderson, stated: 'It is greatly to be desired that we should stir up the feeling of Scotland in favour of this movement . . . I believe that if we can stir up religious feeling in Scotland we have won the battle.'[44] The importance of the Scottish connection was impressed upon the Scottish Liberal Munro Ferguson during a visit to Ulster at this juncture. He was told by a Belfast newspaper editor (perhaps the same James Henderson) that 'there will be fighting . . . there will be no amalgamation, Belfast is Scotch and will remain so.' Ferguson, an associate of Lord Rosebery and thus pro-Home Rule, was nonetheless moved to inform his esteemed colleague: 'I can understand the west of Scotland going more Unionist than the East. Yesterday we could see Wigtown, Ayr and the Clyde much as we see the Lothian from Raith. The people are certainly very Scotch.'[45] Ferguson was proved correct in that the west of Scotland indeed became a centre of Liberal Unionist strength, the commercially-minded elites of Glasgow immediately seeing eye-to-eye with their Belfast counterparts; the presence of the august figure of Lord Kelvin on Liberal Unionist platforms seemed to symbolise their mutual business and scientific admiration society.

Culturally, however, Scotland was still oriented towards the small town and rural hinterland environment which the Liberals had found to be their natural constituency in the country. The argument had to be taken beyond Clydeside with all its obvious industrial and commercial similarities with the Lagan Valley which made it so receptive to Unionist fears about the economic damage an Irish Parliament would wreak in tariffs and taxes. Thus T. W. Russell, an Ulster Liberal tenant-right champion who had been born in Scotland, made his 'kith and kin' appeal in the following terms at Grangemouth in Stirlingshire in May 1886:

What, I ask, have they [the Loyalists in Ireland] done that they are to be deprived of their Imperial inheritance, that in the words of the Apostle they are to be made 'bastards and not sons'? Three hundred years ago Ulster was peopled by Scotch settlers for State reasons. You are bound to remember this. The men there are bone of your bone, flesh of your flesh. The blood of the Covenanters courses through their veins; they read the same Bible, they sing the same Psalms, they have the same Church polity. Nor have they proved altogether unworthy of their ancestry. Two hundred years ago, when the Empire was in peril, the descendants of these Scottish settlers, hunted from post to pillar, remembering that they belonged to an Imperial race, 'turned desperately to bay' under the walls of Derry, and left a by no means dishonourable record of their prowess for the historian. The descendants of these men have made Ulster what it is. . . .[46]

Russell's stress on the Empire suggests that he felt he could stir the Scottish imperial consciousness; however, his use of the term 'inheritance' might be said to have reflected the subtle but significant difference in attitude discussed above. The appeal is also very religious — to their common Protestantism, in this case an undisguised appeal to a sense of Scottish Presbyterian virtue and sacrifice. It was the kind of plea Scots were to hear many more times in connection with the Irish Home Rule political dramas. It was also significant that Russell was a non-Conservative political figure whose career, indeed, was to progress along increasingly radical paths surrounding the question of tenant right.[47] In the view of the Ulster Unionists it was imperative that the message got through to the Liberal and radical political constituencies in Scotland, the dominant force in this era, that the Unionist case was not simply supported by Conservatives, Landowners and what was widely seen as their plebeian tool, the Orange Order. It was necessary to demonstrate that many Liberals and Radicals in Ulster, previously loyal to Gladstone and fierce campaigners for such causes as tenant right, Catholic Emancipation, and the Disestablishment of the Anglican Church of Ireland, were firmly anti-Home Rule. The fact that these Liberals were overwhelmingly Presbyterians of Scottish descent infused their appeals with the moral righteousness and emotive language of such as T. W. Russell's address. If the English tended in general towards compromise and indifference, then the

Scots could be trusted to honour the imperishable bonds and duties of history.

However, it was not a straightforward task to get the level of commitment and backing from Scotland that the Ulster Unionists sought. The extent to which support for Gladstonian Liberalism had become an article of faith in Scotland, drawing primarily on a tradition of popular protest against landlordism and privilege, hindered the Unionist objective considerably.[48] Many Liberals may have been persuaded by the Unionists' arguments and appeals but they still considered Toryism the greater evil.[49] Important Scottish Liberal leaders like Rosebery and Campbell-Bannerman also did a fair job in controverting Ulster Protestant fears and soothing possible Scottish Liberal doubts; 'Ulstermen', said Campbell-Bannerman in 1892, 'would not be slaves but active partners in their own country.'[50] At the General Assembly of the Church of Scotland in 1893, at which the Ulster Liberal Unionist Thomas Sinclair made an impassioned plea for support, there were nonetheless the discordant voices he did not want to hear. The Reverend C. C. MacDonald of Aberdeen, for example, was reported as saying: 'He did not believe in the apprehension of priestly tyranny in Ireland. On the contrary, he believed the Home Rule legislation of Mr. Gladstone would lead to the development of free institutions in Ireland.'[51] Although the great bulk of the Assembly on this occasion seemed to be sympathetic to the Ulster cause — and there were the statutory 'No Popery' speeches — there still lingered a doubt about the extent of Scottish Presbyterian support for Ulster if it came to a 'do or die' struggle. Among Scottish Presbyterians, whether of the established Church of Scotland or the dissenting Free Churches, there were those who believed that Protestants had nothing to fear from Home Rule religiously, and that if they were serious about Empire, Home Rule would not, given the expectation by the 1890s of federalist-type developments, harm that connection either. The Unionist campaign in Ulster had a pronounced Orange colouring which the Liberal Unionist message could not disguise, and which handicapped it in its appeals to many Scottish Presbyterians and English non-conformists. Orangeism was equated with Conservatism and landlordism.

In Scotland too the Orange Order's Conservative/Unionist Party association tainted it in the eyes of many Liberals and Radicals, notwithstanding the fact that the Unionist Party after 1886 which the Orange Order supplied with a strong urban populist flavour, was to a significant extent a Liberal Unionist Party.[52] The Orange Order, as noted in the first chapter, remained essentially an Ulster Protestant immigrant organisation in Scotland, a central part of a community network which was spiritually ministered to by evangelical preachers characterised by Lord Rosebery as 'carrying the Shorter Catechism in one hand and a revolver in the other'.[53] Certainly, this perception of Ulster Protestant militants importing sectarian quarrels to Scotland and allying with reactionary elements in Scottish life to fight their corner, was a significant one in prejudicing much political opinion which considered itself progressive, tolerant and rational. The mood of Liberal Scotland in the late 19th and early 20th century, as expressed through, for example, popular and very literate newspapers like *The People's Journal*, was proudly and assertively Scottish, unassertively and non-jingoistically British, and Protestant but not extreme.[54]

There is no gainsaying, however, the efforts expended by the Ulster Unionists in winning over Scottish opinion, however gradually, and however much there were Conservative and landlord albatrosses around the neck of their cause. The Duke of Abercorn's speech at the massive Unionist Convention in Belfast in 1892 against the second Gladstone Home Rule project referred to placing 'some trust' in 'our Scotch neighbours' and this convention took every pain to present the Unionist campaign as a cross-class, cross-denominational and cross-political phenomenon.[55] Instrumental in organising this event, at which he pledged Unionists to passive resistance in the event of a Dublin Parliament, and prominent in the Liberal Unionist camp since 1886, was the Right Honourable Thomas Sinclair, a leading Presbyterian layman who made much of his Scottish Covenanter roots and of his Liberal political past. Sinclair, in fact, epitomised the Liberal wing of Ulster Unionism throughout this whole period, dying in February 1914 as the crisis of the third Home Rule Bill reached a crescendo.

Sinclair, more than anyone else in successive Unionist campaigns against Home Rule, attempted to give the lie to the Irish Nationalist claim that the Unionists simply sought a sectarian ascendancy over the Catholic Irish. With Scottish Presbyterian Liberal and English Nonconformist opinion always in mind, Sinclair constantly reiterated that a Protestant ascendancy was not their aim, that he and others like him had fought along with Catholics for an end to an Ascendancy system in Ireland which held both Catholics and Presbyterians in thrall. Sinclair claimed that Unionists sought no advantage, no privilege, just the continuation of government from Westminster which gave them the security they believed they could never enjoy under a Dublin Parliament. At the 1892 Convention Sinclair lambasted John Morley for his suggestion that the Unionists wanted to 'trample' on what they considered to be 'an inferior race'.[56] It was, in fact, the (overwhelmingly) Catholic claim that Ireland as a single historic (and historically wronged) nation had the right to control her own affairs, which Unionists consistently rejected. They rejected it in the name of the greater good of Ireland, as they saw it, and out of a proud Irish identity which saw no contradiction in being part of a wider British and Imperial, and possibly British national, allegiance. People like Sinclair, at this time at least, could accept the term 'Irish nationality' but not 'Irish nationalism'; the latter was considered synonymous with ultramontane Catholicism. One of the resolutions at the 1892 Convention appealed to 'our Nationalist countrymen to abandon a demand which only served hopelessly to divide Irishmen, and to unite together under Imperial Parliament in the promotion of measures which would tend to the peace and material welfare of our common country.'[57]

Unionists, including Liberals like Sinclair, could not accept that there were grounds for Irish nationalism as such, and they insisted that the remedy of Irish grievances and social and economic ills would solve the 'Irish Question', a thesis the Conservative governments of the period 1895-1905 attempted to put to the test.[58] In 1895, to a Glasgow audience, Sinclair said that Ireland only needed fair treatment to become 'like Scotland', a 'bulwark to the Empire'; and at the same meeting he drew a Scottish parallel with the proposed Dublin rule as follows: 'it is just as if it were proposed to transfer the interests of shipbuilders and manufacturers of Glasgow from Imperial Parliament to the control of a legislature swamped by the crofters of the Highlands.'[59]

Such statements are revealing of the outlook of Unionists like Sinclair. It was an outlook which thought it progressive to 'dissolve' older nationalist allegiances in a wider British and Imperial whole, and there is a suggestion that Sinclair was assuming that this was happening in Scotland to the extent that he could make an appeal to the sense of regional pride in the west of Scotland which had been fostered by the material benefits of Empire, in contradistinction to the rural and 'backward' Highlands. This may indeed have drawn applause from a Glasgow audience in which the local

Chamber of Commerce membership figured heavily, and there was certainly a strong regional identity in Clydeside and in other parts of Scotland; nevertheless, this did not detract from a profound Scottish national consciousness. Sinclair seems to have extrapolated unduly from the Irish situation, assuming too much about Scottish national identity on the basis of his reluctance to admit to the reality of Irish nationalist feeling.

As stated earlier, Irish nationalism, in the course of the 19th century, became to a significant extent identified with ultramontane Catholicism, and this decisively sharpened the Ulster Protestant sense of apartness. Sinclair and others were on surer ground in Scotland when they made their appeal for support with reference to the Catholic Church's growing strength in Ireland and what was perceived to be its quest for power and privileges, especially in the educational sphere.[60] In the Presbyterian mind, both in Ulster and in Scotland, there was little doubt that Catholicism meant intellectual 'enslavement'. Significantly, in the 1910–14 Home Rule crisis period, the implications of the Catholic Church decrees 'Ne Temere' (1908) and 'Motu Proprio' (1911) aroused excited comment in Scotland.[61] The strongest messages and gestures of Scottish support received by Ulster Unionists tended to be in the spirit of a 'stop Popery' crusade, a good example being the deputation from the Free Church of Scotland to the Irish Presbyterian Church General Assembly in Belfast in 1893.[62] The ministers on this deputation claimed to represent 285 ministers and 386 elders and deacons of the Free Church Presbytery of Edinburgh. Their gesture was the more joyfully received on account of the reputation of the Free Church for a radical political disposition and, indeed, of rumours which had circulated hitherto in Ulster that they were in alliance with the Irish Nationalists.[63] There had been, however, something of a Dissenting rapport between the Irish Presbyterians and the Free Churches in Scotland since the time of the Great Disruption in Scotland in 1843.[64]

If Scottish support for Loyalist resistance to Home Rule was less than full-blooded in the years of the first two Home Rule Bills, the ambiguity remained during the period of the third. In the period 1910–14 the Unionist press in Ulster periodically betrayed very clearly their dismay regarding the measure of support for Home Rule among both Scottish Presbyterians and English nonconformists.[65] In Scotland, Ulster Protestant immigrants and their descendants expressed exasperation with the apparent indifference shown to their cause by some Scottish Protestants. The following outburst by the Reverend Victor Logan, an Ulster-born minister in Scotland about whom Lord Rosebery would have been eloquent, encapsulated their feelings and their view of what Irish Home Rule would mean:

> If the present generation of Scotchmen who wished to force Home Rule, that is to say, Rome Rule, on Ireland, could be lifted out of their glorious little country and set down for about three weeks in some central province in South America, they would come home again cured of their growing indifference for Protestantism and cured of a desire to force Ulster under the tyranny and the foot of the Church of Rome.[66]

Unionist frustrations of this kind were nonetheless tempered by the belief that their co-religionists would eventually come round to their way of thinking, that it only required increased propaganda efforts[67] and increased emphasis on historical and traditional bonds. In an editorial, the *Belfast Weekly News* painted the standard Unionist picture of Irish Home Rule as Catholic sectarian tyranny and stated: 'And this is the system of government which the Nonconformists of England and the Presbyterians of Scotland are to be asked to set up in Ireland. We are confident that when they know the truth they will indignantly refuse to betray their Protestant fellow-subjects.'[68] Referring to a proposed Presbyterian anti-Home Rule Convention in Belfast, a columnist in the *Belfast Weekly News* who styled himself 'Ulster Orangeman' testily declared: 'First the Presbyterian Church will made its protest against the betrayal which the Nonconformists across the water meditate. It should carry weight with the Nonconformists of England and the Presbyterians of Scotland who are up to the neck in the conspiracy to hand their brethren in Ulster over to the powers of Rome.'[69]

Again, as in the previous crises, it seemed to be felt by Unionists that the heterodox nature of their movement was not being appreciated across the water, that, in particular, the Liberal Presbyterian element in the movement needed to make its presence more clearly felt. Again, their Nationalist opponents appeared to be having a great deal of success in depicting Unionism as essentially an ascendancy movement. The Presbyterians moved to counter this, and organised a huge Convention in Belfast in 1912 in the manner of previous Unionist extravaganzas. In a sense, indeed, this mode of demonstration and protest can be viewed as essentially a Presbyterian radical tradition dating back in Ireland to the Volunteer conventions of the 1780s and 90s — a resort to extra-parliamentary means to express what Marianne Elliott has labelled a sense of 'persecuted righteousness'. Within this tradition of protest, Elliott suggests, there was always the suggestion of a Presbyterian elitist belief in their own capacity to know what was best for their country. Just as this was a feature of the United Irishmen, so was it on display throughout the Home Rule crises.[70] In its often 'purist' cast of mind, in its stress on principle, in its mentality of resistance, and in its unshakeable sense of moral righteousness and destiny, the radical Presbyterian spirit of Scottish provenance has infused both Irish republicanism and Unionism.

Moreover, the example of the Convention held by Presbyterians in 1912, which will be looked at in detail, suggests that the Unionist tactic of appealing in a dramatic manner to British opinion was a consistent feature of their campaign in all Home Rule crises. Arguably, Alvin Jackson, in stressing the 'localization' of Ulster Unionist politics in the third Home Rule crisis, overestimates the degree to which this mode of appeal to British public opinion was downgraded as a tactic.[71]

The Presbyterian anti-Home Rule Convention was held in Belfast on 1 February 1912. It was a demonstration explicitly conceived to influence British 'progressive', and in particular Scottish Presbyterian, opinion. In the columns of the Irish Presbyterian journal *The Witness* in the weeks before the Convention, there are many indications of this. It was emphasised that the Convention was not an Orange demonstration, that Presbyterians of all political persuasions would take part but that many would 'favour much of the policy of the Government apart from Home Rule.'[72] It was considered vital to counter the Home Rulers' propaganda among Scottish Presbyterians which was perceived to be systematic,[73] and which was making much capital out of the existence of Irish Presbyterian Home Rulers such as the Reverend J. B. Armour of Ballymoney.[74] The paper also carried a 'Scottish Church News' column and urged the establishment of more links between ministers in Ulster and Scotland.[75] It was admitted that there were lay and clerical Presbyterians unhappy about associating with 'Tories, landlords and Orangemen' but stated: 'If there should be any error at all in such association, we think it would be for the sake of the country better to err with Sir Edward Carson than shine with Mr Redmond or Mr Devlin and those behind them; to err with the Unionist Council than shine with the United Irish League and the Ancient Order of Hibernians'.[76]

In its editorial written just before the Convention, the *Witness* then highlighted what it clearly believed was the heart of the matter: the imperishable Ulster-Scottish bond. It stated:

> The Irish Presbyterians desire to appeal in the first instance to Scottish Presbyterians. The vast majority of them are descendants of the Scottish Presbyterians who were sent over three centuries ago to colonise and develop Ulster in the interests of civilisation and the kingdom . . . One of the resolutions makes a special reference to the Scottish Settlement, and a special appeal to Scottish Presbyterians, not to desert the descendants of those who were sent over to plant Ulster, and leave them to the uncovenanted mercies of Mr Redmond and the Irish Romanists, who threaten them with the strong arm because they are true to Scottish traditions, Scottish religion, and Scottish associations, and who have been systematically taunted and insulted as West Britons, and whom Mr Redmond has threatened to put down with the strong hand.[77]

The Convention attracted an estimated 40–50,000 male Presbyterians to Belfast, half of the adult male Presbyterian population in Ulster according to the calculations of the *Glasgow Herald* which was very impressed by it.[78] The Convention issued an appeal to 'Loyal England and Scotland', but as is clear from at least one of the resolutions passed and the accompanying declaration, the main target audience was Scotland. The resolutions claimed that Irish Home Rule would:

1. imperil religion and civil liberties;

2. injure industrial and agricultural interests;

3. curtail the main philanthropic and missionary enterprises of the Irish Presbyterian Church at home and abroad;

4. endanger the congregations and livelihoods of ministers where Presbyterians (many of them consisting of settlers from Scotland) were in the minority in Ireland; and

5. increase the Roman Catholic hierarchy's power over education, which would result in the 'denominationalising' of education in Ireland leading to children of minorities suffering.[79]

The opening declaration of the convention then went on to state:

> In our opposition to Home Rule we are activated by no spirit of sectarian exclusiveness and we seek for no ascendancy religious or

otherwise. Many of us were active sharers in the struggle which, over forty years ago, secured religious equality and initiated land reform in Ireland; and, if permitted, we are all of us ready to co-operate with Irishmen of every creed in the advancement of the social, moral, and material prosperity of our common country. Our demand is, as a matter of elementary right and justice, the undisturbed continuance of our present place in the constitution under which our Church and our country have so signally prospered.

Our Scottish forefathers, in their struggles for religious freedom and civil right, cast their burden on the Lord Omnipotent, who gave them signal victory. Facing as we do now, dangers similar to theirs, we shall follow in their footsteps and emulate their faith. In the profound belief that God reigns, we commit our cause in all confidence to Him.

Some comments might be made on these resolutions and the declaration. Apart from the explicit reference to Scotland in number four, it might also have been the case that resolution number three in its reference to missionary activities abroad was attempting to strike a chord with Scots who were so proud of their missionary work in the Empire, and that resolution number five was in part an attempt to play on the traditional Scottish Presbyterian emphasis on education and similarly fearful view of Papal power. The declaration, besides identifying with past Scottish struggles, makes pointed reference to the struggle for Church disestablishment in Ireland which was an assault on Anglican/Episcopalian privilege, and to the land reform struggle which was against landlordism. Clearly, Scottish Presbyterian sensitivities were uppermost in the organisation of the Convention. Later speakers returned to these themes: much was made of Catholic educational separatism;[80] of the 'Ne Temere' decree of 1908 which stipulated that mixed marriages were only valid if sanctified by the rites of the Roman Catholic Church and that the children should be brought up Catholic;[81] and of the Presbyterians' wish only for equality and justice and their traditional opposition to ascendancy which had led them to fight battles for Catholics in the past as well as for themselves.[82] Displays of prejudice and crude bigotry were, in fact, conspicuous by their absence with several speakers taking pains to accord brotherly sentiments to their 'Roman Catholic fellow countrymen' while expressing their fears about Catholic Church aspirations.[83]

The Chairman of the Convention, Thomas Sinclair, recalled Scottish assistance for Ulster Presbyterians during the persecutions of 1641 and expressed confidence that they would come to their aid again. Sinclair then went on to predict what a Home Rule parliament would be like and in so doing identified the vehicle through which the Catholic Church would exercise domination: 'a body composed of men the great majority of whom would be the nominees of secret societies like the Ancient Order of Hibernians,[84] and utterly inexperienced in financial and industrial affairs'. The Ulster Presbyterians, as their historians have pointed out, took the view that they had escaped the Anglican ascendancy with its denial of the validity of their marriages and legitimacy of their children, and were thus not going to risk a situation where there would be a Roman Catholic ascendancy leaving Presbyterians again in a disadvantaged position.[85]

The Scottish flavour of the Convention was added to by the contribution of a minister from Edinburgh, Dr Salmond, who claimed that he spoke for a great many Scots in expressing sympathy with the Protestants of Ireland in their quest to avert 'a great calamity to their beloved Emerald Isle, and a source of weakness to the Empire'. Salmond further declared that the Liberal government was dependent on support of people who did not have at heart 'the good of the British Empire', and ended by saying that 'as a Scottish Presbyterian conversant with Irish conditions, and mindful of many ancestral traditions — John Knox, Andrew Melville, Jenny Geddes, Thomas Chalmers — he said, "God shield and prosper you!".' Following Salmond, the Rt. Hon. John Young identified the Irish Presbyterians with the Scottish Church, going so far as to say they were a 'Scottish colony' enjoying in the Parliament of the United Kingdom 'civil and religious liberty such as was enjoyed in no other part of the world.' The Imperial connection was stressed by a Dr. R. Henry and a William Colhoun, the latter declaring that 'they would not be driven out from their share of the heritage of the greatest Empire ever known.'

In Scotland itself there were signs that Scottish Presbyterians were responding to Ulster's appeals — messages were sent to the Convention from Churches and individuals,[86] although one well-wisher, William Whitelaw, the Chairman of the Highland Railway, felt constrained to admit that political factors stood in the way of more solid support:

> In the coming fight the Irish Presbyterians will have the assistance and the sympathy of the majority of Presbyterians in Scotland, but I regret to say that I know that a large number of Scottish Presbyterians are so bound by hereditary devotion to the shibboleths of Radicalism that

they will desert their Presbyterian brethren in Ireland rather than range themselves for once among the supporters of the Unionist party.[87]

As in previous years, the Unionists found it hard to get an enthusiastic Protestant response beyond the West of Scotland industrial heartland. Within that heartland, and especially among the Liberal Unionists of the area, the Ulster cause was depicted in terms every bit as apocalyptic as in Ulster itself. In December 1912, for example, the minutes of the West of Scotland Liberal Unionist Association record the following eulogy to the Ulster Unionists:

> In Ulster the fight is hottest [in 'the battle of the Union against Disruption']. The finest population in Ireland are being driven to extremes, and are imploring our help. They believe that their rights as British citizens, the peace of their homes, the prosperity of their businesses, their religious freedom itself, are all involved in the struggle. No Scotsman could read without deep emotion the narrative of a vast and loyal population, closely united to us by ties of race and religion, flocking to their Churches to implore the most High to avert the threatened danger, and we in the West of Scotland, of all in the British Isles, should hold out a strong hand to them in their hour of distress.[88]

Similarly, the *Glasgow Herald* newspaper, befitting its Unionist disposition of the time, editorialised regularly in favour of Ulster and argued, at the time of the Presbyterian Convention, that if 'Glasgow and Clydesdale' were in the position of Unionist Ulster, 'we should talk and act much as do our kinsfolk across the Irish Channel'.[89]

Later in February 1912, after the Convention, the Glasgow Presbytery of the Church of Scotland passed a motion of sympathy for Ulster,[90] while in October of that year a special meeting of the Presbytery of the more radically-inclined United Free Church (an amalgamation, effected in 1900, of the Free and United Presbyterian Churches) was called to 'correct' the impression given that they were not in sympathy with the Ulster Protestants.[91] This suggests that some movement may have been afoot among Presbyterians of a Liberal and Radical hue in favour of the Ulster cause, but much more work has to be done on the Scottish response to Ulster's propaganda efforts outside Conservative and Orange circles before this issue can be discussed with any assurance. It was certainly the case, however, that developments such as the 'Ne Temere' decree (1908) disturbed Scottish Protestants of all denominations and political views. Moreover, the impact in

Scotland of the massive numbers who signed the Ulster covenant
pledging resistance to Home Rule in September 1912, may have
been heightened by the event's conscious attempt to summon the
historical inspiration of the Scottish Covenant; certainly, the Covenanters were still a central part of Scotland's historical self-image,
and tales of persecution and sacrifice continued to provide much
fuel for Protestant militancy.[92] As a speaker, T. G. Houston, had put
it at the Presbyterian Convention:

> It was beginning to dawn on the people of England and Scotland that
> they had made a serious mistake about Ulster. They thought that they
> were listening only to an ebullition of jingoism. But to their astonish-
> ment and indignation they had found that it was not with the jingo
> spirit, but with the martyr spirit they had to deal. . . .[93]

However, the magnitude of Ulster Unionist demonstrations could
not entirely eclipse the Achilles heel of Protestant Home Rule
support, whether in Ireland or in different parts of Britain. It was
all the more galling, then, that a Scottish Presbyterian should stand
on a Home Rule platform at a by-election in Derry City in January
1913. The candidate, Douglas Hogg, refused to take the pledge of
the Irish Nationalist Party, but they nonetheless campaigned for
him vigorously in the knowledge that such a candidate was grist to
their propaganda mill in relation to Home Rule being a non-sec-
tarian cause. From the reactions of the Unionist press it seems that
they had some success in fomenting divisions between Presbyterians and Episcopalians in Derry, and that they astutely played
up the Establishment Episcopalian credentials of the Unionist
candidate Colonel Pakenham. The *Belfast Weekly News* fulminated
over 'the Scotchman Lundy' whom they viewed as seeking to
deliver them into the hands of 'the pikemen of the Hibernians',[94]
and there were hints that Conservative/Orange disparagement of
the Presbyterian Liberal tradition in Ulster might strain the unity
of Unionism.[95]

Hogg was duly elected by 2,699 votes to 2,642, a majority of 57.
In the *Belfast Weekly News* 'Scots Wha Hae' was rewritten and
dedicated to Hogg as follows:

> What care you for kith and kin?
> Butter's thick and blood is thin
> Majorities are sure to win
> Minorities be hanged.'[96]

Thus, it was as much characteristic of Ulster Unionism as a general movement to allege betrayal and accuse their 'kith and kin' of letting them down, as it was to proclaim the imperishability of these kinship and religious bonds.

The Irish Presbyterian Church, at their Assembly in June 1913, made it more than clear that their opposition to Home Rule was unimpeachable. The vote taken on it resulted in a 921 to 43 result against it. Moreover, the Moderator, in his address, struck an unambiguous note of British patriotism:

> Seldom, if ever, have any of us been ashamed to declare we are Britons . . . whatever quarrels with British policy members of the Assembly may have had from time to time, and whatever their views of the best solution of the Irish problem, the sentiment of loyalty towards and pride in the British inheritance and Commonwealth of peoples has been common to us all.[97]

The *Belfast Weekly News* could have had no complaint about that.

V

Ulster Unionism was a social and political movement difficult to categorise or define, except in the negative sense of its defiance of the perceived Home Rule threat. Jennifer Todd has remarked on the 'multiple, competing, contradictory' versions of Unionism which emerged at the time of the Home Rule crises, an ideological pot pourri which reflected the internal diversity of the movement and the way in which its ideological emphases changed in accordance with the demands of British public opinion, the arguments of Irish nationalists or the internal political requirements of the movement.[98]

However, some scholars and commentators have tried to pinpoint its essence. For Professor Joseph Lee, for example, it was racism.[99] Lee's contention seems to be based on the cultivation of the 'Ulsterman' stereotype referred to earlier. Undoubtedly, there was implicit in this stereotype a suggestion of superiority over the 'other Irish'. The Orange Order, which became increasingly important both organisationally and culturally to the Unionist movement in this era, certainly conveyed something of this in its imagery, its songs, and its catchcries. David Hempton and Myrtle Hill, in their study of evangelicalism in Ulster society, have pointed to the way in which, ideologically, evangelicalism played a significant role in shaping the anti-Catholicism of the Ulster Protestant mind and sharpening it into the defensive 'zero-sum game' type of outlook which came to characterise much of the Protestant-Catholic dialogue in Ulster.[100] However, Hempton and Hill also argue that ethnic stereotyping was based more on religious and cultural assumptions than on scientific or racial observations: 'Irish Catholics were economically and culturally inferior, not primarily because of their racial pedigree, but because of their religion.'[101]

It might be added that, returning to Orangeism, the Order was an organisation less concerned with boasting about racial superiority than with decrying what it viewed as the Catholic Church's striving for ascendancy over Protestantism in Ireland, and the activities of the Orange society's mirror-image: the Catholic sectarian secret society, the Ancient Order of Hibernians.

In many ways the Orange Order viewed the struggle as one between tribal secret societies, a zero-sum game in which there could be no compromises; it was, indeed, a struggle which had its roots in the late eighteenth century when the Orange Order was set up to fight the Catholic Ribbonmen and Defender societies. It is a perspective caught well by T. G. Houston, one of the most skilful of the Presbyterian Unionist propagandists, in a letter to the press in 1913:

> I have followed the controversy since the days of Isaac Butt, and I can find in it only one argument for Home Rule, an argument which was 'summarily comprehended' in the concluding words of an Ancient Hibernian and an Orangeman after a heated discussion on the subject of Home Rule.'We'll raise hell if you don't give us Home Rule.''You'll raise worse hell if we do.' That way of putting the case leaves, perhaps something to be desired in the matter of elegance of language, but nothing in the way of clearness and completeness in stating the point at issue.[102]

The extent to which Unionists feared the AOH has not been appreciated in scholarly accounts of Nationalism, Unionism and the Home Rule era. It was, in fact, the movement's prime bugbear in its perceived role as the tool of the Catholic Church and the Irish Parliamentary Party out to destroy Protestantism. In their propaganda the Unionists painted a vividly demonic picture of it for British consumption,[103] and the Unionist lawyer, A. W. Samuels, claimed both that its object was the 'extermination' of the Protestant community in Ireland,[104] and that it had, in the wake of the removal in 1910 by the Catholic hierarchy of a ban imposed on it, expanded rapidly in Scotland, especially in Glasgow, Lanarkshire and Renfrewshire.[105] Certainly, Scottish Orangeism was preoccupied with a similar perception of the AOH's strength, influence and intentions.

Besides Orangeism being essentially defensive rather than assertive of racial superiority, it might be said that the component of the Unionist resistance exemplified in the Presbyterian Convention speeches quoted above was a powerful influence against Unionism taking on the character of an ascendancy caste protecting privileges. The Nationalist attempts to depict it in this light, while admittedly successful in terms of propaganda impact through the years, were disingenuous in their pretence that Presbyterian liberalism or radicalism was wholly on the side of Home Rule. In fact, much the greater part of it was not, although it has to be said that many Presbyterians of these political leanings in Scotland could not endorse their Ulster co-religionists' willingness to sink their differences with the Conservative and landlord wing of Unionism. It should also be noted that the Orange Order, although still largely identified with the landed class and Established Church ethos of its origins, became a pan-denominational Protestant front organisation in the nineteenth century and was acceptable to many Presbyterians, especially after the disestablishment of the Church of Ireland in 1869. Its main function was to forge Protestant unity which was felt, in the circumstances of Home Rule, to be paramount by a majority in all Protestant denominations in Ireland.

'Race' was a term often used loosely and ambiguously at this time.[106] It is to read too much into terms like 'sturdy race' or 'imperial race' to draw conclusions about Unionism being essentially racist. In the first instance, there were as many Unionist statements disavowing claims to superiority and ascendancy and acknowledging the mixed race characteristics of the peoples of the British Isles in general;[107] secondly, it might be said that statements by Irish Nationalist leaders, such as Arthur Griffith, the founder of Sinn Fein, were more explicitly racist than anything recorded by Unionist leaders.[108]

It is also difficult to sum up Unionism in relation to questions of national identity. A plurality of identities has to be acknowledged, although it has again to be emphasised that there was an unequivocal and positive identification with Britain and the Empire which was complemented, not contradicted, by the cultivation of a spirit of Ulster independence as befitting a people who saw themselves in 'the front line' or as 'under siege', and by a specific appeal, on the part of arguably the most important sector of the Ulster Protestant community,[109] to an historic Ulster-Scottish bond forged through centuries of common religious (Presbyterian) struggle and social and cultural interaction.

What Unionists were rejecting between 1886 and 1920 was the idea that they would be cut off from the rest of the U.K. Their deep sense of attachment was particularly marked in relation to Scotland and things Scottish. Their past link with Scotland and the extent to which Scottish traditions and values had shaped Ulster provided their most glowing testimonial — their right to resist, their right to assert difference although not necessarily superiority.

The Irish Nationalist 'other' was in reality a multi-headed 'beast'. The impact of Fenianism since the 1860s made Home Rule problematic when it took centre stage politically in the 1880s; the Unionists could never simply regard it as an end in itself. Unionists could not trust Nationalists to accept a wider Imperial identity; they always suspected that the Fenian goal of separation would be pursued. Parnell's ambiguities in this respect did not help. Redmond was a more reassuring figure up to a point, but beyond him Unionists saw Joe Devlin and his AOH, and John Dillon, a man quite clearly 'anti-British' in the Unionist mind.[110]

There were many Ulster Unionists who seemed to believe in a British nation; and they probably believed in it more strongly than anyone else. Others probably saw Britishness, as it can be argued most Scots saw it, as a composite identity uniting four different national identities one of which was divided within itself about the nature of the relationship to the others: Unionist wanted no change in it; Nationalists did.

Whatever the internal logic of Ulster Unionism, however, the image presented to the outside world could not avoid seeming insecure and muddled: threats of rebellion mingling with proclamations of loyalty; religious fears cutting across sacred political divisions. For all the appeal to history, the Ulster Protestant sense of what was historically significant could appear too diffuse and incoherent for even Scots Presbyterians to feel affinity with; the essentially Scottish Presbyterian politics and mentality of resistance and protest became obscured to outsiders as it was absorbed into a display of what could appear to be Loyalist special pleading. If the Ulster Presbyterians were the backbone of Ulster Protestantism they did not, ultimately, have a monopoly in defining its overall identity. No neat and tidy mythological narrative of the Ulster Protestants' progress was constructed to match the kind fashioned by such as Patrick Pearse to serve the Irish Nationalist cause.[111] By comparison with the Ulster Protestants, the Catholic Irish story was all the more powerful for its capacity to be reduced to one of an oppressed people rising up and winning their place in the sun.

The Ulster Protestants make their appeal for support in this period with all too apparent anxiety and without the historicist confidence of the Irish Nationalists. Moreover, they make the strongest appeal to a nation, Scotland, which at this juncture is perhaps at its peak in terms of a confident image of itself as a great ancient nation, possessed of internationally renowned traditions and confident of its capacity to carry on achieving greatness and influencing world developments. Scotland saw itself at this time as having the right blend of a working relationship with England, and a cultural distinctiveness which included a Jacobite romanticism to denote potential rebelliousness and independence of spirit, and a thrawn, egalitarian Protestantism which facilitated engagement with the demands and challenges of the modern world at home and abroad.

The Scots' sense of their identity, enhanced through involvement in Empire to which their Protestantism was central, was of an expansive kind in many ways too impatient with the insecurities, the complexities, the narrowness and the defensiveness of Ulster's outlook and preoccupations. In a way, however, this might have been an indication of the Scots' conceit of themselves preventing consideration of the role that large numbers of Irish immigrants (both Catholic and Protestant) were playing in refashioning Scottish society and the overall sense of Scottish national and cultural identity. Beyond the self-proclaimed expansiveness of attitude there perhaps lay an element of insularity which should have caused more critical self-examination than was evident.

VI

The issue of Irish Home Rule was the catalyst for a wider constitutional debate in the U.K. c. 1880–1920.[112] The prospect of a separate parliament for Ireland prompted many politicians and political thinkers, across the political spectrum, to consider the extension of the principle in the direction of some kind of 'federal' U.K., or, as it was more colloquially known, 'Home Rule All

Round'. The Empire loomed large in these deliberations; many British statesmen were concerned about the integrity of the Empire and feared the possible disruptive effects of an Irish measure. Whether out of such anxiety, or on the basis of the more positive visions of Liberal Imperialists like Rosebery, much came to be claimed for 'Home Rule All Round' in relation to the cause of Imperial unity.

Thus federalist-sounding ideas entered British political debate in earnest, although the term 'federal' was used loosely and usually incorrectly; the great majority of participants in the debate envisaged devolution with supreme sovereignty continuing to rest at Westminster, not, as in the proper definition of federalism, a division of sovereignty between the centre and local legislatures. 'Home Rule All Round' meant, therefore, separate devolved legislative assemblies for Scotland, England, Wales and Ireland with an 'Imperial' Parliament at Westminster (in which ultimate sovereignty resided) dealing with issues common to all such as foreign policy and defence. In addition to Imperial concerns, there were arguments for such a development which surrounded the issue of the 'overload' of parliamentary business at Westminster; it was believed by many that local affairs could be dealt with more efficiently by local assemblies. Foreshadowing political debates well into the future, great claims were made about devolution across the board leading to more efficient and accountable government.

The 'federal' debate soon, however, revealed the difficulties of applying devolution all round. England, for instance, was so much bigger and more powerful than the other constituent nations that devolution would be all but impossible to apply in a uniform manner across the U.K. Suggestions that devolution be on a regional rather than a national basis ran the risk of offending nationalist sentiment and faced the problem of creating new regional identities.

Notwithstanding obvious problems, the 'Home Rule All Round' lobby succeeded in stimulating Home Rule sentiment in Scotland and Wales. In Scotland, a significant amount of *administrative* devolution already existed. In 1885 a separate Scottish Office, headed by a Minister (later upgraded to Secretary of State), was established; this was the culmination of years of complaints by senior Scottish politicians like Lord Rosebery that the handling of Scottish business was inefficient. From 1885 functions previously discharged in Scotland by the Home Office, the Privy Council, the

Treasury, and the Local Government Board were transferred to the new department. From 1892 the Scottish Minister had a seat in cabinet.

In 1886 a Scottish Home Rule Association (SHRA) was set up as an extra-parliamentary pressure group seeking further progress towards a measure of self-government. Sympathetic to the new lobby were Liberals like Rosebery and Campbell-Bannerman, cognisant of the nationalist feelings in Liberal strongholds of the Scottish Highlands. The leading light of the SHRA was, in its early phase, a radical crofters' rights champion, Dr. G. B. Clark. However, the coolness of another Scottish Liberal (and Ulster-born) figure, James Bryce, was typical of those close to Gladstone: nothing was to be allowed to detract from the 'Grand Old Man's' Irish 'crusade'.[113]

In Scotland Home Rule was to become a stated political objective of both the Liberal Party and the Scottish Labour Party after its formation in 1888. It was to be taken up also by the Independent Labour Party (formed 1893) which developed a strong base in west-central Scotland. However, Home Rule was part of Scottish political culture on the level of an *idea* which provoked discussion and a measure of controversy; it did not release any wave of nationalist feeling in the country in any way comparable to that in Ireland. Those who favoured the idea were for the most part as or more concerned about the issue of the integrity of the Empire; Rosebery's views quoted earlier were widely held. For most Scots at this time Home Rule was not looked to in any spirit of national regeneration; as argued above, Scottish national self-confidence and security of identity were not in such doubt. Besides boasting their own separate institutions, Scots could, for example, reflect on the way the Westminster Parliament had to adapt Scottish legislation to take account of the Scottish legal system, or on the fact that, in contrast to Ireland, the executive acts of government in Scotland were carried out by Scots.

In 1893 Gladstone introduced his second Irish Home Rule Bill (the first having been defeated in the House of Commons and having split the Liberal Party in the process). The new bill disappointed 'Home Rule All Rounders' in that it was an Irish-only measure. Further, it made no provision for *Ulster*, and it was of course the Ulster difficulty which was to become increasingly intractable in the course of discussions on wider constitutional change. On the other hand, problematic as it was, the Ulster question stimulated wider interest in 'Home Rule All Round' as a means of both solving the Irish question *and* promoting Imperial federation. This will be considered below.

Besides the question of Ulster, Gladstone ran into a storm of controversy by providing for the retention of Irish MPs at Westminster after a Home Rule parliament had been set up in Dublin. This was a question which was to haunt the whole issue of devolution: if, to take the Irish example, a Dublin Parliament was set up to deal with purely Irish business, would Ireland continue to send MPs to Westminster where they could have a say about purely English, or Scottish or Welsh business? Gladstone, having decided in the negative in 1886, reversed his decision in 1893 and thus triggered a constitutional conundrum which was to resurface in the future, most notably in the 1970s debate about devolution for Scotland and Wales. At this time the issue was re-christened the 'West Lothian Question' after the constituency represented by the anti-devolution Labour MP Tam Dalyell who put the issue at the forefront of his campaign against devolution. There was, at least, a neat sense of symmetry about the question being raised, albeit in different ways, by members identified with the Lothian region.

There was also the question of financial provisions, the calculation of Ireland's imperial contribution and estimate of her likely reserves. These bedevilled Gladstone's scheme, both in 1886 and 1893, and foreshadowed the problems there would be when Northern Ireland was given its own Parliament. As perhaps the best analyst of these issues in the Gladstonian era, John Kemble, has put it: 'It was obvious that serious difficulties would always confront those attempting to divide taxing powers in order to meet the needs and responsibilities of a portion of a country which in some matters was self-governing but which, in others, such as defence and foreign policy, was clearly dependent'.[114]

The most serious problems emerging from both Gladstone's attempts at Home Rule for Ireland can perhaps be listed as follows:

1. the issue of Irish representation in the Westminster Parliament after an Irish Parliament had been set up;

2. the issue of Ireland's financial contributions to the Imperial Exchequer; and

3. the issue of the protection of minorities, or specifically in relation to Ireland at this time the issue of the Unionist resistance to Home Rule, concentrated in Ulster.

Gladstone's second bill fell at the House of Lords hurdle, and his government soon fell with it. The constitutional debate went rather into abeyance in the late 1890s and early 1900s, notwithstanding the proposed devolution schemes for Ireland in 1904 and 1907 which were too little for the Nationalists and too much for the Unionists.[115] It was only when, in the period 1910–14, the constitution became the central issue in British politics with the Liberal Government's assault on the House of Lords' power of veto, that interest in 'Home Rule All Round' really revived.

In this period most of the prominent advocates were Conservatives and Unionists who saw the plan as the best way of maintaining the Union. Particularly important, in terms of ideas and the way the case for 'Home Rule All Round' was publicised, was Frederick Scott Oliver, a Scot, and English Unionists such as Lord Selborne and Earl Grey. However, the leader of the Unionists (as the Conservative Party was then commonly called), Arthur Balfour, was a strong opponent of 'federal devolution'. He spoke for those who considered any constitutional tinkering to be a mistake and his objections echoed the arguments of the constitutional lawyer Albert Venn Dicey who had opposed Gladstonian Home Rule for Ireland. Dicey had argued that any kind of federal plan would destroy the sovereignty of Parliament, would diminish the power of Great Britain, and would only increase the likelihood of friction between rival parliaments. To these arguments Balfour added his belief that federation in the U.K. — in contrast to America, Canada and elsewhere — would not be a step to unification (because there already was a unitary system of government) but would instead be a step to separation. These arguments — of Dicey and of Balfour — have been used repeatedly by opponents of devolution and federalism in the U.K. since this pre-first world war period.

However, the reformers argued in turn that what they were seeking was *not* the destruction or the weakening of the sovereignty of Parliament (and therefore not true federalism), and that if constitutional change did not take place it would be too late to save the Union — in other words, it was no use Balfour complaining of the Union being weakened by federalism when his policy would lead to its breakup.[116]

The matter attained a new peak of urgency after 1910 when the Liberal Government — intent on wiping out the veto power of the House of Lords — was dependent on the support of Irish Nationalist MPs at Westminster for its survival. Another Home

Rule Bill — the third — was thus prepared, and the federal devolutionists attempted as far as they could to ensure that the Bill
would be part of a wider scheme of 'Home Rule All Round'.
Scottish Liberal members exerted pressure on the Prime Minister,
Asquith, to this end.[117]

However, Asquith's Irish Home Rule Bill when it appeared in
1912 bore the Gladstonian rather than the federal stamp — its
critics claimed it was incompatible with Home Rule All Round,
although Asquith himself in the House of Commons stated that it
was his hope that the Bill would be followed by others for Scotland,
England and Wales. However, the nature of the Bill ensured that
the *Ulster* problem, rather than questions of wider devolution,
would take up future political energies. The Bill did not provide for
any exclusion of Ulster — which the Ulster Unionists demanded —
and in its financial clauses it was clear that the Unionist arguments
about the revenues of the industrialised North of Ireland being
used to shore up the rural Southern economy, were ignored. The
Ulster Unionist opposition to Home Rule thus intensified, with
Edward Carson and James Craig promising the establishment of a
provincial government in Ulster if Irish Home Rule were forced
upon them, and the Ulster Volunteer Force (UVF) being armed to
resist by force. The 1911 Parliament Act took away the House of
Lords' power of veto which meant that after passing its third reading in the House of Commons, the Irish Home Rule Bill would
automatically become law. Hence the build-up of tension in the
1912–14 period.

To avert possible civil war, which indeed looked likely, the federal devolutionists redoubled their efforts. They argued that *only*
'Home Rule All Round' could satisfy both Unionists and Nationalists in Ireland. However, they underestimated, firstly, the extent
to which the Nationalists felt that Ireland — in their leader John
Redmond's words — was 'an entirely exceptional case', and that
Ireland merited separate priority treatment without having to wait
on Scotland, England and Wales coming round to the idea of Home
Rule. And, secondly, they underestimated the extent to which the
Unionists were determined not to have Dublin rule in any form,
even as part of a wider U.K. settlement; a constant theme in the
Unionist campaign was that they considered 'safeguards' to be
futile, that in *practice* a Dublin Parliament would ride over these
and would defy Westminster. For the Unionists, there was no security in any form of Dublin rule whatever the context.

The First World War effectively transformed the context of the constitutional debate. In Ireland the Easter Rebellion and its bloody aftermath altered the mood of the country towards full independence or Dominion status and away from Home Rule. Sinn Fein eclipsed the Irish Parliamentary Party and won a landslide election victory in 1918. The Irish problem both North and South took on a character which rendered a federal-type solution increasingly unlikely, although efforts continued to be made to find such a solution during the war. After the war a Cabinet committee (of the now coalition Liberal/Conservative government headed by Lloyd George) was formed to draw up new legislation for Ireland. The Government of Ireland Act of 1920 resulted. This did not establish a federal system in Ireland but it did keep the door open for eventual federal unity in the U.K. Ireland was to be given two parliaments — one for the South, one for the six north-eastern counties (Armagh, Londonderry, Fermanagh, Tyrone, Antrim, Down), and a Council of Ireland was to deal with business common to both. Neither Parliament was given significant revenue-raising powers — these were to be retained at Westminster.

The Government of Ireland Act was in fact designed to bring about Irish unity at a later stage *and* to retain the link with Britain, perhaps even leading to a wider U.K. devolved government settlement. However, the Act could not be implemented in the South where a guerrilla war raged from the end of 1919 between the Irish Republican Army (IRA) and the British army, augmented by the notorious 'Black and Tans'. Republican feeling was now strong in Ireland. Eventually the question was resolved by means of the 'Anglo-Irish' Treaty of December 1921 which conferred Dominion status on the 26 county 'Irish Free State', a considerable advance on the Home Rule envisaged in the Government of Ireland Act. However, even this was not securely put in place until a civil war was fought out between those in favour of acceptance of the settlement and those who wanted to maintain the struggle for a republic completely separate from Britain.

The Government of Ireland Act was implemented in the North with the establishment of the Northern Ireland Parliament in June 1921. What is important to stress is that the separate Northern Ireland Parliament was not set up with powers designed for the operation of devolved government as had been originally envisaged in the Irish Home Rule schemes; rather, they had been designed to facilitate the union of Ireland at which time additional powers would have been transferred. The Ulster Unionists had not requested such a Parliament and Carson, indeed, was dismayed by the outcome. All the problems which had bedevilled Gladstone and Asquith were still unresolved in the financial relationship between central and local legislature; the role of Ulster MPs at Westminster; and the minority problem which, in the new 'Northern Ireland' state meant the sizeable Catholic and Nationalist minority (about a third of the population) who were now cut off from their fellow Nationalists and co-religionists in the rest of Ireland.[118]

The devolution, or 'federal', issue in British politics was thus inspired by and linked closely to the demand for Irish Home Rule which emerged in the 1870s and 1880s. It was an idea which sought to provide a logical and tidy political answer to the issue of national diversity in the U.K. The extent to which the idea took root could be viewed as recognition of the strength of these separate U.K. nationalisms, thus indicating caution about the use of terms such as 'British nation'. On the other hand the ultimate failure of the federal idea could be interpreted as evidence of the strength of the British allegiance, excepting of course Nationalist Ireland; or at least of the venerability of Britain's constitution and hallowed notions of the sovereignty of parliament.

It has also been argued that the Liberal Government of the pre-World War I period, and the coalition government after the war *used* the idea of 'Home Rule All Round' as a ploy to get the Irish question settled and out of the way. There is some scepticism about whether these governments really *then* intended to implement 'Home Rule All Round'.[119]

Certainly, it is the case that, despite Bills for *Scottish* Home Rule being put before Parliament, there was not the same degree of serious attention given to it: these bills, with one exception, never reached a decisive stage. The exception was the Bill of 1913 which actually passed its second reading by a substantial majority — if the war had not then intervened and if Irish Home Rule had been put into operation then Scottish Home Rule may have followed.

But this is all hypothetical. After the war Bills for Scottish Home Rule were presented in 1919, 1920, 1922, 1924, 1927 and 1928, but all fell at various parliamentary hurdles. With the Bill of 1928 which was not even debated, an era of more than twenty years, during which a Scottish Home Rule Bill had been almost an annual event except in wartime, was closed. After 1928, Home Rule did not impinge on Parliamentary business for over forty years.

As the new state of Northern Ireland came into being, Scotland was politically drawn more closely into the British State, a development arguably aided by the eclipse of the Liberals by Labour as the party of the left of centre. However, the idea of Home Rule and the question of Scottish nationalism and Scottish identity continued to be a signal feature of Scottish political culture, although in complex and unpredictable ways. Neither were the basic terms, language and concepts of the 'federal' debate before the first world war fated to be anachronistic; much later, as Andrew Marr has pointed out, the threads would be picked up again.[120]

NOTES

1. L. Colley, *Britons*; and L. Colley, 'Britishness and otherness: an argument', *Journal of British Studies*, Vol. 31, no. 4, pp. 309–30.
2. B. Crick, 'Essay on Britishness', *Scottish Affairs* no. 2, Winter 1993, pp. 71–83.
3. See discussion of MacKenzie's views in Angus Calder, *Revolving Culture* (London, 1994) pp. 32–36; also, G. Walker, 'Empire, Religion and Nationality in Scotland and Ulster before the First World War', in I. S. Wood (ed.), *Scotland and Ulster*. Some of the material used in this chapter first appeared in the latter article.
4. J. H. Grainger, *Patriotisms* (London, 1986) p. 51.
5. On the contrary, the heavy industry West of Scotland area in and around Glasgow benefited greatly from the connection.
6. See A. C. I. Naylor, 'Scottish Attitudes to Ireland, 1880–1914' (PhD thesis, University of Edinburgh, 1985), pp. 433–435 regarding the Scots' sense of superiority about their own institutions. See R. Mitchison, 'Nineteenth Century Scottish Nationalism: the Cultural Background', in R. Mitchison (ed.), *The Roots of Nationalism* (Edinburgh, 1980) regarding the Scots' delight in teaching the English about such matters as banking and the management of education.
7. Naylor, 'Scottish Attitudes', p. 435.
8. Quoted in I. McLeod, 'Scotland and the Liberal Party 1880–1900. Church, Ireland and Empire. A Family Affair' (MLitt thesis, University of Glasgow, 1978) p. 144.
9. For 'Home Rule All Round' see J. Kendle, *Ireland and the Federal Solution* (Kingston and Montreal, 1989); there is significant material on Scottish Home Rule and Imperial federation ideas in the papers of Alexander McCallum Scott, Glasgow University Special Collections.

10. Colley, 'Britishness and Otherness: an argument', p. 317.
11. Crick, 'Essay on Britishness'.
12. Calder op. cit.
13. Quoted in J. Adam Smith, *John Buchan* (Oxford, 1985) p. 112.
14. Adam Smith, *Buchan*, p. 318.
15. See W. McGregor Ross, *Kenya from Within* (London, 1927), especially p. 95, pp. 454–459.
16. See McKenzie's points as discussed in Calder, op. cit.
17. Although it has been argued that this did not prevent Scots behaving in racist and exploitative ways, see R. Miles and L. Muirhead, 'Racism in Scotland', *Scottish Government Yearbook* (1986) pp. 108–131.
18. See D. W. Bebbington, 'Religion and National Feeling in Nineteenth Century Wales and Scotland', in S. Mews (ed.), *Religion and National Identity: Studies in Church History* Vol. 18 (Oxford, 1982) pp. 489–503.
19. B. Aspinwall, 'The Scottish Religious Identity in the Atlantic World 1880–1914', in S. Mews (ed.), *Religion* pp. 505–518.
20. *People's Journal for Glasgow and West Scotland* 4 January 1890.
21. The memo was produced by the Committee of the Scottish Unionist Association. Bonar Law Papers, House of Lords Records Office, 32/3/30. See also the minute book of the Central Council of the Scottish Unionist Association, 17 March 1914, NLS Acc. 10424/63.
22. K. Robbins, *Nineteenth Century Britain* (Oxford, 1988) pp. 177–78.
23. Ibid. p. 178.
24. See remarks of John Morley on the Scots and imperialism quoted in L. T. Hobhouse, *Democracy and Reaction* (Brighton, 1972) p. 65.
25. See R. J. Morris, 'Scotland 1830–1914: the making of a Nation within a Nation', in W. H. Fraser and R. J. Morris (eds.), *People and Society in Scotland* Vol. II (Edinburgh, 1990).
26. P. Gibbon, *The Origins of Ulster Unionism* (Manchester, 1975); D. Miller, *Queen's Rebels*; J. Loughlin, *Gladstone, Home Rule and the Ulster Question* (Dublin, 1986); A. Jackson, *The Ulster Party*.
27. Jackson, *Ulster Party* pp. 16–17.
28. D. G. Boyce, *Nineteenth Century Ireland* (Dublin, 1990) p. 207.
29. D. G. Boyce, 'The Marginal Britons: the Irish', in R. Colls and P. Dodd (eds.) *Englishness: Politics and Culture 1880–1920* (London, 1986) pp. 230–253.
30. See T. Hennessey, 'Ulster Unionist territorial and national identities 1886–1893: province, island, kingdom and empire', *Irish Political Studies* Vol. 8 (1993) pp. 21–36.
31. See V. Bogdanor, *Devolution* (Oxford, 1979) p. 80; also L. Paterson, *The Autonomy of Modern Scotland* (Edinburgh, 1994) for an extended discussion of this theme.
32. Most Unionists at this time laid claim to some sense of Irish identity.

Many rhapsodised about Ireland and her beauties. See, for example, speeches delivered at a Glasgow–Ulster Association meeting of Ulster immigrants in Scotland as reported in the *Belfast Weekly News* 25 January 1912.

33. Thomas Sinclair's speech reported in *Northern Whig* 9 March 1895.
34. *Irish Unionist Pocket-Book* (1911), PRONI D989/C/1/11A.
35. See J. Todd, 'Unionist Political Thought 1920–70', in D. G. Boyce et al. (eds.), *Political Thought in Ireland*.
36. *The Covenanter* no. 1, 20 May 1914.
37. See Grainger, *Patriotisms* pp. 252–254.
38. See Loughlin, *Gladstone* p. 156; also the speech by Rev. Sides quoted in Hennessey op. cit.
39. See Kendle, *Ireland* passim.
40. Kendle passim; see discussion in section five of this chapter. Carson actually voiced approval of 'Federal' schemes at certain junctures. See Kendle pp. 190–91, 196, 208, 238.
41. See A. W. Samuels, *Home Rule: What is it:?* (Dublin and London, 1911), PRONI D989/C/1/13.
42. See J. Anderson, 'Ideological Variations in Ulster during Ireland's First Home Rule Crisis', in C. H. Williams and E. Kofman (eds.), *Community Conflict, Partition and Nationalism* pp. 133–166.
43. For whom see R. B. McMinn, *Against the Tide: J. B. Armour, Irish Presbyterian Minister and Home Ruler* (Belfast, 1985).
44. Quoted in H. Kearney, *The British Isles* (Cambridge, 1989), p. 186.
45. Letter from Ferguson to Rosebery, 17 August 1891 quoted in McLeod op. cit. p. 99.
46. Speech quoted in Samuels, *Home Rule*.
47. For analysis of Russell's threat to the Unionists see A. Jackson, 'Irish Unionism and the Russellite Threat, 1894–1906', *Irish Historical Studies* XXV (1986–7), pp. 370–404.
48. Something recognised by the Rev. Lynd (a Presbyterian Liberal Unionist) in an interesting speech to the Irish Presbyterian General Assembly in 1893. See *Northern Whig* 10 June 1893.
49. See McLeod op. cit. p. 110.
50. Quoted in McLeod p.158.
51. Report of speeches in Sinclair Papers, PRONI D3002/1.
52. See I. C. G. Hutchison, *A Political History of Scotland* 1832–1924 chpts. 6, 7 and 8.
53. McLeod op. cit. pp. 161–2.
54. Note the mixture of politics, folklore and popular literature in papers like the *People's Journal and The Glasgow Weekly Mail*. For the Ulster question specifically see editorial of *Glasgow Weekly Mail* 15 April 1893 where it is stated that Scottish churches were not in sympathy with Orange lodges.

55. See report of the Convention in *The Times* 18 June 1892.
56. *The Times* 18 June 1892.
57. Ibid.
58. Sinclair, indeed, worked closely with Sir Horace Plunkett on the latter's Recess Committee. See H. Plunkett, *Ireland in the New Century* (Dublin, 1983) p. 218. For Plunkett's significance in relation to 'constructive Unionism' see A. Gailey, 'Failure and the Making of the New Ireland', in D. G. Boyce (ed.), *The Revolution in Ireland* (London, 1988).
59. *Northern Whig* 9 March 1895. See also T. W. Russell, *Ireland and the Empire* (1901) p. vii.
60. See, for example, controversy over the Irish Universities Bill (1908).
61. See B. Aspinwall, 'Popery in Scotland: Image and Reality, 1820–1920', *Scottish Church History Society Records* Vol. 22 (1986) pp. 252–3.
62. *Northern Whig* 10 June 1893.
63. Ibid. See especially speeches by the Rev. Lynd and Rev. Dr. Brown.
64. See chapter one.
65. See, for example, 'Ulster Orangeman' column, *Belfast Weekly News* 4 January 1912.
66. Quoted in 'Scottish Orange Notes', *Belfast Weekly News* 11 January 1912.
67. See P. Buckland, *Irish Unionism 2: Ulster Unionism* (Dublin, 1973) p. 74, for details of the propaganda efforts of the Unionist Association of Ireland (UAI) in Scotland and England.
68. *Belfast Weekly News* 18 January 1912.
69. Ibid.
70. See M. Elliott, *Watchmen in Sion: The Protestant Idea of Liberty*.
71. See Jackson, *Ulster Party*, 'Conclusion'.
72. *The Witness* 5 January 1912.
73. Ibid. 12 January 1912.
74. McMinn op. cit.
75. *The Witness* 19 January 1912.
76. Ibid.
77. *The Witness* 2 February 1912.
78. *Glasgow Herald* 2 February 1912.
79. See full report of Convention in *Belfast Weekly News* 8 February 1912. I have summarised the resolutions in my own words; the reference to Scotland in number four is as in the original. Quotes from speeches used hereafter are taken from this report.
80. See speech by Sir William Crawford.
81. See speech by Frank Workman. For a discussion of 'Ne Temere', see D. H. Akenson, *Small Differences: Irish Catholics and Irish Protestants 1815–1922* (Montreal and Kingston, 1988); also P. Bew, *Ideology and*

the Irish Question (Oxford, 1994) pp. 31–34, which explains the significance of the subsequent 'McCann case' in relation to Unionist fears.

82. See speech by Rev. J. C. Johnston.
83. See speeches by Rev. J. Gailey and T. G. Houston.
84. For an extended Unionist phillipic against the AOH see A. W. Samuels op. cit. pp. 100–109. On p.107 it is claimed that the AOH was spreading rapidly in Scotland.
85. See R. F. G. Holmes, 'Ulster Presbyterians and Irish Nationalism', in Mews (ed.) *Religion* pp. 535–548; also Finlay Holmes, *Our Irish Presbyterian Heritage* p. 134.
86. *Glasgow Herald* 1 February 1912.
87. Ibid.
88. Minute book of West of Scotland Liberal Unionist Association 5 December 1912, NLS Acc. 10424/22.
89. *Glasgow Herald* 12 February 1912.
90. Ibid. 29 February 1912.
91. Ibid. 21 October 1912.
92. C. Harvie, 'The Covenanting Tradition', in G. Walker and T. Gallagher (eds.), *Sermons and Battle Hymns: Protestant Popular Culture in Modern Scotland* (Edinburgh, 1990).
93. *Belfast Weekly News* 8 February 1912. For Houston, see P. Bew, *Ideology* p. 41.
94. *Belfast Weekly News* 16 January 1913.
95. See 'Ulster Orangeman' column in *Belfast Weekly News* 13 February 1913.
96. *Belfast Weekly News* 6 February 1913.
97. Quoted in Holmes, 'Ulster Presbyterians and Irish Nationalism' p. 548.
98. See Todd op. cit.
99. J. J. Lee, *Ireland 1912–1985* (Cambridge, 1990) chpt. 1.
100. See D. Hempton and M. Hill, *Evangelical Protestantism in Ulster Society*, especially chpt. 9.
101. Ibid. p. 183.
102. Letter reproduced in T. G. Houston, *Ulster's Appeal* (Belfast, 1913). Paul Bew, *Ideology* p. 46, points out that the Orange Order's membership in Belfast more than doubled between 1908 and 1913. It can be safely assumed that many Presbyterians were overcoming their traditional coolness towards it.
103. See the Ulster Unionist Council pamphlet, *The Ulster Question* (1911).
104. Samuels was quoting William O'Brien, the Cork Nationalist and arch-critic of the AOH. O'Brien's speech was dated 13 September 1910.

105. Samuels op. cit.
106. See Hennessey op. cit.
107. See A. J. Balfour, 'A Note on Home Rule', in S. Rosenbaum (ed.), *Against Home Rule* (Port Washington, NY, 1970).
108. See, for example, Griffith's comments in his preface to John Mitchel's *Jail Journal* (London, 1983). Griffith also expressed anti-semitic sentiments — see T. Garvin, *Nationalist Revolutionaries in Ireland 1858-1928* (Oxford, 1987) p. 122.
109. See comments of T. W. Moody quoted in R. F. Holmes, 'Ulster Presbyterians and Irish Nationalism' p. 535.
110. For a brief guide to Parnell see R. Foster, 'Interpretations of Parnell', *Studies* Vol. 80, no. 320 (Winter 1991) pp. 349–357; for Redmond, Dillon and Devlin see P. Bew, *Ideology*.
111. See the writings of Pearse in P. H. Pearse, *The Murder Machine and other essays* (Cork, 1976), especially 'Ghosts'.
112. This topic is scrupulously documented and discussed in J. Kendle, *Ireland and the Federal Solution*; see also J. Kendle, *Walter Long, Ireland and the Union, 1905–1920* (Dublin, 1992).
113. See McLeod op. cit. pp. 139–140. See H. A. L. Fisher, James Bryce (London, 1927) Vol.1, pp. 218–219 for Bryce's view of Liberal Presbyterians and Home Rule in Ireland; see also Bew, *Ideology* pp. 48–9 regarding Bryce's concern that Gladstone had driven Presbyterian Liberal Unionists 'into the hands of the Orangemen' over Irish Home Rule.
114. Kendle, *Ireland* p. 79.
115. See Gailey op. cit.
116. 'Pacificus', *Federalism and Home Rule* (London, 1910). 'Pacificus' was Frederick Scott Oliver.
117. See material in McCallum Scott Papers op. cit.
118. For an account of the tortuous events leading up to partition, see M. Laffan, *The Partition of Ireland* (Dundalk, 1983).
119. For a sceptical reading see E. Dyas, *Federalism, Northern Ireland and the 1920 Govt. of Ireland Act* (Belfast, 1988). Kendle, on the other hand, is persuasive that Long and others around him were in earnest. See Kendle, *Walter Long*.
120. A. Marr, *The Battle for Scotland* (London, 1992) pp. 1–5. See the discussion in chpt. 6 below.

3

Popular Unionist and Protestant Politics in Scotland and Northern Ireland c. 1920–70

I

During the years of devolved government in Northern Ireland, when the Ulster Unionist Party enjoyed continual political dominance, the Conservatives (known as the Unionists) in Scotland also enjoyed considerable political success. The political contexts were significantly different.

In Northern Ireland the politics of the six county State were cut off from those at Westminster, although the Province continued to be represented there in the form of twelve MPs. The Northern Ireland State was brought into being against the wishes of those, overwhelmingly Catholic, who desired a unitary, independent all-Irish State; they comprised roughly a third of the population. From the start this community made it clear that the new State was not an entity to which they could owe allegiance or loyalty. The Ulster Unionist, and overwhelmingly Protestant, majority saw the securing of the State as their first priority. Although less than happy with the terms of the Government of Ireland Act, the Unionists went along with them, and came to view the new State as a bulwark against being forced into a united Ireland. The scene was set for the one-issue politics which followed: the polarisation of Unionists and Nationalists over the question of the State's legitimacy, a political cleavage sharpened by the abolition of a Proportional Representation electoral system for the Province by the Unionist Government in 1929. In the half-century history of the State the Unionist Party won each election by maintaining its hold on sufficient support across the Protestant population. The Catholic Nationalist portion was that of being condemned to permanent opposition. Until the outbreak of 'The Troubles' in 1969, a convention operated at

61

Westminster to exclude from discussion business pertaining to Northern Ireland.

Scotland's politically integrated place in the wider context of the British State oriented her political development to the increasingly two-party, left-right, class-based pattern of the inter-war years and beyond. This might well have been helped by the settlement of the Irish issue in 1921–22; more scope existed for class, or 'secular', politics, and religious divisions were not on the Northern Ireland scale of seriousness. Nevertheless, the Irish issue, as James Mitchell has pointed out,[1] did not decline in significance in Scottish politics as it did in the rest of Britain. There is still much evidence of ethnic or religious sectarian political resonances in Scotland during this half-century. Comparisons with Northern Ireland cannot be direct or precise, but there is a basis, which will be demonstrated, for such exercises.

This chapter will thus consider, comparatively, the subject of popular Protestant and Unionist politics, highlighting both the common ground between Northern Ireland and Scotland, and the ways in which their experiences diverged. In both Scotland and Northern Ireland the principal 'actors' in this sphere were the same: namely, the respective Unionist parties and minor political pressure groups; the Protestant Churches; and the Orange Order. These organisations differed in respect of such variables as numerical strength, political roles, social profiles. However, they were all significant actors in the politics and the political cultures of both places in this era. Moreover, the range of social, economic, cultural and religious themes with which they interacted can be said to match up to a large extent, between Scotland and Northern Ireland.

II

The Unionist Party's iron grip on power throughout Northern Ireland's political history suggests a security they never felt, or allowed their supporters to feel; as a recent scholar has commented, they 'only needed to lose once'.[2] The Unionists perceived an implacable Irish nationalist threat both in the South of Ireland and with Northern Ireland itself; moreover, they considered British governments to be unreliable. Their political success came to rest on their capacity to command sufficient support around the defence of the Northern Ireland State and the Union with Britain.

They succeeded by virtue of an economical message which col-
lapsed all other issues into this overriding one; they could not
afford the luxury of appealing on a broader social and economic or
cultural front. In this sense Unionism did not fundamentally
change in character from its origins as a pan-class, multi-denomi-
national, internally politically protean, Protestant mass movement
pledging solidarity in opposition to Irish nationalism. It thrived,
and held together politically, in relation to a sense of threat and
danger which was defined as the Irish Nationalist and Catholic
'other', and the possible sacrifice to it of the Unionist cause by the
British Government.

The threat took several forms and was represented by several
institutions and organisations. At the time of the State's inception
the threat was a deadly and violent one and was represented by the
IRA. The Unionist answer was to establish a special police force
drawn from the Protestant community, and use its newly devolved
powers to put in place special security legislation. Law and order
was immediately put on a partisan sectarian footing and a host of
grievances began to be stockpiled by the Catholic minority.[3] These
were soon supplemented by allegations of electoral boundaries
being gerrymandered to Unionist advantage, and of discrimination
against Catholics in the provision of housing and employment. The
case against the Unionists' 'hegemonic' use of their power[4] in the
State's history has been put vividly and often emotively in a
plethora of writings, and the case for their defence, or pleas of
mitigating circumstances, in somewhat fewer.[5]

The circumstances of the State's birth set the tone for the
cut-throat sectarian politics which subsequently developed. The
Unionist approach to devolved government was 'minimalist': until
the 1960s no Unionist Government seriously attempted to use the
autonomy granted to it to take a significantly different direction
from Britain. Rather, it was used simply to reaffirm the Unionists'
loyalty to, and pride in, the Union with Britain. This was the peren-
nial answer to the perceived aggression of Irish nationalism.

Similarly, Unionist politics were shorn of ambiguities and possible ideological or doctrinal pitfalls. It was a politics of constant
re-affirmation on a nakedly exclusivist Protestant basis, notwithstanding the strains at Government level between those ministers
who epitomised this 'populist' approach and those who deprecated
it or feared its impact in London.[6] It was a 'zero-sum' politics
which carried over into the Northern Ireland State political arena

an attitude which had characterised the Irish question since the 1880's: that a gain for one side was automatically a loss for the other. In the Unionist outlook there could be no compromise between loyalty and disloyalty.

The legacy of the early years of the State was certainly uncompromising: the bonds of Unionist solidarity had been strengthened by fire. In the 1923 Yearbook of the Ulster Unionist Council (UUC) Carson exhorted all Unionists to rally round Unionist Prime Minister James Craig and 'rely upon yourselves!'; a special mention was also made of the 'liberal' contribution to the Loyalist Relief Fund set up for the dependants of the victims of Sinn Fein 'bombers and gunmen', made by 'the working classes in the Shipyards, Mills, Factories and Warehouses'.[7] It was to these Unionist supporters that the party had to take care to reciprocate politically.

The same yearbook, in its breakdown of delegates to the UUC, demonstrates the influence on the Unionist movement of the Orange Order: it possessed approximately 20 per cent of the places. From the beginning it functioned as probably the most powerful pressure group in the political life of the State. By 1935 a high-ranking civil servant was of the view that the Order's influence on the Government was akin to 'the tail [wagging] the dog'; 'No Unionist politician dare say anything against them or their excesses or he would lose his seat', he added.[8] The Orange Order's concerns were, to a large degree, the Unionist Party's concerns. Within the Orange Order there were, moreover, a large number of clergymen of all Protestant denominations, and while there were individual churchmen who were dismayed by the Order's influence, there was an absence of a collective Protestant Church voice in favour of a different political tone or policy or approach. In 1930 an alliance of Orangemen and Protestant Churchmen secured amending education legislation which reversed the secularising intentions of the original (1923) piece of legislation.[9] This was a good example of Orange influence and of the Unionist Government's readiness to appease its well-organised and collectively vocal supporters. Other more isolated and dissident Protestant voices did not get the same hearing from a governing party which did not feel itself under the same pressure to respond to them.[10]

III

Popular Unionist politics in Scotland after the first World War bore many Irish (or Ulster) traces. In the industrial central belt at least, there existed among many Protestants a similar baleful regard for the Irish Catholic 'other'. There was considerable IRA activity in Scotland in the 1920-22 period, and genuine alarm about civil unrest spreading from Ireland.[11] With the removal of the Irish constitutional question from the political agenda by 1922, the issue of Catholic Irish immigration into Scotland became politically focused in terms of a threat or a danger. In the inter-war period this issue was highlighted by the Unionists who responded to pressures from the Scottish Protestant Churches and the Orange Order in Scotland. At several junctures during the 1920s and 1930s Unionist politicians made interventions on the basis of claims of escalating numbers of Irish Catholics in Scotland; these were invariably accompanied by dire prophecies of the ruin this would bring to the nation's fabric and character if left unchecked. The work of scholars such as Tom Gallagher and Richard Finlay has brought these political interventions to light and indicated the extent to which the issue was also a source of concern to certain Scottish Nationalist and even Labour figures in the same period.[12]

Hostility to Irish Catholic immigrants was not new, but the social tensions and economic problems of the inter-war era helped to politicize it in a lurid fashion. There also seemed to be a sense of the Scottish people taking stock after the traumas of the Great War and the onset of a new straitened economic era and pondering questions of identity. It was a period in which a cultural re-shaping process opened up opportunities for a range of individuals and organisations to press the claims of their own perceptions and definitions of Scottishness. Some sought a reaffirmation of old certainties, others a radical new departure or spiritual and cultural revival.

Official statistics on Irish immigration prepared by the Census Office in Edinburgh in 1933 showed that it fell consistently after 1900, and that in the period 1921–31 it was probably out-weighed by those Irish who emigrated from Scotland.[13] However, the figures did not differentiate between Catholic and Protestant Irish immigration, and did not attempt to speculate on the number of people living in Scotland of Irish descent. It was, indeed, the perception of a large community differing in religion and proclaiming an Irish nationalist sense of identity, regardless of actual place of birth, which exercised some Protestants. Moreover, even if the analysis is restricted to those in the statistics who were Irish-born immigrants, the official papers highlight matters which were central to the concerns of those who raised the issue. These matters were the effects of Irish immigrant competition for increasingly scarce employment; and Irish immigrants who received poor relief and who were alleged to be a 'drain' on public assistance.

In a separate memorandum by a health department civil servant, Sir John Jefffrey, it was pointed out that during the 15 years preceding the 1931 census date, the majority of immigrants came from the Irish Free State, and thus were overwhelmingly Catholic, whereas many Protestants had been numbered among the immigrants in earlier periods. Jeffrey went on:

> Under normal conditions an annual accession of about 2,000 immigrants from Ireland would be immaterial but with trade and industry heavily depressed, as it has been during the past ten years, even that number must have had an effect in aggravating an otherwise difficult situation.

Jeffrey pointed out that the great majority of the recent Irish immigrants were persons within the most effective working period of life, and as in previous times they settled mainly in the West of Scotland, in for example Glasgow, Greenock and Clydebank. Such areas had been heavily hit by unemployment and even a small number of incomers was enough to make a material difference in their economic position. Jeffrey concluded:

> To the extent to which the immigrants have obtained employment, they have kept other, probably Scotsmen, out of work and to the extent to which the immigrants are themselves out of work they have probably added to the burden of expenditure on public assistance.[14]

Along with long-held stereotypes about the Irish Catholic poor and crime, and perceptions of the Roman Catholic Church using its Irish community base to build up its power and influence, for example in education,[15] the economic effects of Irish Catholic immigration were thus mixed to produce a heady cocktail of scapegoating in an austere era. The Orange Order, and important figures in the Unionist Party and the Churches, combined to depict the Catholic community as a threat to the Scottish way of life and, in its stubborn insistence on its Irish identity, as 'disloyal' and 'unBritish' and 'unScottish'. In doing so they brought a style of politics to Scotland very reminiscent of Northern Ireland.

It will be argued that the political rhetoric and imagery employed owed much to the Orange Order, which even into the 1930s retained its Irish Protestant immigrant character.[16] The Order had, predictably, been at the centre of the anti-Irish Home Rule campaigns in Scotland before the first World War and had been politically active with varying degrees of success through the Conservative/Unionist Party from the 1870's.[17] In the socially turbulent period following the Great War it presented itself as a bastion of British loyalty and patriotism and the social and economic order. It confronted the powerful political challenge mounted by socialism and the Labour movement in Scotland, as well as its traditional foes the Catholic Church and Irish nationalist activity. Its populist appeal and growing strength in the years after World War One[18] made it impossible for the Unionists to ignore, even if it was a relationship which past history suggested would be an uneasy one. The Order had a formal position in the Western Divisional Council of the Party from before the war, and, although these links were broken by the Order in protest at the Irish Treaty of 1921 and an 'Orange and Protestant Party' (OPP) set up, the estrangement proved short-lived. The OPP never got off the ground and the leading Orange figures such as Grand Master (after 1925) Archibald McInnes Shaw, remained Unionist Party members and, in Shaw's case, a Unionist MP between 1924–29. Senior Unionist politicians such as Sir John Gilmour, Scottish Secretary of State for periods in the 1920s and 1930s, and Lt Col T. E. R. Moore, were members also of the Orange Order. The link may have embarrassed other Scottish Unionists, but in the inter-war era at least the Order's value to the Unionists as a grassroots electoral machine capable of delivering crucial votes in certain working class constituencies in Glasgow and the industrial heartlands of west-central Scotland, was gratefully acknowledged.[19]

The post World War One period also saw the Unionist party draw closer to the Protestant churches in Scotland. Stewart J Brown has noted that socially progressive elements in the Churches who had been influential before the Great War became increasingly marginalised after it.[20] This was partly a result of political changes which saw the emergence of Labour to fill the progressive vacuum left by a divided Liberal Party; the prospect of alienating the Churches' predominantly middle class membership by allying with Labour's programme, proved to be a constraining force. So too did the risk of antagonising the Government when the movement for Church union (between by this time the Church of Scotland and the United Free Church) would require parliamentary sanction. The union was duly effected in 1929 by which time Presbyterianism in Scotland was led by a new set of divines typified by the professed Conservative John White. White and other leading ministers shared the alarm of Orange leaders about the effects of Irish Catholic immigration, and Brown has brought out clearly how doggedly the issue was pursued, politically, by Presbyterian delegations intent on legislation restricting Irish Catholic immigration, how intensely it was debated at Church assemblies, and how essentially racist the terms of this debate were.[21]

As the kirk drew closer to the Unionists and lost much of its social reforming zeal, so Catholics began to perceive the operation of a powerful political network linking the Churches, the Unionist Party and the Orange Order, and extending out to embrace other secret societies like the Freemasons (in Scotland overwhelmingly Protestant) and militarist offshoots from the kirk like the Boys Brigade which recruited largely from the ranks of urban Protestant working class youths.[22] In the inter-war period there also existed a clutch of Protestant associations of one kind or another, usually locally based such as the Shettleston Protestant Club or the Protestant Vigilance Society in Motherwell. These may have been mainly social clubs or Church-associated bible study groups, but it is also possible that they were politically motivated. Certainly, the Protestant Vigilance Society was politically energetic on the issue of mixed marriages and the Catholic Church's position on them.[23] On top of these groups there was the Scottish Protestant League (SPL), an organisation founded by Alexander Ratcliffe in 1920 which made inroads in Glasgow municipal politics in the early 1930s; and Protestant Action (PA), the vehicle for an Edinburgh Protestant militant John Cormack, which also enjoyed municipal success in that city. The SPL and PA were the most significant Protestant political forces in addition to the Unionists and the Orange Order; indeed, in their political outlook, the Unionists and the Order were weak-kneed and supine representatives of Protestant interests.[24]

IV

In Scotland, therefore, a sense of threat requiring eternal vigilance was at the heart of popular Unionist politics as in Northern Ireland. In both places the notion of 'disloyal' Catholics working to undermine state and society in the interests of their Church was deeply embedded in the political culture and assiduously fostered. It was often enlivened in both places by means of rumours about Catholic activity and Catholic influence. This will be explored below. However, standing out amidst the rumours, speculation and conspiracy theories, and in a sense appearing to give them credence, was the substantial fact of State support in both Scotland and Northern Ireland for Catholic education. This issue was perhaps the most solid plank in the platform of Protestant politics, yet it was also a very problematic one for the Unionist parties.

In Scotland Catholic schools were granted full State support by the terms of the Education Act (Scotland), passed during wartime by the Conservative-dominated coalition government in 1918. In addition, these schools remained under the control of the Catholic Church which ensured that Catholic religious education would be provided where possible by Catholic teachers. On the other hand, the other State schools, which had been turned over to the State in many cases by Protestant Churches, were largely secular; only a general and denominationally unspecific religious education element was included in the curriculum. The objection came immediately from outraged Protestant opinion: the Catholic Church was being allowed to propagate its teachings at the State's expense ('Rome on the Rates') while Protestants in State schools were not receiving the form of spiritual instruction they were entitled to. Protestant anger went far beyond traditionally militant quarters, and the Orange Order undoubtedly owed much of its membership boom in the 1919–20 period to the impact of the controversy.[25]

At the elections to the Glasgow Education Authority in April 1919 the Orange Order put up eight candidates and got five elected. Leading Unionist politician and Orangeman, Sir Charles Cleland, became the Chairman of the new Education Authority. The Order has continued to stress the educational issue from this period on; it has campaigned for amendments to be made to the legislation, so far unsuccessfully. Until at least the 1950's, influential elements in the Protestant Churches campaigned for the same objective. In the 1920s and 1930s such elements openly accused the Catholic Church of pursuing the conversion of Scotland using their educational 'privileges' as a means of 'propaganda'. It was agreed that control of education gave the Catholic Church a powerful base from which to build, and that its doctrinaire stance on mixed marriages was calculated to increase the number of its adherents. All this, added to the generally higher Catholic birthrate, aroused fears among many Protestants of a growth of Catholic numbers and influence amidst Protestant apathy and a decline in Protestant Church attendance and membership. Such themes were a staple of orange platform orations. Calls to Scotland to 'wake up' to the 'encroachments of the Church of Rome'[26] jostled with statistics attesting to rising Catholic numbers; in 1934, for example, the Orange leader Frank Dorrian claimed that the number of Catholic school pupils had increased from 88,096 in 1913 to 113,292 in 1931 and that the total number of children attending school in Scotland over the same period actually decreased.[27] A year later a Church of Scotland minister, the Rev W. A. Guthrie, provided figures denoting a 28% increase in the Catholic school population against a 5% Protestant increase over the period of the previous 20 years.[28] Moreover, as Brown has argued, the Presbyterian Churches were certainly anxious about their declining influence and authority in Scottish life in the inter-war era.[29]

In Northern Ireland a similar education controversy developed. In 1923 the first Unionist Government led by Craig introduced legislation secularising the State school system but conceding to the minority Catholic community State support, without State control, of their schools to the extent of payment of teachers' salaries and 50% of the schools' maintenance costs. These terms were not as favourable as in Scotland, where there was full State support, but many Protestants, as in Scotland, viewed them as all too favourable. They echoed the objections of Scottish protesters about the lack of what they considered essential bible teaching in State schools for Protestants; and about unfettered Catholic Church control of subsidised Catholic schools. As noted above, a concerted Protestant Churches-Orange Order campaign was launched in pursuit of amending legislation, and the Unionist Government conceded the issue of 'bible teaching' in new legislation in 1930. However, the Catholic schools' position was left unchanged.

In 1947 there was a replay of this controversy when a new education measure secularised the State schools while increasing the

State support to voluntary (for the most part Catholic) schools from 50 to 65% of capital costs. The Unionist Government and Party were hit by another combined churches and Orange Order backlash. The Government, led by Basil Brooke, sacrificed the Minister of Education, who was not a member of the Orange Order, replacing him with one of the Bill's most outspoken populist critics.[30] However, notwithstanding speculation about amendments, the legislation remained intact and was a source of grievance to elements of the Protestant community for years afterwards. Dissatisfaction among grassroots Unionists with the Government in the 1950's tended to focus on the education issue. In the proceedings of the Orange Order resolutions reprimanding or warning the Government on the issue were passed regularly.[31]

In the view of the disgruntled Protestant lobby in Northern Ireland, separate Catholic schools were symbolic of the Catholic Church's quest for political power and influence. They viewed the schools as transmitting disloyal attitudes and as hotbeds of partisan Irish Nationalist and Republican thinking, particularly in relation to the teaching of history. They considered Catholic educational demands to be insatiable. The Unionist Government, far from properly conceding minority rights, were, in the view of the objectors, facilitating the perpetuation of a large, disloyal and politically disruptive minority in the State. In the outlook of the Protestant protesters, and among even those who considered it politic to provide State support for Catholic education, there was not so much the arrogant, contemptuous and supremacist view of the Catholic minority as is so often suggested, but a fearful and agitated and embattled mentality which saw a powerful Catholic Nationalism around every corner. The nature of Ulster Unionism was always too anxious and never relaxed enough to be truly supremacist in the manner it has so often been accused of. Nor did working class Protestants feel 'privileged' in the way imagined by some historians.[32] Notions of the Catholic church and community as 'underdogs' were greeted with derision; in 1930, amidst the education controversy in which the leading Catholic church figure in Ireland, Cardinal Joseph MacRory, had made a typically out spoken intervention, a Unionist press commentator remarked; 'A church that threatens to make Ulster's Education Act unworkable unless it gets free support for its sectarian schools is no "underdog"'.[33] Thus, in their baleful perception of Catholic power-accumulation, sizeable numbers of Protestants in both Scotland and Northern Ireland shared a common impulse, one which had important political ramifications in both places.

V

If education was viewed as the core symbol of Catholic power by disaffected Protestants in both Scotland and Northern Ireland, of no less significance to them were signs of what they considered Catholic 'aggression' in other areas of public life. In both places the slogan 'peaceful penetration' was a recurring theme in the respective Unionist and Protestant political networks, used to describe a perceived catholic 'take-over' conducted often by stealth but deeply insidious and irrepressible.

In Northern Ireland such a perception was basic to Unionist fears throughout the history of the State. Year by year at Orange Order meetings and 'twelfth' demonstrations, there came resolutions about such matters as 'the increasing number of shops, farms and small holdings passing out of the hand of Protestants',[34] and land and property falling into Catholic hands for the purpose of school or chapel building.[35] Any increase in Catholic population statistics was translated as a loss in *territory* for Unionism; Catholics spreading into territory once exclusively Protestant, or building up a strong presence in areas where they had previously been weak, were automatically taken as signs of a stronger Nationalist challenge to the Unionist way of life. The Catholic Church and the Catholic community were viewed as *aggressive*.

In this Protestant outlook Catholic aggression took many forms. In times especially of economic harshness it took the form of Catholics getting jobs which it was claimed should have gone to Protestants as a reward for their 'loyalty'. In the 1930s, notwithstanding the objective reality of massive Catholic social and economic deprivation in Northern Ireland, many badly-off Protestants believed that Catholics were using influences, for example their priests or secret societies like the Ancient Order of Hibernian (AOH), to secure scarce jobs or an unfair share of welfare benefits or resources. In this period the Unionist Government came under severe pressure from supporters alleging that it was not doing enough to 'look after its own', but instead was appeasing the minority. Extremist Protestant politics in the form of the Ulster Protestant League (UPL)[36] which demanded jobs for Protestants and a premium on loyalty, caused great difficulties for Craig's Government in the 1930s.[37] Indeed, the Unionist Government's own Protestant tub-thumping of these years, and before and after, has to be viewed in the context of the militant Protestant opinion it was always attempting to keep in check as a political threat. A Unionist education minister in the 1930s, Lord Charlemont, tried to explain the rabble-rousing speeches of Government ministers such as Sir Basil Brooke at this time as follows: 'It's not entirely religious fervour — it's the gradual increase of pressure from independent organisations, leagues, socialism; all the political expressions of Ulster individualism'.[38] Charlemont was fully aware of why Unionists took every opportunity to buttress their position, and how this left little room for conciliatory approaches towards the minority. The dangers of such groups as the UPL, as well as disaffected elements within the Orange Order and the Unionist Party itself, had to be constantly attended to; as, indeed, did left wing political appeals to the Protestant working class, something considered below. But the Unionists would also have considered Catholic and Nationalist attitudes, displayed in areas such as education and the constitutional questions, to be intransigent to the point of making political dialogue impossible.[39]

In the 1930s there were also Protestant allegations concerning the seizure by Catholics of new public housing,[40] of physical assaults on Protestants celebrating the Royal Jubilee in 1935,[41] and on Protestants travelling to places of worship.[42] Hair-raising threats to Protestants in supposed Catholic secret society oaths were a staple of Protestant folklore.[43] The IRA, of course, did not cease to be regarded as the main military threat to the Unionist cause; Denis Kennedy has charted well the extent to which its activities, if only sporadic for the most part in the State's history, were presented by the Unionist press in a tone which helped to maintain a mood of deep wariness among Protestants.[44] The perception of the IRA as a constant danger was of more significance than its actual condition which was often virtually moribund. The Catholic perception of the IRA as a defence against *Protestant* aggression, and abuses by the 'B' Specials, only serves to highlight the extent of the gulf between respective popular attitudes and assumptions in the Province. The Unionist political leaders had their actions shaped less by a coherent political philosophy than by a reaction to political pressures brought upon them by such phenomena as the 'peaceful penetration' perceptions. More thought was given to coping with these pressures and appearing to defend territory, position and so on than to formulating sophisticated political theories and justifications.

In Scotland the perception among groups of Protestants of a Catholic 'take-over' in areas of public life fed off, and focused on, the same kind of tensions and material circumstances as in Northern Ireland. When unemployment was high, as in the depressed early 1930s, similar speeches were made by Protestant orators in Scotland about 'loyalty' counting for little against the power and influence of a well-organised and aggressive Catholic community. As in Ulster, the respective perceptions of the situation on the part of Protestant and Catholic could not have been more contrasting. In the Catholic view it was they who were discriminated against in several occupational sectors, and the Protestant network alluded to earlier operated to keep a firm grip on certain jobs and positions of power. Objectively, the evidence concerning unemployment, poor living conditions and badly paid employment certainly bears out a story of Catholics being particularly disadvantaged, a state of affairs unaltered since the arrival of large numbers of Irish Catholic immigrants in the early 19th century.[45]

However, objective statistics mattered little to those Protestants whose own grim experience led them to be receptive to a zero-sum message of Ulster vintage. Thus Digby S. Brown, a high-ranking Orange Order official, reportedly addressed his audience in 1930 as follows:

> He asked them who were in public works if they thought for a moment that they would get employment when there was a preponderance of Roman Catholics. The moment a Roman Catholic became foreman then from that moment Roman Catholics only would be employed in their public works.[46]

Implicit in this declaration was the argument that it was necessary for Protestants to remain in positions such as foreman in work-places so that they could regulate employment, and that if they were not it would be Catholics who got hired. In economically depressed times, in days before fair employment legislation, the powers of such people as foremen could be formidable, and it was a fact of life in industrial Scotland as well as Northern Ireland that in such a situation a 'connection' through an organisation could be an advantage.[47] Both sides, in both places, tended to believe that the other side was better at using influence than themselves. In another speech at an Orange occasion in Glasgow, this time in 1931, the Rev R. F. Whiteley was reported to have said:

They lived in difficult times, difficult because of the lack of employment, and he would speak a word to any who had influence in that connection that they would not forget their brethren of the Orange Order, because they knew only too well that those of the other side had their passwords and such like which they could well use, so that it was necessary for Protestants and Orangemen to defend themselves and to see that they got a fair chance in any work that was available.[48]

Around the same time, there were claims made about Catholic foremen hiring other Catholics on instructions from priests.[49] The 'peaceful penetration' allegations were made in Orange Halls, political platforms, and Church assembly rooms, in relation to symbolical occupational sectors such as the shipyards on the Clyde, and labour unrest was depicted as a bolshevik *and* Irish Catholic 'rebel' conspiracy.[50] In Scotland, as in Northern Ireland, tensions were fuelled by *rumour* — rumour that jobs and housing and favours were going to the 'other side', that the 'other side' was intimidating 'our side' into selling up land and property and moving out of an area, that 'our side's' leaders were ineffectual compared to 'theirs' and so on.

Such tensions resulted in bloody riots in Belfast in 1935, riots in which Glasgow Orangemen, over for the 12th of July celebrations, played a lively role.[51] Street riots of a religious kind also broke out in Edinburgh in the same year, and wild scenes accompanied the Orange celebrations in Glasgow which took place a week before those in Belfast. Glasgow's religiously-based football rivalry between Rangers and Celtic intensified between the wars. In Scotland, as in Northern Ireland, enough Protestants took seriously the concept of 'peaceful penetration' of important areas of public and social life by Catholics, to believe that their own position was at risk and that militancy and aggression were called for to turn back the tide.[52]

However, in Scotland as in Northern Ireland, all of this caused political tensions which did not fall straighforwardly to the Unionists' advantage, notwithstanding the Party's clearly-demonstrated Protestant and 'loyal' image. Such was the depth of sectarian feeling and material deprivation in Central Scotland in the interwar years, that the Unionists struggled not to be outflanked by extremist rivals such as the SPL and PA pressing sectarian buttons, and, of course, by the class politics of the Labour movement.

It is the first that will be discussed at this juncture. Both the SPL and PA with their populist, demagogic leaders played on the sectarian tensions of the period in a way the Unionists could not.

Ratcliffe and Cormack demanded a revision of the 1918 Education
Act, and lambasted those Scottish (and in some cases Orange
Order) Unionists who either voted for or abstained in Parliament
during the passing of the Catholic Relief Act in 1926. The Act was
passed by a Conservative Government which then went on to
establish diplomatic links with the Vatican. Howls of militant
Protestant protest, using the argument that the Roman Catholic
church placed itself above the law of the land in matters such as
mixed marriages, could not alter the situation. It was a good illustration of the uncomfortable position Orange leaders like McInnes
Shaw were in as Unionist MPs and members of a British-wide
party. On Orange platforms McInnes Shaw attempted to pre-empt
the appeal of such as Ratcliffe by giving voice to the 'peaceful penetration' anti-Catholic argument in terms every bit as strident and
uncompromising as his populist rival. Thus, in 1932, he raised the
spectre of a 'Roman Catholic State' in Scotland and went on:
'Almost every week in their city [Glasgow] they saw houses being
taken over by the Church of Rome. In a certain district there
seemed to be an attempt to set up a citadel of the Roman Catholic
church, and Protestants allowed them to go on doing these things.'[53]

However, Ratcliffe was probably correct in suggesting that
McInnes Shaw and others took care not to have their 'blood and
thunder' Orange speeches widely publicised in Scotland.[54] Being
members of the broader Conservative Party imposed restrictions
on Scottish Unionists' exploitation of religious divisions. As has
been argued, they *did* capitalise on them in their willingness to co-
operate with the Orange Order in certain constituencies. However,
the Party did not want to be beholden to the Order, and did not
want its appeal narrowed down to sectarian issues. In Government,
as Secretary of State for Scotland, Sir John Gilmour, although an
Orangeman, resisted the pressure for legislation to prohibit Irish
Catholic immigration. In 1933 an attempt by the Orange Order
to get a bill introduced to Parliament on the subject of mixed
marriages was unsuccessful. Sir Charles Cleland, as leader of the
Glasgow Education Authority in the 1920s, took a far from anti-
Catholic line.[55] The Unionists in Scotland, in short, could not
always deliver to those of its supporters who believed that 'Protestant interests' had to be looked after.

This point illustrated a contrast with the situation in Northern
Ireland, something illuminatingly discussed by Steve Bruce.[56] The

Unionists in Northern Ireland were, by virtue of the 'pork barrel' of patronage accruing to their own parliament and devolved government set-up, better placed to appease militant Protestant opinion. By setting up the Special Constabulary in 1921, for example, they gave jobs to their supporters as well as helping to secure their State. In 1930, as has been pointed out, the militant Protestant lobby were given the concession of bible teaching in State schools. The Unionists in Scotland did not have the same patronage resources, and were part of a wider (British) party which officially frowned on religious loyalties being mixed in with political ones. McInnes Shaw in sounding off to an Orange audience in 1932 as above, was indulging in the same sort of exercise as Basil Brooke in 1934;[57] the difference was that Brooke could afford politically the publicity he sought. The Unionist Government in Northern Ireland, although troubled, withstood the UPL threat rather better than the Unionists in Scotland coped with Ratcliffe and Cormack if local government election results are taken as a guide.[58] Bruce also argues that there was a lack of the same sense of threat drawing together Protestants in Scotland as in Northern Ireland.[59]

Politically, then, the Scottish Unionists, far less the Conservative Party in Britain as a whole, were not a one-issue or 'one-theme' party like the Ulster Unionists. There were marked limits to how far they could use or benefit from Protestant-Catholic divisions. These divisions in turn were not nearly as entrenched or widespread as in Northern Ireland; the Orange Order's role in Scottish society was on a far smaller scale than its Ulster counterpart.

That said, the Unionists in Scotland still used the *language of loyalism*, and used it at least to an extent up to the 1960's. Concepts of 'loyalty' and 'disloyalty' were part of Scottish as well as Ulster political culture. In Scotland, as in Ulster, the terms referred to loyalty to the British crown and constitution, although in Northern Ireland from 1921 there was also the question of loyalty to that State as well as Britain. Bruce's points about the Northern Ireland Unionists' 'pork barrel' and the element of threat are important, but they should be qualified by an acknowledgement that possession of their own State structure and resources did not prevent the Unionists being challenged and accused of betrayal at different times by disaffected Protestants; and an acknowledgement that strenuous and at least partly successful efforts were made in Scotland, at least in the inter-war period, to present the Catholic

Irish as a very real political threat to Protestant Scotland. This *did* rebound to the Unionists' advantage in certain key constituencies, and it was an important factor in the Unionists' political successes in Scotland at this time.[60]

VI

There were, on the other hand, clear limits to the Unionists' ability to draw support from the Protestant working class in Scotland. These limits were not just marked by a failure to satisfy extremist appetites; they were also set by the growing appeal, from the beginning of the century, of labour politics based on class interest. Over this half-century time-span it is equally valid to stress the political successes of labour in constituencies where either a working class Orange tradition was a strong cultural presence, or where there at least existed a preponderance of Protestant working class voters. Thus both at national and local elections Labour rivalled, and often surpassed, the Unionists in areas such as Govan, Partick, Bridgeton and Springburn in Glasgow, and industrial towns such as Larkhall, Motherwell and Paisley. Valuable as the Catholic working class support was to Labour after 1918, it required even more Protestant working class support to attain the electoral breakthrough of 1922, and to sustain the Party as the force it became thereafter. Some of this Protestant support seems to have been of an Orange colouring if clear tensions between the leadership and the rank and file of the Order are taken as evidence.[61]

It might be argued that the Orange Order fought the propaganda war against socialism on behalf of the Unionists in west-central Scotland for a long period. It was, after all, an overwhelmingly proletarian organisation with roots in communities which the Unionist Party hierarchy naturally lacked. It also appeared to have among its lodge activists representatives of that strand of working class opinion which considered a paternalist relationship between boss and worker a 'natural' one, and which distrusted trade unionism and the Labour movement in general as a vehicle for self-seeking 'professional agitators'. In addition, of course, there was the notable presence of Catholics in trades unions and the Labour Party. To such working men and women, it had to be part of a Catholic plot of some kind as well. Certainly, speeches at Orange functions in the inter-war period implicated Labour in the perceived Catholic campaign to bring ruin to Protestant Scotland.[62]

There was, in fact, something of a propaganda war between the Orange Order and the Labour and Communist Parties in the immediate post first world war period. The Independent Labour Party (ILP) newspaper in Scotland, the *Forward*, claimed that 'thousands' of Orangemen were joining them[63], and although this was probably a mischievous exaggeration the ILP clearly had built a strong popular base on Clydeside across religious divisions. The party's central role in the wartime rent strikes in areas like Partick and Govan had given it a purchase on at least some of those Orange men and more importantly women who took part in that struggle.[64] Issues like housing and rents, school meals, and public health which were identified with the ILP in Scotland at this time were issues which transcended sectarianism. Attacks on capitalist profiteers and greedy landlords struck chords in 'Orange' and 'Green' households alike. It was no accident that the appeal made by Ratcliffe and the SPL involved similar irreverent lampooning of wealthy public figures (often Unionist), and a portrayal of the Unionist Party as antagonistic to Protestant working class interests. The same appeal was made in Northern Ireland in the 1930s by the UPL and other Independent Unionist politicians; and from the 1960's onwards by the Reverend Ian Paisley. Ratcliffe, interestingly and shrewdly, contributed to debates in the *Forward* and did not attempt to argue that Protestants should not vote Labour on account of the number of Catholics in that party.

This *was* the stance taken by the Orange Order, and it was to prove mistaken. The shrill and panicky tone of Orange warnings about Labour and socialism betrayed the fact that Orange members and supporters were being attracted to it. 'The Unionist Party', advised the anti-Catholic Reverend Duncan Cameron in 1927, 'will not rouse the industrial area of Scotland with the Cry of Anti-socialism. It leaves our Scottish people — I mean of the industrial class — quite cold'.[65] In 1924 the Orange Order invoked the ultimate sanction — expulsion — for members who also joined the Labour or Communist parties, but even this did not, apparently, have the desired effect. By the early 1930s Orangemen and women were participating in Communist-led unemployment demonstrations and hunger marches.[66] By this time Orange leaders like McInnes Shaw and Frank Dorrian were admitting that members sought welfare aid from socialist parties[67] and were being 'led away' by what such groups promised them.[68] The harsh uncompromising anti-socialist sub-thumping had, by the onset of the depression, given way to a more emollient political message emphasising the 'welfare of the workers'. McInnes Shaw spoke in such terms at a meeting of the Ulster Unionist Labour Association (UULA) in Belfast in 1934.[69]

The Order was in many ways battling against the tide, not least in the realm of industrial relations. Developments during the Great War and after in the heavy industry sector of the economy rendered the chances of paternalistic employer — worker relations less likely. Industrial disputes over workplace practices, workplace bargaining, and control of the day-to-day workshop processes proliferated, and defeats at the hands of employers over such issues in the early 1920s generated much bitterness and resentment among workers. Relations between employers and workers on Clydeside became increasingly adversarial and remained so through the decades, culminating in the dramatic Upper Clyde Shipbuilders' (UCS) work-in in 1971.[70] Many workers in industries like shipbuilding, most notably the boilermakers, had strong Orange and masonic allegiances. However, Orange loyalties did not prevent these workers acting collectively and combatively against employers on matters concerning pay and conditions, and they certainly did not prevent the expansion of trades unionism. Such factors as changing workplace developments ensured that Protestant sectarian loyalties did not translate, in a significant number of cases, into Conservative political loyalties. A sense of workers' solidarity among skilled occupational groups in which Catholics were rare might also have reinforced *Protestant* solidarity. In mining areas in the central belt where the Orange Order was strong, religious feelings co-existed with Labour militancy; this was as true of such areas which were heavily Catholic.[71] Certainly, it seems to have been the case that many workers kept different sets of loyalties apart to a great extent and that if they recognised contradictions in them, then this was something they were prepared to live with. There were thus important limitations to both class and sectarian loyalties and behaviour.[72]

If class loyalties and bitterness led to the Orange Order's Conservative political message being ignored by some of its rank and file in Scotland, then it might also be said that the Orange leadership's craving for a socially 'respectable' image was often frustrated by the defiantly robust expression of fervour on the part of sections of its membership. The street fighting engaged in by Orange Order members was part and parcel of working class culture in many areas.[73] Displays of raucous celebration on the '12th' or fighting back against violent attacks by outraged Catholics on marches were out of the leadership's control. The movement was not socially, culturally or politically quiescent or pliable. Orangemen damned by middle class opinion in the press and the courts as 'trouble-makers' may have felt a sense of class bitterness to accompany their anti-Catholic prejudices. Certainly, this dual sense of religious and class identities has been recently expressed by elderly Orange Order members recalling their experiences through the decades in Bridgeton in Glasgow, a traditional Orange stronghold; these men and women express Orange and Protestant sentiments *and* use the language of community and class consciousness.[74] Historically, Orangeism has been, albeit ironically, a context in which class consciousness has been expressed, both in Scotland and in Ulster.[75] This theme will be taken up in relation to a discussion of the relationship between socialism and national and ethnic identity in a later chapter.

In Northern Ireland the Unionists worried about the appeal of left wing politics as well as about Nationalism. Lord Charlemont's comments about the pressures on Unionism noted above included socialism. Two years earlier he had voiced the opinion that only the Orange Order had prevented Belfast becoming socialist in its politics.[76] In 1937, Sir Wilfrid Spender, head of the Northern Ireland Civil Service and a prime mover in Government circles, echoed this point of view. He wrote: 'I am strongly concerned that the Ulster working classes appreciate the benefits of the British connection, but if this were severed, a large proportion of those resident in Northern Ireland would change to socialistic tendencies'.[77]

The Unionists' electoral position was never secure in Belfast. In addition to those seats in the city, parliamentary and municipal, which were Nationalist, working class Protestant constituencies like Woodvale and Shankill for long periods returned Independent Unionists whose opposition to the Unionist Government and Party was often venomous and often couched in terms of class resentments. In addition there was the Northern Ireland Labour Party (NILP) which trod a delicate middle way on the constitutional issue until 1949 (when it plumped for the Union) and attempted to unite Protestant and Catholic workers on the basis of a social and economic programme which was usually a local version of the British Labour Party's programme of the day. The NILP was formed out of the ILP which had emerged in Belfast, as in other

British cities, back in the 1890's. The Party never achieved its goal of breaking the Unionist — Nationalist polarisation of Northern Ireland politics, but it won occasional election triumphs and was a constant source of anxiety to the Unionists as the most credible political alternative for disaffected Protestants. The Charlemont and Spender quotes may exaggerate the extent to which the Unionists were worried about socialist doctrines as such; rather, they saw Labour as the most substantial part of an 'oppositional' political culture affecting Protestants. It did not matter so much whether people voted against the Unionist Party for socialist or for extremist sectarian reasons (as in some votes cast for Independent Unionists and UPL candidates); the point was that any kind of defeat for the Governing Party could be interpreted beyond Northern Ireland as an indication of weakness in the basic Unionist position. The constant Unionist Party propaganda about the need for unity and loyalty to the Party was inescapably self-interested, but the Unionist leadership had cause to be alarmed by the possible effects of any electoral setback. It was clear that Nationalist or Republican propaganda would not miss the change to inflict damage by exploiting any such result, however little basis there might have been in reality for a Nationalist or Republican interpretation of it.

Steve Bruce's argument about the Unionists' 'pork barrel' is clearly pertinent to the Unionist difficulties with the demands of its working class supporters. Having leeway to reward them directly or play to their fears and prejudices concerning Catholic nationalism was obviously a help. But this leeway was not unlimited, and could not of itself resolve class tensions. As in Scotland sectarian attitudes could co-exist with a pronounced sense of class consciousness. Charlemont's belief that the Orange Order stood in the way of socialism may contain some truth; the Order was a more socially heterogeneous body in Ulster than in Scotland and it perhaps helped to foster class harmony. In 1970 the Unionist historian, Hugh Shearman, expressed the view that the Order in Ulster had been traditionally more 'orderly and restrained' than in Glasgow or Liverpool, and was drawn from 'a wider sector of society'.[78] The Order's role as a unifying force across the different Protestant denominations as well as classes has to be acknowledged; its importance in this regard far surpassed that of its Scottish counterpart which was not so denominationally or socially mixed. However, there still must be a question mark over how far the Order influenced the lives of many working class Protestants beyond the annual marches; arguably it was more socially influential in rural areas where it assumed the role of a communal focal point. This was not so true in Belfast where class grievances took most obvious and persistent form. We have, therefore, to look elsewhere for a fuller explanation of how the Unionists still managed, albeit with difficulty, to prevent such grievances splintering the Party and fatally damaging the Government.

Even before the establishment of the Northern Ireland state Ulster Unionism had institutionalised a Labour dimension to its party structure. The Ulster Unionist Labour Association (UULA) was in formal existence by 1918, with Carson its President, although it seems to have been the result of Unionist working men banding together earlier and demanding recognition.[79] The Unionist leadership valued the Association in the period of social unrest after the Great War when Belfast was affected by the mood of class warfare in heavy industry, along the lines of Glasgow. Similarly in the post Second World War period, in the wake of a record amount of industrial disputes and much Communist activity in the trades unions, the UULA took on a high profile. An editorial in the newspaper it probably controlled urged that it be in closer unity with the rest of the Unionist Party machine and said: 'There is nothing wrong with a healthy "Labour" movement — there is everything to be said for the encouragement of Labour views in side the Unionist Party, and the development of our present Labour wing should be the very first plank in the new Unionist policy'.[80]

The Unionist Party leadership, worried about the marked swing to the left in public opinion in the Province during the war as reflected in the voting total, if not the seats, in the Northern Ireland election of 1945,[81] were only too happy, as in the 1920s, to be seen to accommodate this Unionist Labour interest. It was undoubtedly one of the major reasons why the British Labour Government's welfare State legislation was reproduced in Northern Ireland after 1945, and why a tendency in the party against it which favoured greater autonomy for the Northern Ireland Parliament instead, was unsuccessful.[82] A leading member of the British Labour Government, Herbert Morrison, expressed himself hopeful in this post-war period, of a Labour Government coming to power in Northern Ireland.[83] Morrison's was a kind of small 'u' Unionist Labour viewpoint combining acceptance of the constitutional position of Northern Ireland with the enthusiastic propagation of left wing politics. The Northern Ireland Labour Party in effect took up this position in 1949, and could be said to have eventually reaped significant electoral benefits among the Protestant working class; in 1958 and 1962 it won four predominantly Protestant constituencies and in the latter election polled some 60,000 votes in Belfast against the Unionists' 66,000. This was a good indication of the potential for Labour politics in Northern Ireland in the right circumstances, that is at a time when the National Question had somewhat receded. The problem, of course, was that such times were rare: all the progress of 1945, for example, when the National Question had looked as if it could be 'manageable' for a left of centre political party like the NILP[84], was swept away by 1949 against a resurgence of the issue brought about by the powerful anti-partitionist campaign waged by the Anti-Partition League (APL) and drawing support from across the political parties of the South.

The Government figure with whom the UULA had most contact in the inter-war period was John Miller Andrews, successively Minister of Labour, Minister of Commerce, and Prime Minister (1940–43). Andrews came from a Liberal Unionist Dissenting and business background, and typified the strain of paternalism in Unionism.[85] It was Andrews more than anyone who strived, with a great degree of success, to keep the appearance of the Party broad and inclusive and to sell the message that the Government cared about the worker's welfare and material interests. In the person of Andrews the tradition of Liberal Unionism stretching back through to Thomas Sinclair, lived on, although its 'progressivist' impulses were in a broader sense severely circumscribed by the politics of the lowest sectarian common denominator which characterised the State.

Until he became Prime Minister, in succession to the equally benign Craig in this respect, Andrew's main political objective was to establish Northern Ireland's social services on the same level as Britain. This policy was dubbed 'step by step' and it was completed in such a fashion by Andrews from 1921 till 1938 when parity had been effectively attained. Shortly after the State's inception, in September 1921, in the midst of a trade depression and increasing unemployment, Andrews addressed the UULA and spelled out the 'step by step' creed which he and Craig largely made the cornerstone of Government policy.[86] According to this outlook, if Northern Ireland people paid the same taxes as people in Britain they should receive the same level of welfare benefits; in the view which prevailed in Craig's time as Premier,[87] it was vital to the Unionist cause that workers in Northern Ireland should receive full benefit of the British connection. Anything less, it was believed, would weaken the Unionist Party's central contentions and articles of faith.

What this added up to was an unadventurous approach to the devolved structures of government Northern Ireland possessed. Neither Craig, Andrews, nor the latter's successor Brooke (who remained Prime Minister till 1963) wished to use the powers devolved to Northern Ireland to diverge significantly from Britain, at least in the crucial area of social and economic policy. From the point of view of accommodating the Unionist Labour interest this made a lot of sense. In addition, it furnished the Government with the argument that if Ulster workers were guaranteed the same welfare standards and social legislation then there was no point in them voting for another party, such as the NILP, and thereby sending out the wrong message on the constitutional position — it was a potent and winning political formula, notwithstanding the difficulties they encountered in Belfast constituencies.[88]

The Unionists thus in effect removed much of the provincial basis for class politics. The absence of political debate concerning social welfare policy, and indeed about the big questions of public finance in general,[89] hardly helped Stormont's reputation as a serious political arena, but to the Unionists this was of secondary importance to the need to strengthen the Union. In the history of Northern Ireland no Government had the will to expand the powers of the State and adopt innovative policy directions, until the accession of Terence O'Neill in the 1960's. And, notwithstanding the right-wing Conservative views of most senior Ulster Unionists down the years, the Party had the political sagacity to behave largely in accordance with the view put by a young John Taylor in 1959: 'Our Party must never appear to be solely a right wing party but it must continue to be the party representative of Ulster loyalists of all classes'.[90]

VII

So far populist Protestant and Unionist politics in Scotland and Ulster have been compared in terms of how they were shaped by perceived threats and antagonists, and in terms of their relationship with class politics and social and economic questions. They can also be looked at in relation to questions of identity, including national, local and group forms, questions explored for the period before the Great War in the previous chapter.

In their struggle against Home Rule Ulster Unionists, in contrast to Southern Unionists,[91] came to base their case on the idea of *difference* from the majority on the island of Ireland. Various arguments were advanced to illustrate the sense of difference: a religious and culturally homogeneous community geographically concentrated and independent of the rest of the country; a distinctive economic basis to this way of life; a racial distinctiveness based on the settlement of the 17th century; a loyalty to the British crown and constitution and Empire and a concomitant and deeply felt sense of British nationality which might be said to have overshadowed a sense of Irish nationality. Whatever the differences in emphasis or interpretation concerning such arguments, the upshot of the anti-Home Rule campaign was the idea of Ulster as a 'place apart', a notion which has troubled as well as buttressed Unionism since, whether in terms of self-perception, or in the view of outsiders. The 'settlement' of the Irish question in 1921–22 was not a triumph for either Nationalism or Unionism. For the latter it also brought, or reinforced, feelings of ambivalence and doubt, reflected perhaps in the Unionists' regard for the Parliament they were given to keep Northern Ireland affairs out of British politics. Of itself this compromised the Unionists' 'Britishness' if only in the perception of many people outside Northern Ireland. Hard as successive Unionist Governments thereafter tried to minimise the political disjunction by 'step by step' policies, the situation created by the British Government entailed a difficult twin-track project for the Unionists: firstly, the necessity of ensuring that Northern Ireland's 'British' identity and connection remained meaningful and potent; and, secondly, that the political entity of 'Northern Ireland' be made workable and that the Northern Ireland people, or at least the majority, be proud of their local identity through it.

The result, it may be argued, was that Ulster Unionism came to stand for, and cultivate assiduously, both a heightened sense of British loyalty and patriotism, the displays of which began to appear increasingly at odds with the changing nature of post-imperial Britain itself in the half-century period 1920–1970; and also a narrower and more self-conscious 'Ulsterness' with 'Ulster' now synonymous with the six-county area of the State and the outlook of the majority within it.

Both British and Ulster identities eclipsed the sense of Irishness that at least some Unionists had been willing to proclaim even at the height of the Home Rule controversy. The more Irish nationalism or republicanism seemed to be essentially anti-British, and it did seem so after de Valera and Fianna Fail came to power in the South in 1932 and remained dominant,[92] the more Unionists left the designation 'Irish' aside for fear of being misunderstood. In the earlier Home Rule period it was always potentially likely that the Unionists' Irishness would weaken as others laying claim to it defined it in such a way as to threaten the Unionists' Britishness — which was proclaimed more resoundingly. The period of the Northern Ireland State only served to realise this possibility, although it should not be forgotten that some 20 per cent of Protestant respondents to a survey in 1968 were prepared to assert an Irish identity while, for the most part, still favouring the Union.[93]

Certainly, the Unionists devoted a significant amount of political energy to questions of identity. Todd has highlighted the Unionist *Belfast News-letter's* encouragement to the BBC in Northern Ireland to think of Ulster 'as a country, like Scotland, with some articulation of its own'.[94] Much irritation was felt by Unionists when outsiders failed to draw a distinction between North and South, or between 'Ulster' and 'Irish'. Unionists, especially in the post-war era when the benefits of the British Welfare State made 'compare and contrast' exercises with the South politically telling, were pleased to see signs of a regional patriotism. The notion of 'Ulster' as the most truly British of places in its values and tradition tied both sentiments neatly together. But Britishness was the real bedrock: a Unionist Government spokesman, Colonel Topping, conceded in a debate on partition in 1954, that there might have been practical advantages to the elimination of the border and that there was 'the sentimental appeal of being Irish throughout (a sentiment which the Scotsman and the Welshman proudly maintain)', but that these things could only have occurred if being Irish had not been made 'incompatible with being at the same time British'.[95]

Politically, the Ulster Unionists reflected the ambiguities of their position in the UK as a constitutional anomaly. Some Unionists took a quasi-federal view of their devolved parliament and warmed to the idea of greater regional autonomy. This was particularly evident in the post–1945 period when a group of Unionists including a couple of cabinet ministers argued the case, in effect, for

'Dominion Status' for Northern Ireland. They based their case on
the proposition that the Northern Ireland people had not voted for
the socialist measures which were being implemented by the British
Labour Government at Westminster and that the Northern Ireland
Parliament should have the powers to diverge from Westminster and
respond to local demands and needs.[96] This lobby were defeated in
their quest with the Brooke government unwilling to risk the possible alienation of Protestant working class votes which might be
entailed in any decision to reject the Labour welfare measures.
However, tensions between those who regarded the Northern
Ireland Parliament as decidedly a subordinate assembly to Westminster, and those who thought of it more in federal terms, were
discernible at various junctures in Northern Ireland's history, and
Terence O'Neill's approach after 1963 was in the direction of
greater autonomy and imbued with the evident belief in the potential of devolution which his predecessors had not evinced.

Over the history of the State the picture is one of a dual assertion of British loyalty and Ulster pride, accompanied by doubts
about the trustworthiness of British Governments — attitudes
often viewed as stemming from the Unionists' fundamentally 'contractarian' definition of their loyalty[97] — and a readiness to fall
back, if need be, on a sense of separate Ulster identity. This latter
sense of identity was an idea of cultural difference long in the
making — to which the 'Ulster-Scottish' bond was central — and
largely held in political check. However, the Unionists were
increasingly made aware that it was an idea of difference which
could bring unwelcome political pressures upon them to question
the Britishness that most of them continued to insist was at the
heart of their identity, even after the fall of the Northern Ireland
State in 1972. The whole area of national identity continued to
pose awkward ideological problems for Unionists after the establishment of the State; whenever lured or forced into debate on such
questions Unionists tended to reveal inner tensions and a lack of
clarity — in many ways understandable and hardly unique —
which could confuse or alienate outsiders. They were happier when
affirming loyalty and demanding that their position vis-à-vis the
minority be understood in terms of loyalty and disloyalty, but this
was usually the beginning rather than the end of debate on the
problems, and sooner or later definitions of identity were called for.

The Unionists in Scotland, as discussed in the previous chapter,
were well aware of the political significance of a strong sense of

Scottish national identity, and pride in Scottish national institutions. They themselves took a pride in their distinctiveness within the Conservative Party. However, their political appeal had at its heart an equation of healthy Scottishness with a pride in the Union and in the Empire. They stood for, and profited by, for a long period, the assertion of a dual sense of Scottish/British national identity. They used straightforward arguments about the Union and the Empire bringing benefits and opportunities to Scotland. They were careful to use 'British' in its proper sense, unlike many of their English colleagues who equated it with 'English'. They were well aware that Scottish Nationalist sensibilities had to be catered for.

As has been shown, they attempted to make anxiety over Irish Catholic numbers an indicator of concern for the Scottish national interest on the basis that the assumed 'disloyalty' of the Catholic community struck at the Union and thereby at what benefited Scotland. Implicit in this was an appeal to Protestant voters, although this had to be kept strictly within limits and explicit sectarianism was officially discountenanced. On the other hand, the Orange Order, on which it unofficially depended in certain constituencies, was more than willing to be explicit. The Order infused the Party's political message with a quintessentially Irish 'zero sum' attitude in various localities in relation to the Catholic community. In so doing the Order was making manifest the extent to which it was also part of an Irish, largely Ulster, immigrant culture, although it was also enthusiastic about the propagation of an Ulster-Scottish bond which had survived the trials of history, be it amidst the persecution of the Covenanters in 17th century Scotland or the siege of Derry in 1688. Indeed, the Orange Order in Scotland played regularly on the history and legacy of the Covenanters in order to unite Ulster and Scotland in a shared bond of martyred Protestantism.[98] The Order stood for a celebration of Scottishness which revolved around the Covenanters, Robert Burns and David Livingstone. A simple equation was made between Scottish patriotism and the upholding of Protestantism, which for Orangemen and women meant fidelity to the Union.[99]

The Unionists' willingness to exploit Scottish national sentiment was also demonstrated in the post-Second World War era. Their behaviour in this period invites an interesting parallel with that of the 'Dominion Status' advocates in the Ulster Unionist Party in the same period. For, in accordance with the same anxiety about the Labour government's programme, elements lent support to the

Scottish Convention movement for Home Rule which made a powerful impact on Scottish public opinion in the late 1940s.[100]

Both in Scotland and Ulster, Unionist and Protestant politics negotiated a path between different identities, and for a time were the stronger for their advocacy of a *blending* of such identities. Thus in Northern Ireland the Unionists cultivated a pride in 'Ulsterness' within the framework of 'Britishness', much as Unionists in Scotland preached that the wider British context provided the perfect foil for Scottishness. However, in general Northern Ireland Unionists' Britishness was more emotionally and defiantly proclaimed than Scotland's; the sense of being politically under pressure from Irish nationalism, and 'cut off' from the rest of the UK was clearly seen as necessitating a compensatory celebration of British national and imperial symbols, most obviously the monarchy. Correspondingly, the sense of 'Ulster' identity on the part of the Unionists was far more ambiguous than the Scottish Unionists' sense of Scottishness; Colonel Topping's statement presented above suggests an awareness of an Irish identity being compromised and nowhere mentions an Ulster identity as a substitute.

In the Post Second World War era, moreover, a far starker contrast between the two places became evident in relation to the perception of Britishness. In Scotland it can be argued that gradually until the 1960's, then rapidly thereafter, the popular appeal of Britishness declined and was overtaken by a more pragmatic and functional interpretation of Scotland's relationship to Britain.

Historians and sociologists have identified several key factors combining to diminish the potency of a British sense of identity and the strength of its link with Protestantism and Unionist/ Conservative politics. Such factors include the decline of the Empire, the process of secularisation in Scottish society, and the decline of sectarian friction between Protestants and Catholics through such developments as increased intermarriage and ecumenical relations between churches.[101] It is in this context that political commentators have put the decline of Unionist/Conservative politics in Scotland.

This decline was not precipitate or strictly continuous after 1945. The Unionists performed well in Scotland in the 1951 and 1955 elections; in the latter they won over half of the total Scottish vote, a political achievement unique to them. Neither did religion cease suddenly to have a significant bearing on political behaviour; a survey in the mid–1960's suggested a relatively strong correlation, in the British context, between the two with the relatively high Protestant working class Unionist vote and the solid Catholic Labour vote the most salient features.[102]

However, it is from this point — the mid 1960's — that crucial factors such as the end of Empire and the clear prevalence of sec- ularising tendencies in Scottish life, make political change more likely, especially when considered alongside the effects of popular discontent over economic issues. This was a time of anxiety as attempts, on the part of both Conservative and Labour Govern- ments, to re-shape Scotland's economic base away from traditional heavy industry faltered or fell prey to inflation, industrial relations strife or bad planning. By this time the glory days of the West of Scotland industrialists were long gone, and with them much of the political clout they had wielded through the Unionist Party; as David McCrone has pointed out, the social base of Scottish Unionism had been the alliance of industrial and business interests with a significant measure of Protestant working class support.[103] On the back largely of the economic flux, the Scottish National Party (SNP) made its breakthrough in the late 60's, early 70's, cul- minating in the winning of 30% of the vote and 11 seats in the General Election of October 1974. Studies have shown that the vast majority of SNP voters at this time were Protestants,[104] and some were clearly defectors from the Unionists/Conservatives. It may even be hypothesised that the SNP picked up a protest vote in 1974 from some Protestants disgusted by the Conservative Government's prorogation of the Northern Ireland Parliament in 1972. For a decade before being stripped of its power, the Unionist Party in Northern Ireland was itself undermined by the sense of uncertainty created by O'Neill's quest for modernisation. As with the Scottish Unionists, there were tensions between rival economic outlooks and interests;[105] but, unlike Scotland, Protestant extrem- ist politics remained potent, demagogic and populist, and were able to exploit the gathering fears and the revitalised hatreds which were to spill over into open conflict in 1969.

By the late 1960's more Scots were questioning the benefits of the Union. The end of Empire meant the end of the appeal of empire loyalism and the case for Scottish talents finding a global showcase. It should not simply be assumed that the end of empire implied an automatic decline in the political significance of the idea of Britishness;[106] however, that idea arguably changed its form suf- ficiently to make it difficult for the Unionists to continue to strike a populist note on the basis of it. This ability seems to have been further impaired by the decision in 1965 to dissolve the distinctively Scottish Unionist Party identity by changing the name of the party officially to Conservative.[107]

The secularisation factor has caused more debate among scholars,[108] but Steve Bruce's stress on it at least relative to Northern Ireland is surely beyond dispute. On the basis of such variables as Church attendance, opinions on moral issues, and sabbatarianism, Scotland was more oriented towards the broader British trends, while Northern Ireland was a society which defied them.[109] Intermarriage was far more prevalent in Scotland than in the much more rigidly segregated social life of Northern Ireland, while Scotland, Jack Glass notwithstanding, produced no-one to arouse popular opposition to ecumenism in the 1960's, in the fashion of Ian Paisley in Northern Ireland. On the other hand, as has been indicated, Scotland's political situation offered no parallel to the impact made by Terence O'Neill's 'modernising' project which sought to kill off communal friction by the kindness of economic prosperity for the whole Province. O'Neill's gestures to the Catholic minority allowed Paisley to characterise his new approach as the political equivalent of the religious ecumenism which he claimed was a betrayal of Protestantism.

Equally, the end of Empire hardly registered on the political scale in Northern Ireland. As in the period of original opposition to Irish Home Rule, it was essentially an extension of the affirmation of British loyalty which was the main justification for the Unionist position. Empire meant the greater glory of all things British, but the end of it left the Unionist position in Ireland unaltered. That was still defined in terms of the struggle against being forced into a united Ireland. The 'privileges' supposed to be incumbent on the Unionists having their own Parliament were also taken away in 1972 with the same result. Unionist *politics* was thrown into turmoil by the rise of the civil rights movement and the Unionist party splintered under the impact of 'the Troubles'; however, Unionism remained as a popular Protestant ideology, a mass movement communally adhering to the unwavering perception of Irish nationalism/republicanism as a threat to their liberties and identity. Neither Imperial symbolism nor economic prosperity was at the heart of Ulster Unionism. Both, it might be said, were more integral to the success of Scottish popular Unionism, and the decline of both hastened the Unionist political decline there. However, the decline in Unionist/Conservative political fortunes in Scotland did not imply a similar decline in the social significance of religious identity and the popular culture of sectarianism; from the 1970's the question becomes more one of finding an explanation for the disjunction between the social and cultural reality of religious tensions in Scotland, and their relative lack of political expression. This theme will be taken up in the last chapter, along with the impact of the Northern Ireland troubles on Scotland.

NOTES

1. James Mitchell, *Conservatives and the Union* (Edinburgh,1990) p.41.
2. J. Todd, 'Unionist Political Thought 1920–72' in G. Boyce, R. Eccleshall and V. Geoghegan (eds.), *Political Thought in Ireland Since the 17th Century.*
3. See M. Farrell, *Arming the Protestants* (Dingle, 1983) passim.
4. See B. O'Leary and J. McGarry, *The Politics of Antagonism* (London, 1993) chpts. 3 and 4, for the most recent scholarly attack.
5. See J. H. Whyte, *Interpreting Northern Ireland* (Oxford, 1990) for an incisive summary of the field. Unionist perspectives are illuminatingly discussed in Denis Kennedy's study of the Unionist Press, *The Widening Gulf* (Belfast, 1988).
6. See P. Bew, P. Gibbon and H. Patterson, *The State in Northern Ireland* (Manchester, 1979).
7. UUC Yearbook 1923, PRONI D1927.
8. Brigadier H. D. Young quoted in P. Bew, K. Darwin and G. Gillespie (eds.), *Passion and Prejudice* (Belfast, 1993) p. 20.
9. See W. Corkey, *Episode in the History of Protestant Ulster* (Belfast, 1947).
10. Bew et al, *Passion and Prejudice,* passim.
11. See documents held in SRO, HH55/68 and 69; Tom Gallagher, *Glasgow: the Uneasy Peace* pp. 90–98; and Iain D. Patterson, 'The Activities of Irish Republican Physical Force Oranisations in Scotland, 1919–21', in *Scottish Historical Review* LXXII, 1, April 1993, 39–59. See next chapter.
12. For examples of how the issue made an impact on Unionist politics in Scotland see the following: Minute book of Central Council, Scottish Unionist Association 13 March, 26 July 1939, NLS Acc. 10424/64; Minute Book of Glasgow Unionist Association 21 Dec 1926, 29 August 1927, NLS Acc. 10424.73.
    See Gallagher, *Glasgow* chpt. 4; T. Gallagher, 'Scottish Catholics and the British Left', *Innes Review* XXXIV no. 1 (Spring 1983) pp.

17–42; R. Finlay, 'Nationalism, Race, Religion and the Irish Question in Inter-war Scotland', *Innes Review* XLII, no. 1 (Spring 1991) pp. 46-67. See also Mitchell, op. cit. pp. 8-14; and S. J. Brown, '"Outside the Covenant": The Scottish Presbyterian Churches and Irish Immigration, 1922–38', *Innes Review* XLII, no. 1 (Spring 1991), pp. 19–45.

13. SRO 37110/1.
14. Ibid. Figures for Poor Law relief are also enclosed in these papers.
15. See below, chpt. 4.
16. See G. Walker, 'The Orange Order in Scotland between the Wars', *International Review of Social History* XXXVII, no.2, 1992, pp. 177–206. See also chpt.1.
17. E. McFarland, *Protestants First!* chpt. 9.
18. There were some 400 lodges in Scotland by 1914, and it is generally thought that membership numbers climbed to between 30,000 and 40,000 in the 1920s. See Walker, 'Orange Order'.
19. Such constituencies included Kelvingrove, Maryhill and Partick in Glasgow, and Rutherglen and Motherwell in the City's industrial hinterland. See Walker, 'Orange Order'.
20. See S. J. Brown, 'Reform, Reconstruction, Reaction: The Social Vision of Scottish Presbyterianism c. 1830–1930', *Scottish Jrl. of Theology* vol.44 (1991) pp. 489–517.
21. Brown, '"Outside the Covenant"'.
22. See Steve Kendrick's review of Gallagher's *Glasgow* in *Radical Scotland* no. 30 Dec 1987/Jan.1988.
23. See previous chapter re 'Ne Temere'; also Walker, 'Orange Order'.
24. For Ratcliffe and the SPL see Gallagher, *Glasgow* chpt 4; and S. Bruce, *No Pope of Rome* (Edinburgh, 1985) chpt 2. For Cormack and P.A. see T. Gallagher, *Edinburgh Divided* (Edinburgh, 1987); and Bruce, op. cit. chpt 3.
25. Walker, 'Orange Order'.
26. Speech by Rev. James Deans at an Orange social, reported in *Belfast Weekly News*, 9 January 1930.
27. *Belfast Weekly News*, 14 June 1934.
28. *Belfast Weekly News*, 6 June 1935.
29. See Brown, '"Outside the Covenant"'.
30. See G. Walker, *The Politics of Frustration: Harry Midgley and the Failure of Labour in Northern Ireland* (Manchester, 1985) pp.190–195.
31. See, for example, half-yearly report of Orange Order 8 June 1949, PRONI D2222 Box 8.
32. See, for example, J. J. Lee, *Ireland 1912–85* (Cambridge, 1989) chpt 1. For a critique see G. Walker, 'Old History: Protestant Ulster in Lee's *Ireland*', *The Irish Review* no.12, Spring/Summer 1992, pp. 65–71.
33. *Belfast Weekly News* 16 January 1930. See also comments of Lord

Charlemont (Minister of Education in N.I.) in Bew et al, *Passion and Prejudice* p. 5 and p. 49.

34. Half-yearly report of Orange Order 14 June 1933, PRONI D2222 Box 8.
35. Ibid. 8 June 1949.
36. See G. Walker, '"Protestantism before Party!" The Ulster Protestant League in the 1930's', *Historical Journal* vol.28, no.4, (1985) pp. 961–967.
37. Ibid; see also Bew et al, *Passion and Prejudice* pp. 22-23.
38. Bew et al, *Passion and Prejudice* p. 50.
39. See views of Father McShane in correspondence recorded in Bew et al, *Passion and Prejudice* pp. 69–82.
40. A. C. Hepburn, 'The Belfast Riots of 1935', *Social History*, vol.15 (Jan.1990) pp. 75–96.
41. Bew et al, *Passion and Prejudice* p. 37.
42. Ibid, p. 52.
43. See oath printed in *The Ulster Protestant* May 1939. This was the paper of the UPL.
44. See D. Kennedy, op. cit. passim.
45. Gallagher, *Glasgow* chpt.2; also J. E. Handley, *The Irish in Scotland* passim and *The Irish in Modern Scotland* passim. See evidence of Scottish Office documents, SRO 37110/1 and discussion in next chapter.
46. *Belfast Weekly News* 30 January 1930.
47. See Walker, 'Orange Order' for examples of Orange Order influence in employment and discussion of Order's perception of general employer indifference to questions of religion and 'loyalty'.
48. *Belfast Weekly News* 26 March 1931.
49. Ibid. 18 September 1930.
50. Walker, 'Orange Order'; Brown, '"Outside the Covenant"'. See also Minute Book of Glasgow Unionist Association 26 Nov 1934 (NLS Acc. 10424/74) for comments of Sir Charles Cleland on Catholic vote in Glasgow.
51. See Hepburn op.cit.
52. See Walker 'Orange Order' for further discussion.
53. *Belfast Weekly News* 10 November 1932.
54. *Vanguard* 21 March 1934 — This was the paper of the SPL.
55. See J. McCaffrey, 'Irish Issues in the 19th and 20th Century: Radicalism in a Scottish Context' in T.M. Devine (ed.), *Irish Immigration and Scottish Society*.
56. S. Bruce, 'Sectarianism in Scotland: A Contemporary Assessment and Explanation', *Scottish Government Yearbook* (1988) pp. 150–165.
57. For details of Brooke's speeches and an assessment of their significance see B. Barton, *Brookeborough* (Belfast, 1988) pp. 84–89.

58. See Gallagher, *Glasgow* pp. 151–3, and *Edinburgh Divided* Chpt 6 re Protestant parties' local election successes — the SPL vote in 1933 in Glasgow was enough to damage the ruling Moderates and give control of the council for the first time to Labour. The PA vote in the Edinburgh Council election of 1935 was 32% of the total.

    See also Minute Book of Glasgow Unionist Association 27 Nov 1933, 22 Oct 1934 (NLS Acc. 10424/74).

59. Bruce, 'Sectarianism'.

60. See Walker, 'Orange Order' for electoral details.

61. Ibid.

62. See examples of speeches in Walker, 'Orange Order'.

63. See *Forward* 3 February 1923.

64. See J. Melling, *Rent Strikes* (Edinburgh, 1983) pp. 70–71.

65. Quoted in Brown, '"Outside the Covenant"'.

66. See I. MacDougall (ed.), *Voices from the Hunger Marches* Vol 1. (Edinburgh, 1990), testimonies of Phil Gillon and Michael Clark

67. *Belfast Weekly News* 16 June 1932.

68. Ibid. 3 November 1932.

69. Ibid. 6 December 1934.

70. See J. Foster and C. Woolfson, *The Politics of the UCS Work–In* (London, 1986) p. 188 regarding Orange sympathy for the strikers.

71. Examples of 'Protestant' mining areas could be said to be Broxburn and Bo'ness in West Lothian; a 'Catholic' example is that of Croy in Stirlingshire.

72. See discussion in Walker, 'Orange Order'.

73. The gang warfare of 1930s Glasgow had a pronounced sectarian character, particularly in the East end of the city.

74. See Joan McAlpine, 'New Defenders of King Billy's cause', *The Scotsman* 11 July 1992.

75. See H. Patterson, *Class Conflict and Sectarianism* (Belfast, 1980); E. McFarland, *Protestant First*.

76. Bew et al, *Passion and Prejudice* p. 3.

77. Ibid. p. 116.

78. H. Shearman, 'Conflict in Northern Ireland', *The Yearbook of World Affairs* Vol. 24 (1970), in PRONI D3816/15.

79. See papers of Joseph Cunningham, PRONI D1288/1

80. The *Unionist Worker* March 1947

81. See G. Walker, 'Ulster's Forgotten Radical Ferment'. in *Fortnight* no. 275 July/August 1989.

82. See P. Bew et al, *The State in Northern Ireland* Chapt. 4; G. Walker, *The Politics of Frustration* Chpt. 9; J. Ditch, *Social Policy in Northern Ireland* 1939–50 (Avebury, 1988) Chpts. 4 and 5.

83. See D. W. Dean, 'Final Exit? Britain, Eire, the Commonwealth and the Repeal of the External Relations Act, 1945–49', *The Journal of*

Imperial and Commonwealth History, Vol. XX, no. 3, pp. 391–418.

84. See comments of W. McCullough (a communist) in his pamphlet, *For a Prosperous Ulster* (Belfast, 1945) about Northern Ireland now having the scope to develop along 'democratic lines'.

85. See biographical material in Alex Riddell Collection, Belfast Central Library, AA2.

86. See *Belfast News-Letter* 5 September 1921.

87. But see Bew et al, *The State in N.I.* for discussion of internal divisions.

88. See G. Walker 'Labour in Scotland and Northern Ireland: The Inter-war Experience' in R. Mitchison and P. Roebuck (eds.), *Economy and Society in Scotland and Ireland* (Edinburgh, 1988).

89. Northern Ireland's budget was drawn up by civil servants in London. See V. Bogdanor, *Devolution* (Oxford, 1979) Chpt. 3.

90. See Taylor's article in the Yearbook of the Queen's University Unionist Association (1958–59), PRONI D3816/15. It should, however, be noted that a foreword to the Yearbook was supplied by Tory Prime Minister Harold McMillan.

91. P. Buckland, 'Irish Unionism and the New Ireland', in D. G. Boyce (ed.), *The Revolution in Ireland* 1879–1923.

92. See quote from the *Northern Whig* in Kennedy op. cit. p. 174.

93. See R. Rose, *Governing Without Consensus* (Boston, 1971) Appendix.

94. Quoted in Todd op. cit.

95. Quoted in *Why the Border Must Be* (UUC, 1956), PRONI D3816/15.

96. See D. W. Harkness, 'The difficulties of devolution: the post-war debate at Stormont', *The Irish Jurist* Vol. 12 pp. 176–186; J. Ditch op. cit. Chpt. 5; B. Barton 'Relations between Westminster and Stormont during the Attlee Premiership', *Irish Political Studies* Vol. 7 (1992) pp. 1–20.

97. See D. Miller, *Queen's Rebels* passim; see also issues raised in chapts. 2, 4 and 6.

98. See speech by Digby S. Brown reported in *Belfast Weekly News* 10 January 1929.

99. See discussion of this theme in Walker, 'Orange Order'.

100. See J. Mitchell op. cit. pp. 48–50.

101. See Gallagher, *Glasgow* Chpt. 8; S. Bruce, 'Sectarianism'.

102. See I. Budge and D. Urwin, *Scottish Political Behaviour* (London, 1966) pp. 60-65, 68-71.

103. D. McCrone, 'Towards a Principled Elite: Scottish Elites in the Twentieth Century', in A. Dickson and J. H. Treble (eds.), *People and Society in Scotland* Vol. III (Edinburgh, 1992).

104. See J. Brand, *The National Movement in Scotland* (London, 1978) pp. 150–154.

105. Bew et al, *The State in N.I.* pp. 187–200.
106. See K. Robbins, 'This Grubby Wreck of Old Glories: The United Kingdom and the End of the British Empire', in *Journal of Contemporary History* XV (1980) pp. 81–95.
107. See views of Teddy Taylor as recorded in G. Walker and T. Gallagher, 'Protestantism and Scottish Politics', in G. Walker and T. Gallagher (eds.), *Sermons and Battle Hymns: Protestant Popular Culture in Modern Scotland* (Edinburgh, 1990).
108. See summary of this debate in C. G. Brown, *The People in the Pews*, Studies in Scottish Economic and Social History no. 3 (1993), Chpt. 5.
109. Bruce, 'Sectarianism'.

4

Nationalisms, the Politics of Identity, and the Catholic Experience in Scotland and Northern Ireland c. 1920–70

I

This century has seen an escalating crisis surrounding the idea of 'Britishness'. As the decades have passed the factors which historians such as Colley have identified as having shaped it have disappeared or declined in significance. In the last chapter it was noted that in Scotland the mileage in Britishness for popular Unionist politics had been drastically reduced by the 1960s. In Northern Ireland its vitality was the result of a continuing community division — an ethnic conflict in which conceptions of national identity took on a timeless and fossilised character. Northern Ireland Catholics, by and large, as will be discussed in this chapter, clung tenaciously to an ideal of Irish unity which owed everything to their plight in the Northern Ireland State and nothing to the discrete development of the independent Irish State in the rest of the island. Northern Ireland Protestants defined their unionism in terms of the threat they believed Irish nationalism or republicanism constantly posed to the survival of their identity; that the latter looked increasingly out of place as ideas of Britishness underwent significant change did not weigh as heavily in their consciousness as the importance of opinion in the rest of the U.K. suggested that it should.

The Northern Ireland Protestants, as the six-county state took root, allowed their sense of Irishness to diminish to a trivial level; the teaching of English, rather than Irish history in the 'Protestant' schools was one of the crucial ingredients in the process.[1] However, in laying claim to Britishness as a priority, the Unionists only framed themselves in the eyes of most British onlookers as something of a 'misfit'. Exaggerated displays of loyalty, couched in increasingly archaic religious language, when added to the fact of the Province's detachment from British politics, seemed to define Northern Ireland as irredeemably 'a place apart'.

This may in turn have reflected the narrowness of the average English, and indeed Scottish, perspective; as Boyce has argued, following recent seminal work by historians like Kearney, Northern Ireland ought to have been viewed in the context of the cultural interaction which was in many ways the key to understanding the 'Britannic' historical experience.[2] However, the fact remained that for Ulster Unionists, the wider British hinterland to which they sang praises, was problematic. More than anything the lack of dialogue between Ulster Unionists and British opinion in general, reinforced the Unionists' defensiveness and contributed to their tendency to substitute an historically-fabricated abstraction for a highly complex and rapidly-changing reality.

Scotland did not, of course, experience the detached political existence of Northern Ireland. However, in many ways her British identity became strained in the fifty year period when devolution was applied to the Province. If Scotland was not a 'place apart' in the sense in which Northern Ireland was commonly viewed, then she was at least a place more restless and unsure about the benefits of the constitutional status quo. Economic adversity partly explains this: the Scottish industrial bourgeoisie seems to have suffered a loss of confidence in the inter-war period from which it never truly recovered.[3] By the 1960s the end of Empire and the decline of Scotland's heavy industrial base prompted the 'break up of Britain' analysis of the Marxist Nationalist Tom Nairn: for Nairn Britishness had turned on the Scottish middle class being suborned in the classical age of nationalism in the nineteenth century by the blandishments of capitalist opportunity in Britain and the Empire. Nairn thus considered it inevitable that a crisis of capitalism would issue, in this case in the first instance, in a nationalist direction.[4]

Other factors seemed also to point to such a development. The capacity of religion — Protestantism — to be employed in the service of the British ideal, shrunk in accordance with the decline in the number of its adherents. This fall was steepest in the 1960s.[5] Lowland Scotland had by this time become integrated into a wider British secular trend. Even an apparent popular reverence for the monarchy in Scotland could not be taken as a declaration of political enthusiasm for the British state. All in all, the 'props' of Britishness seemed to have been removed or eroded.

Yet Nairn and those who have followed his outline analysis[6] have neglected other developments which may have served to counter-balance these factors to a significant degree. The issue of secularisation, for example, could be said to have cut two ways. It weakened a 'Church and State' appeal but it simultaneously brought Scotland more firmly into line with modern British popular culture. Secularisation was part of increased social and cultural interaction between different parts of Britain. Another vital force in this regard was the media: from the shared experience of radio from the 1920s, through the advent of the mass popular press of the 1930s and 1940s, to the impact of television in the 1950s and 1960s, a wider British leisure culture forged more 'customs in common' between Scotland and England than had existed before. Only the Scottish Highlands and Islands, and Northern Ireland, can be said to have significantly defied the secularist trend and retained their religiously-oriented way of life.

The 'end of Britishness' school has also tended to pass over the impact of the experience of World War Two and the ways in which it might have restored an ailing sense of British identity among many. In terms of myth-making and the power of myth to shape identities, the war against Nazi Germany has been a cornerstone of the positive image of latter-day Britishness; through the mass media and film it has entered the collective consciousness vividly and stirringly. Notions of collective sacrifices in the cause of democracy and civilisation have done much to counter critical reflections on Britain's role as an imperial aggressor and oppressor through the centuries. Moreover, the subject of war serves to highlight the enduring strength of British military culture in Scotland. This was the kind of factor which transcended the loss of Empire and cut across a Nationalist interpretation of the economic results of the Union being bad for Scotland; many people's livelihoods were bound up with the British military machine. Genuinely popular campaigns to protect Scottish regiments have been features of the country's post-war politics that even the Scottish Nationalists have not hesitated to back.[7]

Finally, there is also the shared experience of British institutions, perhaps most importantly the Welfare State in the post-World War Two era. This in turn points to the heritage and political objectives of the British Labour movement which has such deep roots in Scotland, and, in the post–1945 era, has drawn on a steady and vital mass electoral support base in Scotland. This topic will be explored in depth in the next chapter.

Such factors serve to caution against too ready an acceptance of 'End of Britishness' analyses. They can be said to have balanced those which have weakened older ideas of Britishness. Thus the Empire's decline has not led axiomatically to the end of the Union. 'Britishness' has remained one of the 'nationalisms', or at least one of the national identities, in the political equation. It has remained, in relation to Scotland, one of the central loyalties in relation to which the range of variables which shape identity have operated;[8] moreover, it has been an identity to which many people in Scotland have emotionally looked as well as functionally held.[9]

II

Yet it is equally important to stress and explain the rise, politically, of Scottish nationalism within this fifty year period. It may indeed be equally valid to argue that many of the variables taken as indications of a wider British identity can be interpreted as contributing more obviously to a sense of Scottish distinctiveness. As the historian Keith Robbins has noted, there have been competing forces in the matter of identity in the modern era towards British integration on the one hand and towards diversity, or even separation, on the other.[10]

Scottish nationalism, however, has been a variable political force and a problematic cultural movement. It is not, as McCrone points out,[11] a national movement of the age of nationalism; as a political party it dates officially from 1934. It many ways it is a study in contrasts with Irish nationalism which did emerge at the 'classical' 19th century nationalist moment.

Irish nationalism was based to a great extent on linguistic, religious and cultural distinctiveness; it could be labelled an 'ethnic nationalism' cohering as it did around the homogeneity of Catholic Ireland outside the North-East, and drawing strength from grievance: from a deep-rooted sense of historical injustice and resentment over misgovernment. Irish nationalism was also a movement with a deep awareness of history, and it was adept at *using* history — at drawing upon past heroes, past acts of rebellion, past acts of national consciousness-raising, to build up a powerful propagandist message.[12] It was — and is — a movement which, as Bob Purdie has commented, has had a central concern with *territory*, and with the concept of a sovereign state embracing the geographical wholeness of the island.[13] And Irish nationalism is a tradition with both moral and physical force dimensions to it: force has been employed at various times in an attempt to secure political objectives.

The character of Scottish nationalism has been overwhelmingly that of a movement preoccupied with constitutional, or practical, politics.[14] It has evolved as a political force out of the small beginnings of the 19th century Scottish Home Rule Association (SHRA) and was, until the 1960s, more often identified with the goal of Home Rule than outright independence or separation. In contrast to Ireland's system of government following the Act of Union of 1800 Scotland's governance was administered *by* Scots, albeit from the lowland Scottish ruling elites, and, in the twentieth century, increasingly *in* Scotland. Perceptions of misgovernment were often held, but were not wedded to the Irish notion of being dealt with in 'colonial' fashion. Only on the cultural nationalist fringes of the movement since the 1920s, have the Irish traits of grievance-fuelled interpretations of history, assertions of a racial or ethnic form of national identity, and advocacy of physical force methods, been in evidence.

In the 1920s the cultural nationalist voice was an articulate and eloquent one, finding expression through the literary 'renaissance' of the time; maverick 'gurus' such as Erskine of Mar and the poet Hugh MacDiarmid (Christopher Murray Grieve) attempted to raise consciousness in the manner of the romantic figures of the Irish tradition. Patrick Pearse's example inspired them; in Pearse there was the appeal to history and the spiritual and sacrificial traits required to build a similarly virile nationalist resistance to British imperialism in Scotland.[15] Parnell's jibe about Scotland having sold its soul struck deep chords in the thoughts of envious Scottish 'fundamentalists'.[16]

The best efforts of the cultural nationalists to present Scotland's cause as bound up in a racial struggle between the Saxon and the Gael[17] found little response in the densely populated urban and industrial heartlands of central Lowland Scotland. Wisely, the political wing of nationalism, when underway by the late 1920s, distanced itself from the racial exclusivism of the 'Celticists' and were more cognisant of the complexities and contradictions of Scotland's modern historical development and contemporary social and cultural reality.

Most nationalists resisted the Celtic reductionism of the cultural movement of the 1920s. Simplistic readings of history in this vein were avoided. But something of the potential of history to sharpen the nationalist appeal, as in Ireland, was also lost.[18] The past, indeed, has always been an awkward tool for Scottish nationalists to work with: there has been a reluctance to dwell on what intellectuals like Nairn have identified as a 'deformed' past — the way in which Scots have been induced to accept a risible image of themselves as tartan-bedecked jesters at the court of English sophistication. During our 20th century period, this 'Lauderesque' caricature blended with, and trivialised, the Jacobite tradition of popular imagery and song. This has been an additional matter of regret for intellectuals who have discerned in Jacobitism a useful ideological antidote to Unionism.[19] However, Jacobitism had long been largely a recreational pursuit on the margins of Scottish discourse; any analysis of Scottish identity which places it so centrally, as in Pittock's work, has a lot to explain away in relation to the impact made on the national consciousness by competing ideological strands which derive from such phenomena as Presbyterianism and the Scottish Enlightenment.[20]

The dominant tone of Scottish nationalism, then, derived from a constitutionalist, and indeed civic, imperative. It was a nationalism which remained institutionally-based, which fed off the proclaimed distinctiveness and excellence of the legal, educational, and local government systems, and the perception of a religious tradition — Presbyterianism — which was deeply righteous, moral and character-building. Scots felt they could *negotiate* their way to whatever degree of independence they desired, that the Union was a contract which could at any time be revised.[21] The bias in nationalistic thinking was thus legalistic rather than subversive; the Irish perception of the Union as a repressive and constraining force found only a faint echo in Scotland where there was a general recognition that their distinctive civil society had been allowed to flourish.

Above all, there was no unifying ethnic identity to underpin a 'romantic' nationalism: the fundamentalists' anglophobic quest to convince lowland Scots that they were part and parcel of a Celtic nation, flew in the face of centuries of racial mixing and cultural interaction within the British Isles; repudiation of the idea of a

British nation might have persuaded more but it too had to confront the contemporary experience of British empire-building to which the Scots were so central and out of which most developed some sense of British identity.

The cultural nationalists were grouped together in the Scottish National League (SNL) during the 1920s, and they stood for full-scale independence. They joined up with the National Party of Scotland (NPS) which was formed in 1928 by SHRA members who were dissatisfied with the lack of progress towards Home Rule through the medium of Westminster. By 1933 the fundamentalists had been expelled and the NPS entered into talks with the largely conservative Scottish Party which had been set up shortly before to pursue devolution. The result was the formation of the Scottish National party (SNP) in 1934, a party committed to the moderate goal of Home Rule within the Empire. This was an indication of the continuing strength of ideas about Imperial federation, so much part of the constitutional debate before 1920.

The ex-Scottish party element in the SNP was, in fact, more concerned about the greater glory of the British Empire than the cause of a distinctive Scottish national identity.[22] There were soon tensions between them and those who favoured something more substantial than Home Rule, namely Dominion status — a concept which probably aroused opposition in the Imperialists for its contemporary Irish connotations and implications, among other factors. For the Imperial element was also notable for their fervid anti-Irish Catholic outlook; academics and writers of this persuasion such as Andrew Dewar Gibb and George Malcolm Thomson painted lurid pictures of the baleful effects on the Scottish national character of Irish Catholic immigration.[23] Taken along with the similar outbursts emanating from the Scottish Protestant Churches already noted, this amounted in Catholic eyes to the equation of Scottish nationalism with anti-Catholic bigotry. The marginalisation of the cultural nationalists — some like Erskine of Mar were Catholics and their ideological stance indicted the Reformation for many of Scotland's ills — only helped to reinforce this impression. For Gibb and the rest racial blending had produced an unbeatable *British* mongrel, to which the ethnically Celtic Irish Catholics were clearly inferior.[24]

The SNP's electoral fortunes in the 1930s, 40s and 50s were largely dismal; the exception was a bye-election victory at Motherwell in 1945. The party's significance, as Finlay has argued, lay in its role as a pressure group providing a 'catalyst' to important public debates on the Scottish economy and the administrative governance of the nation.[25] With regard to the latter, the 1930s saw an accretion of government business situated in Edinburgh, and the performance of Tom Johnston during the Second World War pointed to the possibilities of the Secretary of State's role in winning important legislative reforms and increased autonomy for Scotland.[26]

Post-war, it was John MacCormick (a former SNP figure who had split from the party in 1942) and his Covenant movement for self-government which took the political limelight. The impact of this movement was an interesting reminder of the sensitivities of the Scots to the whole constitutional issue at a time of increasing centralisation on the part of the Labour Government at Westminster. Moreover, its symbolical character and appeal seemed again to identify the Scottish national cause with an essentially Protestant mode of protest and argument.[27] In as much as moderate Nationalists considered the Northern Ireland devolution experiment, there was a belief that it provided a good illustration of their case for self-government,[28] and critical perspectives more likely to engage Scottish Catholic sympathies were always confined to the fundamentalist and separatist elements which continued to agitate from the wings.

When the SNP emerged as a formidable political force in the 1960s, it is generally agreed by academic commentators of different ideological persuasions that they did so in response to the failure of the regional economic planning schemes of successive Conservative and Labour governments; as McCrone has put it, there occurred a 'Scottishing' of the economic agenda.[29] Rising economic expectations which were unfulfilled resulted in the SNP enjoying the benefits of protest votes, and making headway with its own message that Scotland could only properly re-structure her economy when the levers of power were in her own hands. The discovery of North Sea oil in the early 1970s convinced many that she now had the resources for the task — self-government was thus vital to ensure that the resources were deployed to this end.

III

The cause of Scottish Home Rule trailed a long way behind that of Irish Home Rule up to 1920, not least in Scotland itself. The Irish

Catholic experience in Scotland in the preceding century had largely been one of an immigrant group resisting — and being denied — assimilation; whatever the precise dynamics, active Scottish hostility or at the very least ambivalence reinforced a deep-rooted sense of introspective clannishness. Religion was the most clearly distinguishing badge of identity, but the preponderance of Catholic over Protestant immigrants during this century contributed in practice to the equation of Catholic with 'Irish'. This was in turn reinforced by the political mobilisation of the Catholic community around Irish nationalism, notwithstanding the prominence in Irish nationalist political circles in Scotland in the late nineteenth century of the Belfast-born Protestant, John Ferguson.

As scholars such as Gallagher and Gilley have made clear, the Irish Catholic community in Scotland, heavily concentrated in the industrial West, was marked by a temporally as well as spiritually dominant Church. Much of this socially and economically disadvantaged community's social life was directed by the Church. Politically, relative poverty did not notably translate into support for the nascent Labour movement of the late nineteenth and early twentieth century;[30] rather, the United Irish League directed political activity according to the interests of the Home Rule cause, and in this period the Liberal Party were thus the electoral beneficiaries. A blending of the social and the political distinguished the appeal in Scotland, as in Ireland, of the Ancient Order of Hibernians and the Gaelic League.[31]

If constitutionalist Irish nationalist politics were dominant in Scotland before the First World War, the events in Ireland during the war were to be reflected to some extent in Scotland in the form of increased Irish republican support and activity. Sinn Fein held only a toe-hold among the Irish Catholics in Scotland until 1916; from the aftermath of the Easter Rising till the mid–1920s its impact in Scotland did much to enliven the Irish ethnic identity of some of those born in Scotland, and to further prejudice perceptions of the Irish Catholics on the part of Protestant Scots. Irish Republican Army (IRA) activity in Scotland during the War of Independence (1919–21) and the Civil War (1922–23) in Ireland was significant if, in the view of one historian, relatively ineffectual from a military point of view.[32] It led, for example, to pressure being put on certain Scottish MPs to raise with government officials the issue of Irish immigration and the number of Irish immigrants in receipt of poor relief and in employment. The Chief

Constable of Paisley wrote to the Scottish Under-Secretary of State on 12 July 1922:

> It is true that a large number of men and women came to the Clyde district from Ireland to work in the Munitions Factories during the war and many of those remained in Scotland, and they now prove strong competition against the native workers.[33]

The anti-Irish Catholic campaigning of the inter-war period, as discussed in the previous chapter, revolved around notions of Irish Catholics coming to Scotland (as Protestant emigration from Scotland rose steeply[34]) and taking jobs which were 'rightfully' Scottish Protestant, or making themselves a burden on the rates by claiming poor law or unemployment relief. The publicity generated through IRA operations in Scotland in the 1919–22 period, or through the trials of those arrested and charged with such activity,[35] helped some to draw a portrait of an organised takeover of vital industrial jobs by Irish republicans who subsequently ransacked their workplaces for munitions and materials for IRA purposes. The incidents in which policemen were shot, in Glasgow and Bothwell in 1920, while interrupting IRA operations, seemed to lend credence to such alleged conspiracies. Many hostile observers took no notice of constitutionalist nationalist/physical force republican divisions, or the more recondite animosities within and between the Catholic secret societies the AOH and the Knights of Columba, an organisation formed in Glasgow in 1919.[36]

The image of a monolithic, politically disloyal and rebellious and violent community, directed by an authoritarian Church, was irresistible to many Scots, even without Orange prompting. As the Paisley Chief Constable wrote:

> At the outbreak of war the young men of the Catholic religion in Paisley enlisted in greater proportion than the rest of Paisley's inhabitants; they were then apparently loyal, but their attitude has changed since the Dublin Rebellion of 1916, and while many support Collins and the Free State, De Valera and his Republic have many supporters, and the majority of both sides are against the Crown and Constitution of this country.[37]

Arguably, the upsurge in Irish republicanism in Scotland, corresponding to the situation in Ireland itself, was a key factor in reinvigorating anti-Irish Catholic prejudice and populist politics, and in keeping the community's concerns fixed on Ireland, whatever the divisions within it on the upheavals taking place there.

Internal divisions were certainly the keynote theme in relation to the effects of the partition settlement on the Catholic community of the new Northern Ireland state after 1921. Politically, the main fault line ran between the supporters of the old Irish Parliamentary Party, led in the North by Joe Devlin, and Sinn Fein, but the civil war caused a further split in the ranks of republicans.[38] As the new Northern Ireland State found its feet, the Catholic community was fragmented in relation to the crucial issues of participation in it, and strategies of opposition to it. Such a confused political situation enabled the Church to enhance its role as community fulcrum, and in the early 1920s the Church was central to the provision of community needs and infrastructure, and to Nationalist political evolution. The Church more than any other single agency, shaped the 'State within a State' which the Catholic community became; the Church also played a critical role in the gradual process by which Nationalist political forces became more coherent and began to play an (unofficial) oppositional part in the State's politics.[39]

The Church was prominent in relief provision for Catholics in the troubled period of the State's birth, and it was a mouthpiece of anti-partitionism to the point of non-cooperation with the Northern Ireland Government in key public policy areas in the early months of the State's existence. However, one issue eclipsed all this: the securing of unfettered control of education for Catholic school-children. Against the background of uncertainty which marked the State's early years, the Catholic Church attempted to ensure that secularisation of schooling stopped at the Catholic community; the schools were seen as the key to the maintenance of the faith and a separate identity. Thus in the Education Act of 1923 the Catholic schools were permitted to remain outside local authority control. The Catholic Church, indeed, even rejected the '4 x 2' governing committees proposal under which there would be two statutory lay members; they feared any potential dilution of their own authority in the realm of education. The price of being free of state control or influence was to receive only 50% of the running costs of the schools from the State. Even this, however, was viewed as an injustice, a penalising of Catholic schools for insisting on the preservation of their own ethos and identity.[40]

Defiance, such as was displayed by the Catholic Church over education, defined the mood of the minority in general. It persisted after the Boundary Commission's report in 1925 had confirmed the border between North and South as stipulated by the

Government of Ireland Act, and it had ample cause to feed off Unionist tunnel-vision. However, the more the Catholic minority, politically and culturally, were seen to accept the 'disloyal' designation, the more Orange populism made claims on Government attention and indulgence. The political culture was thus shaped by the extent of alienation engendered.

In Scotland the Irish Catholic community faced a body of opinion which regarded them as aliens, yet the organising theme of scholarly inquiry into their experience has been the question of assimilation.[41] Central to this question, just as it was central to Northern Ireland Catholics' quest to maintain their identity in a hostile environment, was education. The 1918 Education Act (Scotland) brought Catholic schools into the State sector; although unsure at first about the permanence of the legislation and its benefits, the Catholic Church in Scotland came to regard this, in contrast to Northern Ireland, as a satisfactory arrangement.[42] Historians have viewed the Act as a significant factor in the eventual assimilation of the Catholic community, although the issue's capacity to provide ammunition for anti-Catholic campaigners may have helped to ensure that this process has been a gradual one.[43]

The Act clearly gave the Catholic community a stake in Scottish, and indeed British, society, but in confirming in practice Catholic Church control over the schools, it also provided conditions in which a distinctive ethnic identity and self-enclosed communalism could thrive. Indeed, the story of the Irish Catholic community in 20th century Scotland was both one of interaction with wider Scottish society and one of the reinforcement in important ways of a separate profile. Assimilation was never allowed to imply a disintegration of cultural distinctiveness. In this too a certain defiance and rebelliousness, reminiscent of Northern Ireland Catholics, was evident.

On the basis of the returns of the 1931 Census the Scottish Office, in response to politicians' inquiries, prepared a report on the Irish in Scotland which sheds much light on their numbers and social profile.[44] The report concerned those Irish-born, as opposed to those of Irish descent, and so is of limited value in helping us appreciate the numbers who considered themselves part of the Irish community. The figures for the census do not, in addition, distinguish by religion.

The report provides figures for Irish immigration since census records began. Thus a pattern of high Irish immigration to Scotland in the 1860s and 1870s, followed by another steep rise till the turn of the century, can be traced. The 20th century figures were over-all much lower, although the First World War seems to have been the main cause of an increase in the second decade of the century. After 1921 the report concluded that the balance was one of net *emigration*, it being presumed that a substantial number of Irish immigrants of former years were included in the emigration total of 392,000 between 1921 and 1931.

In 1931 the total number of Irish-born persons enumerated stood at 124,296. Of these, residents numbered 122,944, some 2.5% of the population of Scotland. 67,216 (55%) were born in what was now Northern Ireland, 54,854 (45%) in the Irish Free State. It appeared, however, that the bulk of the most recent immi-grants, since 1915, had come from what was now the Irish Free State area. The Northern Ireland figures remind us that a significant portion of Irish immigrants to Scotland, at least in the nineteenth century, were Protestant.

The Irish-born population, and those of Irish descent, were heavily concentrated in industrial west-central Scotland, particu-larly in Glasgow but also in industrial towns such as Greenock, Clydebank, Coatbridge and Motherwell. This concentration of their numbers seems to have distorted the impression of many contemporaries; it fostered the belief that their presence was a far greater proportion of the total population than was the case. Significantly, of course, popular anti-Irish Catholic politics were largely a feature of the industrial west, although the case of Edinburgh in the 1930s should not be overlooked. Notable too, in relation to the interplay of sectarian perceptions, was the triumph-alist reporting in the Catholic community newspaper in Belfast, the *Irish News*, of the rise of the Catholic population in Scotland and the decline in Protestant numbers.[45]

The 1931 census figures also indicate that the occupational pro-file of the Irish in Scotland had hardly changed much in a century: the largest proportion of the Irish-born in work (27.8%) belonged to the category of 'Other and Undefined Workers' which included labourers and unskilled workers. Lack of skills had disadvantaged many Irish immigrants from the start, and in this respect the Irish Catholic experience differed sharply from the Irish Protestant.[46] The numbers of Irish-born in the 'Metal Workers' occupational category (14.5%) probably included quite a few Protestants, even by 1931. The other occupational categories in which the Irish-born were significantly represented in 1931 were those of 'Transport Workers' and 'Workers in the Mines and Building Trades'.

Partition and the erection of two new States in Ireland in 1920–22 has also been taken as a watershed in the development of the Irish Catholic community in Scotland. Gilley argues that by this time the strongest binding force in the community was religion rather than nationality.[47] Gallagher too perceives the identity of the community as having been re-oriented in this period away from 'Irish' preoccupations towards 'Catholic' ones. Central to this process, he argues, was the transfer of Catholic political activity and allegiance from Irish Nationalist politics to the Labour Party's cause in British politics.[48] The resolution of the Irish question in this respect coincided almost precisely with the Labour electoral breakthrough in Glasgow and the West of Scotland in the general election of 1922: the Labour vote, it has been clearly demonstrated,[49] owed much to the Irish Catholic community, many of whom were newly enfranchised.

The theme of Labour and the Catholic vote will be more thoroughly explored in the next chapter. At this point what needs to be stressed is the extent to which the Labour movement in its widest sense, encompassing political and industrial wings and local government spheres of influence, proved to be a vehicle for the assimilation of the Irish Catholic community into public life, while becoming another medium through which a distinctive Catholic ethnic identity was expressed in Scotland. Participation in the Labour movement meant interaction with Scottish Protestants and those of no religion, politically and industrially, around issues of class interest. The assumption of positions of responsibility, as trade union officials or local government workers, became a symbolical act of social and cultural integration on behalf of a whole community. On the other hand, the very concentration of Catholic support for labour and participation in its affairs as the one political force perceived to be sympathetic to specifically Catholic interests in such areas as education, and Irish nationalist aspirations, tended to fashion 'fresh assertions of ethnic identity'.[50]

Certainly, as studies of the Irish in England have also shown,[51] the Labour Party took care not to set ethnicity at odds with class. In Scotland, as in certain parts of England, Labour soft-pedalled or abandoned liberal lines on moral issues such as birth control in its appeal to Irish Catholics and was prudent enough to recognise that the Catholic Church line on birth control and education was central to the cultural identity of the community and could not be opposed without a serious price being paid in terms of the vital votes of that community. The reward for appeasing Catholic sensibilities in these respects was in Scotland a virtual monopoly of the community's support; a specifically Catholic political party did not materialise in spite of rumours and threats of one in the 1920s and 1930s.

However, Gallagher's work has demonstrated that groups such as the Catholic Union and Catholic Action were politically energetic into the post Second World War period; the former played a crucial role in mobilising Catholic votes for the Local Education Authority elections in Scotland until their curtailment in 1929.[52] During World War Two the Catholic Workers' Guild was formed to combat Communism; this organisation seems to have built on the vocational guilds which had been formed out of Catholic workers since before the First World War.[53] Pressure groups such as these defended Catholic interests regarding education, attempted to counter communist influence in the workplace, and campaigned against what they saw as Protestant and secularist influences in public life more generally. All in all, the effect of such groups' preoccupations was to strengthen the religious dimension over the national in relation to the overall ethnic community identity, although it should be noted that the Catholic Union campaigned for a public enquiry into the political situation in Northern Ireland after the communal riots in Belfast in 1935.[54]

A more specifically *Catholic* profile was also the result of the Church's efforts to encourage a popular devotionalism in Scotland, particularly in the inter-war period. The Legion of Mary, a movement of Irish origin, was successfully transplanted to Scotland, and the Knights of Columba grew at the expense of the less pious and definitively Irish Ancient Order of Hibernians. Above all, in terms of its impact on the wider Scottish consciousness, the construction of a grotto at Carfin in Lanarkshire proclaimed the Catholic spiritual presence.[55] Fully in control of its schools, whose rolls rapidly increased in the inter-war period, and delighted by the devotional displays of the faithful, the Catholic Church exuded a certain confidence. Amidst a socially and economically depressed community there was nonetheless fostered a sense of moral righteousness and superiority. The Church, as in Northern Ireland, seemed to turn the suffering of many of its adherents into a test of faith; sacrifice meant spiritual ascendancy.[56]

The Catholic sense of its own spiritual superiority was conveyed

occasionally through its publications. In *The Aloysian* (the maga-
zine of a Glasgow parish), for example, the following comment was
passed on the subject of Protestant Churches taking up the practice
of midweek services:

> If the kirk orators have so frequently to preach to empty benches on
> the Lord's Day, what chance is there of their getting congregation in
> mid-week?[57]

A certain triumphalism could accompany public conversions to
Catholicism in Scotland,[58] but consolidating the allegiance of the
flock was given priority over proselytizing. As another issue of *The
Aloysian* on the topic of mixed marriages put it:

> Loyal Catholics who contemplate entering the holy state of matrimony
> should always make it clear that they cannot marry anyone but a
> Catholic. There should be no promise of marriage to anyone but a
> Catholic. The fact that a non-Catholic promises to go under instruction
> is no guarantee that such a person will become a Catholic. It sometimes
> happens that the non-Catholic is unwilling to give up certain false
> principles and practices which are impossible in a true Catholic life,
> and may wreck the sanctity and happiness of wedded life.[59]

To some Protestants in Scotland, the combination of public displays of devotion, the existence of a plethora of Catholic pressure
groups, the evidence of Catholic intransigence and exclusivism, the
terms of the Education Act, and the perception of the social and
economic effect of Irish immigration (seen as largely Catholic), was
proof of a powerful social, political and cultural force intent on the
alteration of Scotland's Protestant character and the subversion of
the wider British constitution.[60] As was noted in the previous chapter, popular Protestant and Unionist politics made ample use of
the essentially Irish political discourse of 'loyalty' and 'disloyalty'.
If the Catholic religion was the prime target of their charges, much
of a pejorative and racist nature was made of the 'Irish' dimension.
This anti-Irish Catholic campaign reflected the loss of influence
suffered by the Protestant churches since the First World War,[61]
fears over high emigration from Scotland on the one hand and a
higher Catholic birth-rate in Scotland on the other,[62] and a loss of
economic confidence in the context of ailing heavy industries in the
1920s and 30s. It was a period, in the words of one historian, of
'profound social, cultural, economic and political dislocation'.[63]

The crucial period from 1918 to 1922–23 when political
events in Ireland reached a climax and political re-alignment took

shape to a large extent in Scottish and British politics, does seem to have marked a turning point in the development of the Irish Catholic community in Scotland. Irish developments found a clear echo in Scotland and Irish ethnic consciousness, and nationalist allegiance, were strong. However, the establishment of the two States North and South and the consequent departure of the issue from British politics, effectively closed off channels for the political expression of Irishness. Instead, political energies seemed to have been transferred overwhelmingly to the arena, and through the vehicle, in which the community's social, economic and indeed cultural interests could be successfully pursued. As energies became more collectively focused on the Labour movement,[64] and on the wider political scene at local government level in Scotland and at Westminster, ethnic goals were reoriented from nationality to religion, and class began truly to rival ethnicity in terms of political priorities.

This is not to say that Irishness quickly ceased to have meaning; Catholic communal identity was still clearly Irish to an important extent until the Second World War. However, a number of factors, chiefly political ones, had decisively altered the course of the community's development. Expressions of Catholic hostility to Scottish Protestants tended to be on the basis of religion: a reaction to perceived religious sectarianism or discrimination. It was not generally voiced in terms of Protestants' Unionism or Loyalism or Scottish nationalism, or even an assumed Loyalist view of the Irish situation. From the mid–1920s attacks on the Catholic religion became increasingly more frequent than attacks on Irish nationalism or Irish ethnicity, notwithstanding the racism which was a feature of political and cultural debate in inter-war Scotland. Correspondingly, Catholics were more vigilant in their response to religious slights than solicitous on behalf of Irish nationalist or republican objectives.[65] This included the cause of the Catholic minority in Northern Ireland; in relation to their plight only the Catholic Union protest of 1935 seems noteworthy.

Catholics in Scotland, quite simply, had their hands full in fighting for their own social and economic advancement, or in many cases, survival. Indeed, imbalance in employment opportunities bore many similarities to the situation in Ulster: Protestant domination of the skilled heavy industry sector was self-perpetuating, and Catholic professionals were largely confined to serving their own community. On the other hand, particularly after the Second

World War, the Catholic presence in local government employment became more noticeable, a reflection of the extent to which they had been able to use the Labour Party as a means of social mobility.[66] The Catholic middle class grew more rapidly in this post-war era than its Northern Ireland counterpart, and was able to exploit the far more pronounced atmosphere of religious toleration in Scotland which had set in by the 1960s. Inter-church relations, for example, moved a long way from the tense stand-off of the interwar period in which mutual suspicion was rife. Active discrimination in employment in Scotland became largely confined to the small business sector, although some folk memories and fears on both sides of the sectarian divide were much less sanguine.[67] Rumblings of such issues persist through to the present.

Scotland, moreover, became more secularised than Northern Ireland, as noted in the last chapter. The process seems to have affected the Catholic Church and community much less than its Protestant counterparts until at least the 1970s,[68] but the Catholic Church in the same period lost its 'Aloysian' grip on mixed marriages and started to fight a rearguard action in defence of its schools in the face of an onslaught of liberal opinion against educational 'apartheid', dating from the 1960s. Post-war demographic changes, which led to the break-up of inner-city communities, served to weaken the Irish Catholic communal identity as well as that of the 'Orange' working class, although arguably in lesser measure. They certainly did not adversely affect the solidity of the Catholic Labour vote. Crucially, Irish immigration ceased to be an issue in post Second World War Scotland; the vast bulk of the heavy outflow from the Irish Republic in the 1950s settled in England rather than Scotland.

IV

The Northern Ireland Catholic experience after 1922 was altogether more politically hopeless and somewhat more socially and economically dismal than that of their co-religionists in Scotland. In Scotland the Labour Party proved to be a safety valve; in Northern Ireland Catholics did not find opportunities for political redress of grievances. The grievances in turn, even when social and economic, became inextricably bound up with the 'National Question', with the existence of the Unionist-controlled Northern Ireland State. The prospects of Protestant-Catholic working class cooperation in the context of the Northern Ireland State always faced the obstacle in the Catholic community of the belief, held by a sufficient number, that social justice could not be achieved within the State.[69]

This is not to deny that there was often impressive support given to Labour candidates, of whatever party or none, particularly in Belfast. But Catholic communal solidarity, pan-class in nature, like its Protestant counterpart, was seldom broken with lightly or without baleful repercussions. Experience of discrimination much more systematic and politically calculated than anything practised in Scotland,[70] bred a flinty collective resistance which could often express itself in the same antagonistic sectarian language as the other side. Certainly, from the 1920s through to the 1960s the Nationalist Party, as the main political standard-bearers of the minority, merely answered Protestant intransigence with Catholic defiance. Rallying support for the Nationalist Party cause at local election time in Belfast in 1928, the *Irish News*, the main newspaper of the minority in the North, commented of the Falls and Smithfield wards:

> . . . they never returned any member who was not an avowed and professed Catholic, standing as a Catholic and returned because of his fidelity to Catholic principles . . .[71]

The Nationalists, indeed, often made it clear that their agenda was a limited one. They most assiduously pursued the interests of the Catholic Church whose influence on the party at local level was profound.[72]

Catholic religious belief and practice were clearly central to the minority's identity, and a powerful cultural resource employed politically by extreme Republicans through to conservative constitutional nationalists. The Church's role in maintaining the cultural identity of its community, particularly through the schools it controlled, was vast. Yet notwithstanding its all-pervading presence, religion was not generally identified by Catholics as the issue around which their grievances revolved. On the part of Catholics, the 'National Question' was consistently defined as a political question, a state of affairs which persists to the present. The issue in their view concerned the right to self-determination of the Irish nation which was proclaimed as being self-evidently 'one and indivisible'; religion was simply used as a tool of the meddling British to create division and prevent this happening.[73] Thus, in some contrast to Scotland, Catholic antagonism in Northern Ireland towards Protestants tended to be on account of their proclaimed Britishness, Unionism or Loyalism rather than their religion *per se*, although Protestants regarded such claims sceptically and remembered the slights against their faith by Cardinal MacRory and others.[74] To Protestants in Northern Ireland, as in populist Protestant circles in Scotland, the Catholic community was driven by the contemptuous attitude of its Church towards Protestantism into adopting aggressive postures against what Protestants held dear. Where some Catholics may have seen devotion to their faith as part of the wider resistance to partition, Protestants more generally saw a triumphalist, 'our day will come' message which equated the political with the religious in their minds.

It is widely agreed that the impact of the Welfare State and the increased educational opportunities after 1945 at least encouraged many Catholics to revise their relationship to the Northern Ireland State and the British connection.[75] In some ways it led a sizeable part of the community to adopt a pragmatic identification with the Union if Rose's findings of 1968 are any guide: some 20% of Catholics in this survey of community attitudes were prepared to state that they were British or identified with 'Ulster', and 30% stated that they 'approved' of the proposition that the border should be regarded as final.[76]

Such a pragmatic outlook, based on calculation of superior material benefits in comparison with the Irish Republic, could be said to have mirrored to an extent the attitude which was far more common among Catholics in Scotland since the 1920s in relation to British identity. It was an identification which involved little or no sentiment, and no flag-waving or jingoism. However, in the Irish case the sentimental appeal of the goal of a united country ensured that pragmatism only took hold so far, while in Scotland there was among most Catholics no such sentimental regard for the goal of Scottish independence, and detached romantic views of Ireland were compatible with a more developed Britishness or less inhibited unionism.

The issue is an important one for it is linked to any assessment of the nature of the civil rights movement which convulsed Northern Ireland late in 1968, and lifted the curtain on the present 'Troubles'. The difficulty with such assessments is that strong arguments can be made firstly for viewing the movement as a radical break with traditional anti-partitionist politics of protest and a movement for 'British rights for British citizens' within the Northern Ireland State and, by extension, the Union;[77] and, secondly, for viewing it as essentially oriented towards the traditional anti-partitionist goal of the destruction of the State.[78] The extent of Catholic acceptance of the State, albeit reformed in accordance with the civil rights' demands, is thus a crucial measurement to determine. Rose's findings may help; they certainly suggest a community quite evenly divided between those willing to accept the State, those opposed to it, and those unsure.[79] However, there is no way of knowing how firmly Catholic pragmatism was by this time rooted, and Todd has reminded us that one of the most important civil rights in the eyes of many Catholics was the full expression of their Irish national identity,[80] something which implied constitutional change and brought them inexorably into confrontation with the State as defined by the Unionist ethos.

Within the wider U.K. State the expression of an Irish identity might have been accommodated, but not within the narrow sectarian confines of the Northern Ireland State. The civil rights movement found to its cost that the still prevalent view that Catholic grievances could not be redressed without an end to partition only encouraged many Protestants to believe that any attempt to deal with those issues would endanger the very existence of the State. As Frank Wright has argued, Protestants did not defend privileges because they were privileges but because they were locked into everything else that they believed had to be defended.[81] As it was, Protestant Unionist reaction ensured that whatever pragmatism had developed among Catholics paled beside a renewal of communal solidarity and new levels of national and ethnic conflict.

Overall, then, Catholics in Scotland and Northern Ireland constituted in many ways disadvantaged communities in this fifty year period. Nevertheless, they were communities in which there was abundant talent and energy to ensure that in the Scottish case the community was put on the map, and in Northern Ireland that it maintained its identity against majority domination. Social and economic misery was rife among Catholics in both places, but it co-existed with community vigour and purposefulness. Small middle classes made an impact out of proportion to their numbers and exhaustive propaganda and organisational skills were politically in evidence to such a degree that Protestant fears and suspicions in both places were aroused, and not just at the extremist point in the spectrum.

V

The question of the Ulster Protestants and national identity has been discussed in previous chapters. Clear conclusions have been difficult to draw, and while some scholars have been in no doubt that the Ulster Protestants have evinced an ethnic 'Ulster nationalism' more or less since the plantations,[82] most are more cautious and either reject the concept or view it as an embryonic form of nationalism which has never politically developed.[83] If, indeed, the Ulster Protestant sense of national identity can be said to have been British, then in theory this was not an ethnic nationalism; it was, at least technically, a multi-ethnic identity to which, if Irish Catholics had subscribed, Ulster Protestants could not have objected. Yet, in cultural terms, a distinctive Ulster identity has been a reality; and, as in the other 'nationalisms' discussed, there have been competing interpretations and definitions of it.

Most common has been the assumption that 'Ulster' identity is a synonym for Protestant ethnic or communal identity. Less common yet still significant definitions have attempted to make Ulster a common identity to be shared by Protestants and Catholics in the area covered by the Northern Ireland State.[84] Such ideas have drawn on the 'regionalist' thinking of the Ulster poet John Hewitt during the 1940s,[85] a period in which some Unionist politicians, as discussed above, argued in the direction of greater regional autonomy for Northern Ireland as a political unit.

In the 1960s, Terence O'Neill's modernising vision for both his Party and the Province entailed greater regional planning and economic powers, a cultivation of the image of a progressive and prosperous Ulster showing the way to the rest of the U.K. rather than just demanding to be kept upsides. Calvert has contrasted the vigour with which O'Neill and his ministers asserted themselves against any 'trespass' by the central government with the lack of enthusiasm shown for devolution by O'Neill's predecessors.[86] Implicit in this was the potential for political nationalism, and O'Neill's rhetoric suggested that it was an identity which could be shared by both Protestant and Catholic.

In the event, O'Neill's raising of expectations only to leave them unfulfilled contributed to the resurgence of full-blown Irish nationalism among Catholics, and his raising of fears among Protestants ensured that 'Ulsterness' would be re-confirmed in terms of anti-Catholic, 'Not an Inch' intransigence. As in Scotland, the failure of programmes of economic modernisation and a new language of regional development contributed to the emergence of the national question;[87] in the case of Northern Ireland, however, the form this took pre-empted any prospect which might have existed of bi-confessional Ulster nationalism on the basis of economic aspirations. 'Ulster nationalism', since the fall of O'Neill and the onset of the 'troubles', has developed exclusively within Protestant communal circles, a phenomenon to be taken up in the final chapter of the book.

NOTES

1. See T. Brown, 'British Ireland' in E. Longley (ed.), *Culture in Ireland: Division or Diversity?* (Belfast, 1991).
2. G. Boyce, 'A Place Apart?', in E. Hughes (ed.), *Culture and Politics in Northern Ireland* (Buckingham, 1991); H. Kearney, *The British Isles*.
3. See Kearney's point (*The British Isles* p. 199) regarding the economic decline of the 'periphery' in the inter-war period, and the growing dominance of the South-East of England. This he sees as contributing to the elision of 'Britain' into 'England'.
4. T. Nairn, *The Break-Up of Britain* (London, 1981).
5. See C. Brown, 'Religion and Secularisation', in A. Dickson and J. H. Treble (eds.), *People and Society in Scotland* Vol. III (Edinburgh, 1992).
6. For example, see P. H. Scott, 'The End of Britishness', in *Cencrastus* no. 456, Autumn 1993, pp. 7–9.
7. I. S. Wood, 'Protestantism and Scottish Military Tradition', in G. Walker and T. Gallagher (eds.), *Sermons and Battle Hymns*; also T. C. Smout, 'Perspectives on the Scottish Identity', *Scottish Affairs* no. 6, Winter 1994, pp. 101–113.
8. Smout op. cit.
9. See J. Mitchell, 'The 1992 Election in Scotland in Context', *Parliamentary Affairs* Vol. 45, no. 4 (Oct. 1992), pp. 612–626.
10. K. Robbins, 'Varieties of Britishness', in M. Crozier (ed.), *Cultural Tradition in Northern Ireland* (Belfast, 1990); and K. Robbins, *19th Century Britain* (Oxford, 1988).
11. D. McCrone, *Understanding Scotland*, especially the discussion in chpts. 1 and 8.
12. See G. Walker, 'Irish Nationalism and the Uses of History', *Past and Present* no. 126 (February 1990).
13. B. Purdie, 'The Lessons of Ireland', in T. Gallagher (ed.), *Nationalism in the Nineties* (Edinburgh, 1991).

14. C. Harvie, 'Nationalism, Journalism, and Cultural Politics', in Gallagher, *Nationalism in the Nineties*.
15. See M. Pittock, *The Invention of Scotland* (London, 1991) p. 145; also R. J. Finlay, 'Nationalism, Race, Religion and the Irish Question'.
16. See J. Hunter, 'The Gaelic Connection: The Highlands, Ireland and Nationalism, 1873–1922', *Scottish Historical Review* Vol. 54 (1975) pp. 184–5.
17. Finlay, 'Nationalism, Race, Religion'. See also R. J. Finlay, *Independent and Free* (Edinburgh, 1994) p. 193 regarding the hostility towards English immigrants on the part of Scottish cultural nationalists — and admirers of Irish nationalism — like Archie Lamont.
18. See M. Ash, *The Strange Death of Scottish History* (Edinburgh, 1980). The Highland Clearances provided explosive material for later popular nationalist historiography — see especially the works of John Prebble.
19. See Pittock op. cit. passim.
20. These themes can be followed up in works such as Pittok op. cit.; C. Harvie, *Scotland and Nationalism* (Routledge, 1994); C. Beveridge and R. Turnbull, *The Eclipse of Scottish Culture* (Edinburgh, 1989); T. Nairn op. cit.; C. Kidd, *Subverting Scotland's Past* (Cambridge, 1993).
21. See Lindsay Paterson, 'Ane end of ane auld sang: sovereignty and the renegotiation of the Union', in *Scottish Government Yearbook* (1991) pp. 104–22. See also chpt. 6.
22. R. J. Finlay, 'For or Against? Scottish Nationalists and the British Empire, 1919–1939', *Scottish Historical Review* LXXI (1992), pp. 184–206.
23. Finlay, 'Nationalism, Race, Relgion'; Gallagher, *Glasgow*, pp. 168–173.
24. Finlay, 'For or Against?'
25. R. J. Finlay, 'Pressure Group or Political Party? The Nationalist Impact on Scottish Politics, 1928–1945', *Twentieth Century British History* Vol. 3, no. 3, 1992, pp. 274–97.
26. See G. Walker, *Thomas Johnston* (Manchester, 1988) chpt. 6.
27. G. Walker and T. Gallagher, 'Protestantism and Scottish Politics', in Walker and Gallagher, *Sermons and Battle Hymns*.
28. Finlay, 'For or Against?'
29. McCrone, *Understanding Scotland* pp. 159–164; M. Keating, *State and Regional Nationalism* (Brighton, 1988) pp. 175–6; H. Patterson, 'Neo-nationalism and class', *Social History* Vol. 13, no. 3 (Oct. 1988) pp. 343–349; M. Hechter, *Internal Colonialism* (London, 1975) pp. 298–310.
30. See discussion in next chpt.
31. Gallagher, *Glasgow* p. 54; S. Gilley, 'Catholics and Socialists in

Scotland', in R. Swift and S. Gilley (eds.), *The Irish in Britain 1815–1939* (London, 1989).

32. I. D. Patterson, 'The Activities of Irish Republican Physical Force Organisations in Scotland, 1919–21', *Scottish Historical Review*, Vol. LXXII, no. 193 (April 1993), 35–59.
33. SRO HH55/68.
34. See Dickson and Treble op. cit. 'Introduction'.
35. Patterson op. cit.
36. For AOH — Knights of Columba rifts see letter from Chief Constable (Lanarkshire) 4 Sept. 1920, SRO HH55/69.
37. SRO HH55/68.
38. For a detailed examination of the divisions among Nationalists and Republicans see E. Phoenix, *Northern Nationalism* (Belfast, 1994) chpts. 4–8.
39. Phoenix op. cit.; M. Harris, 'The Catholic Church, minority rights, and the founding of the Northern Irish state', in D. Keogh and M. H. Haltzel (eds.), *Northern Ireland and the Politics of Reconciliation* (Cambridge, 1993).
40. Harris, op. cit.; see also F. O'Connor, *In Search of a State* (Belfast, 1993) p. 312.
41. Gallagher, *Glasgow* passim.
42. See F. Wright, *Northern Ireland: A Comparative Analysis* (Dublin, 1987) p. 186.
43. Gallagher, *Glasgow*; for a detailed study of Catholic education see J. H. Treble,'The Development of Roman Catholic Education in Scotland 1878-1978', *Innes Review* XXIX, no. 2 (1978) pp. 111–139.
44. SRO 37110/1. This is the source for the information which follows.
45. *Irish News* 3 May 1933.
46. See chpt. 1.
47. Gilley op. cit.
48. Gallagher, *Glasgow* especially chpt. 4; also T. Gallagher, 'Scottish Catholics and the British Left'.
49. See I. McLean, *Legend of Red Clydeside*, chpt. 14.
50. O. D. Edwards, 'The Irish in Scotland', in D. Daiches (ed.), *The New Companion to Scottish Culture* (Edinburgh, 1993).
51. See S. Fielding, *Class and Ethnicity* (Buckingham, 1993), especially chpt. 6.
52. Gallagher, *Glasgow* p. 106, and chpts. 5 and 6.
53. Ibid. p. 124.
54. Ibid. p. 119.
55. Ibid. pp. 108-9.
56. See O'Connor, op. cit. p. 315, 322.
57. *The Aloysian* no. 72, March 1932.
58. Gallagher, *Glasgow* p. 121, 135, 140.

59. *The Aloysian* no. 85, April 1933.
60. See Walker, 'The Orange Order in Inter-War Scotland'.
61. See S. J. Brown, 'Outside the Covenant'.
62. C. Brown, 'Religion and Secularisation'.
63. R. J. Finlay, 'National Identity in Crisis: Politicians, Intellectuals and the "End of Scotland", 1920–1939', *History* lxxx (Summer 1994) pp. 243–259.
64. There had been significant Irish Catholic involvement in the Labour movement in Scotland since its emergence. See next chpt.
65. Although there was some activity on the part of the Anti-Partition League in Scotland in the late 1940s, early 1950s.
66. S. Bruce, 'Out of the Ghetto: The Ironies of Acceptance', *Innes Review* XLIII, no. 2 (Autumn 1992) pp. 145–154.
67. See also Finn's points regarding the perception of a Masonic anti-Catholic agenda in relation to employment etc., in G. P. T. Finn, '"In the Grip": A psychological and historical exploration of the social significance of freemasonry in Scotland', in Walker and Gallagher, *Sermons and Battle Hymns*.
68. Dickson and Treble op. cit. 'Introduction'.
69. See J. Todd, 'Northern Irish Nationalist Political Culture', *Irish Political Studies* Vol. 5 (1990) pp. 31–44.
70. See J. H. Whyte, *Interpreting Northern Ireland* (Oxford, 1990) pp. 61–4, 164–9, for a judicious summary of the debate on the extent and nature of discrimination in Northern Ireland.
71. *Irish News* 9 January 1928.
72. See J. Todd, 'Northern Irish Nationalist Political Culture'.
73. See, for example, O'Connor op. cit. pp. 170–171; Wright op. cit. p. 158.
74. See D. Kennedy, *The Widening Gulf* (Belfast, 1988) pp. 165–6.
75. See J. Ditch, *Social Policy in Northern Ireland 1939–50* (Aldershot, 1988), p. 138 ff.
76. R. Rose, *Governing Without Consensus* (London, 1971) Appendix.
77. For a discussion of this theme see B. Purdie, *Politics in the Streets* (Belfast, 1990).
78. For which see C. Hewitt, 'The Roots of Violence: Catholic Grievances and Irish Nationalism during the Civil Rights Period', P. J. Roche and B. Barton (eds.), *The Northern Ireland Question — Myth and Reality* (Aldershot, 1991).
79. Rose, op. cit; see also Wright op. cit. p. 211.
80. Todd, 'Northern Nationalist Political Culture'.
81. Wright op. cit. p. 18.
82. See, for example, A. Birch, *Political Integration and Disintegration in the British Isles* (London, 1977) pp. 61–68.

83. Loughlin op. cit. rejects it; Gibbon op. cit. sees it as undeveloped politically.
84. See J. W. Foster, 'Radical Regionalism', in *The Irish Review* no. 7, Autumn 1989.
85. J. Hewitt, 'Regionalism: The Last Chance', in *Ancestral Voices* (Belfast, 1987); see also Tom Clyde, 'A stirring in the dry bones: John Hewitt's regionalism' in G. Dawe and J. W. Foster (eds.), *The Poet's Place*.
86. H. Calvert (ed.), *Devolution* (London, 1975) p. 9; see also D. Gordon, *The O'Neill Years* (Belfast, 1989) pp. 47–51.
87. H. Patterson, 'Neo-Nationalism and Class'.

5

A Study in Contrasts: Labour Politics in Scotland and Northern Ireland c. 1920–70

I

Earlier chapters have glanced briefly at the way class politics have interacted with the national question in both Scotland and Ulster; the theme is considered in more depth here. First, there will be a brief discussion of the relationship between socialism and nationalism in both places in the era of the emergence of the Labour movement in Britain and Ireland, a discussion which will focus on ideological figures whose legacy is still fiercely debated. This will be followed by an examination of the contrasting fortunes of Labour politics in Scotland and Northern Ireland in the period c. 1920–70.

II

In the late 19th and early 20th century a Labour movement developed as a political and industrial force in the British Isles. It is often forgotten how much Belfast and its environs (and indeed Dublin) were part of that movement. Trades unionism grew in strength in the heavy industrial employment sector, a fact recognised by the decision of the British TUC to hold its conference in Belfast in 1893. The 1890s also saw the Belfast Trades Council develop an important political profile, and branches of the Independent Labour Party (ILP) set up in the city. In 1907 the British Labour Party (which had changed its name from the 'Labour Representation Committee' in 1906) held its conference in Belfast.

Between Belfast and Clydeside there was a great deal of interaction in the cause of labour and of socialism.[1] Many Ulster workers belonged to trade unions which at this time had their base in Scotland. There were many other factors pulling the two places together: Scottish labour leaders like Keir Hardie paid regular speaking visits to Belfast; others, like Bob Smyllie, born in Ulster, personified the cultural interaction which had so long been a feature of Ulster and the West of Scotland; municipal socialist ideas made a striking impact on both Glasgow and Belfast; and in both places there were heavy industry economies, a profusion of skilled manual labour, and a great deal of craft sectionalism which was somewhat at odds with the 'New Unionism' of the 1880s and 1890s which saw the organisation of much unskilled labour in the U.K.

There were important contrasts too. By the time Labour was pushing its way into the political arena in Ulster, radical liberalism had been confused and then diffused by the Irish Home Rule controversy;[2] no such political struggle between Labour and Liberalism for the 'progressive' banner took place in Ulster as it did in Scotland. Instead, Labour in Ulster had to face, from the start, the challenge of promoting 'progressivism' within the problematic political context of ethnic and national divisions sharpened by the issue of Home Rule. As Purdie has pointed out,[3] no such Unionist-Nationalist polarisation troubled the Labour movement in Scotland, notwithstanding the presence of Scottish Home Rule on the wider political agenda from the late 19th century.

The outstanding Labour leader in Belfast in this formative period was William Walker.[4] Walker was a trade unionist, a local councillor and the leading light of the ILP organisation in the city. He stood unsuccessfully for election in North Belfast on three occasions — 1905, 1906, 1907 — contests which resulted in defeat but conferred on Labour a much higher political profile. Walker saw the way forward for the Irish working class as a whole (not just the Ulster part of it)[5] as lying within the British Labour movement; like many British socialists of the time he believed that the U.K. was evolving 'naturally' in a socially progressive direction and that the wider Empire provided a context for truly international working class unity. Walker was anti-Home Rule, believing that it would make no difference where the seat of government was situated; rather it was necessary to change the people who governed. Walker therefore challenged the assumption that an Irish socialist must also be a nationalist.

This idea — the fusing together of socialism and nationalism — was best epitomised by James Connolly, the Edinburgh-born founder of the Irish Socialist Republican Party in 1896, and one of the most influential social and political thinkers in modern Ireland.[6] Connolly's analysis contradicted that of Walker. For Connolly, the struggle for socialism was also an anti-imperialist struggle. In his major work *Labour in Irish History* (1910) he asserted that the struggle for the liberation of a subject nation must keep pace with the struggle for the liberation of the most subject class in that nation. Thus the social and the national were linked. So while Walker stressed that the Irish working class interest was bound up in the British Labour struggle, Connolly insisted that it was bound up in the struggle to break the British connection.

Connolly and Walker, in fact, debated this issue in 1911 through the pages of the Scottish Socialist newspaper, *The Forward*, and the Belfast Labour movement effectively split over the national question along Connolly/Walker lines at this time. This was a debate which highlighted the problems in the relationship between socialism and nationalism in Ireland, and which was to echo down the years within Labour and socialist circles in Ireland, North and South. In many ways the issue was further complicated by Connolly's participation in the Easter Rising of 1916: this raised questions about the extent to which he had remained a socialist or had subordinated his socialism to the demands of the Fenian republican tradition. Some people have viewed his participation in what was an act of rebellion by a small minority as a decisive break with his doctrine that the liberation of the nation had to keep pace with the liberation of its most subject class.[7] Others have raised questions about who exactly constituted the 'most subject class'; after all, in a Marxist sense the most important part of the working class, the industrial workers of the North-East, were overwhelmingly anti-Nationalist and hostile to Connolly's analysis.[8] Connolly, indeed, failed totally to persuade the Ulster Protestant working class to identify with his vision of an Irish workers' republic, heavily grounded in Gaelic (and Catholic) values,[9] and this merely reflected his refusal along with that of mainstream nationalists and republicans, to take their proclaimed sense of British identity seriously, an identity, it might be said which owed much to Scottish ties including those of a Labour and Socialist nature mentioned above.

However, Connolly, in his own time as well as posthumously, was an inspirational figure to many on the left. One who was inspired was John MacLean, a leading Marxist thinker in Scotland in the same period. MacLean, it seems, was influenced by Connolly to move towards an analogous theoretical position which combined socialism and nationalism in Scotland.[10] In the last years of his life he stood for a Scottish workers' republic and considered Scotland to be, like Ireland, a nation oppressed by British imperialism. Like Connolly, MacLean espoused what he believed were the communal, socialistic virtues of Gaelic society in both Scotland and Ireland. Since his death in 1923 MacLean's legacy, like that of Connolly, has been a matter of intense ideological dispute. Some have played down his nationalism and concentrated on his earlier career as a British socialist;[11] others have stressed it and argue that it complemented his socialism.[12]

At the very least, as with Connolly, MacLean's analysis invited a lot of theoretical problems. For instance, it required a highly selective set of criteria to judge Scotland an oppressed nation at a time when her 'junior partner' status in the Empire was still a highly meaningful concept; neither was more than a fraction of the Scottish working class 'anti-imperialist' in the way that has fancifully been suggested by one well-known Scottish historian;[13] and there were serious gaps in both Connolly's and MacLean's perception of a 'golden age' of 'Celtic communism': an acknowledgement of the slavery system which was part of it, for one.

Criticisms aside, Connolly and MacLean remain towering figures in the landscape of Irish and Scottish political thought and political history. The importance of their contribution is testified to by the endurance of their legends and the continual reassessment of the men, the myths and the legacies they bequeathed. On the other hand, for all their magnetism, it is important not to lose sight of the fact that in Scotland and in Ulster the main vehicle of socialist or Labour politics before, and indeed for a short time after, the Great War, was the ILP, which was organised on a British basis.[14]

The ILP was very much an inheritor of 19th century radical traditions which emphasised ethical and moral issues, voluntary grassroots political participation and democratisation. In Scotland it was to a large extent successful in appropriating the ethical and anti-privilege view of the world represented by strands of Liberalism.[15] In Ulster the evangelistic, crusading character of the ILP was a necessary motivating force in an often hostile and violent political environment. The ILP, indeed, was in both places, and in Northern England and parts of Wales, more than a party — it was a culture.[16] It was a culture of socialist idealism which sought to provide moral uplift to working men and women. It was high-minded and less doctrinal than the emerging forms of Communist politics.

In a context more favourably prepared by deep-rooted Liberal and radical traditions, the ILP made a profound impact in Scotland. It tapped into religiously-based precepts of egalitarianism and popular democracy,[17] it espoused self-help schemes, it promoted municipal socialism, and it propagandised brilliantly through newspapers and pamphlet literature. In the years immediately before and during World War I it built up a working class base of support on key issues such as housing — it organised the successful rent strike of 1915[18] — and brought together Protestant and Catholic working people around such issues. Although the militancy of the Clyde Workers' Committee and the revolutionary charisma of John MacLean have featured prominently in 'The Legend of Red Clydeside' forged during the war, it was the ILP which struck deepest roots, and chords, in the working class, and which emerged best placed to channel class frustrations and aspirations into electoral results.[19]

In theory the ILP was also committed to Scottish Home Rule, as well as Irish, but this was not put to the fore in the way that social issues were. Had the rapport between Highland and Lowland Scotland been closer, had there been a stronger identification between urban industrial worker and highland crofter, then the Scottish national question might at this point have been more politically potent. But the sense of identity between urban and rural, Highland and Lowland Scotland was vague and somewhat romantic; the crofter community was shrinking, and both the Highland Scottish and the Irish migrations to the Lowlands had resulted, from a Labour point of view, in absorption into an overwhelmingly urban industrial culture, a culture oriented towards other such communities in the rest of Britain. The *Irish* national question, on the other hand, caused sectarian friction among Protestants and Catholics in certain industrial Lowland areas, and serious problems for the Labour cause as the testimonies of ILP activists bore witness.[20]

Such problems were serious to the point of being insurmountable for Labour in Ulster. For a while, though, the prospects looked more favourable. Trade union strength and organisation grew during World War I, and a 'Belfast Labour Party' based on the existing ILP in the city won around one fifth of the Protestant vote in the 1918 general election, notwithstanding its support for Irish Home

Rule.[21] ILP activists, largely drawn from the majority community, were anti-partitionist for socialist reasons, and few could have been termed nationalist or republican. The 1919 '44 Hour' strike, which was virtually general, indicated the strength of the industrial (largely Protestant) working class and of the craft trade unions, and Belfast witnessed a huge May Day procession that year. The 1919 strike, indeed, spread to Glasgow where it prompted the intervention, as in Belfast, of troops. There was evidence of workers' solidarity between the two cities and a call for the release of Glasgow strike leaders was issued at the May Day rally in Belfast. The climax of this Labour surge then came in Belfast in January 1920 when the local Labour Party won 12 municipal seats. All in all, Belfast very much shared in the post-war atmosphere of class discontent which characterised many parts of the U.K.

At this point in mid–1920, however, the pendulum in the Protestant working class swung back from Labourism to militant Loyalism, a process occasioned by the impinging of the 'national revolution' and the IRA war and the channelling of unemployed ex-servicemen's agitation to loyalist rather than left wing ends.[22] In Scotland the breakdown of the ex-servicemen's factor was much more evenly distributed between left and right.[23] Soon, loyalist ex-servicemen's organisations along with the UULA,[24] had violently upstaged Labour activists in the workplaces, and the latter ('Rotten Prods') were summarily expelled from their work along with thousands of Catholics. The 'troubles' were to last till late in 1922 and left sectarian scars which have never healed. In this period of communal violence the Northern Ireland State was established and with it the 'zero sum' politics of ethnic imperatives. Labour did well just to survive. And, as Morgan has put it,

> it was in 1921, when political labourism was physically suppressed by loyalism, without any restraint from the Ulster bourgeoisie, that Belfast broke from the political history of the industrial triangle[25],

the triangle being the cities of Belfast, Glasgow and Liverpool.

The removal of the Irish issue from British politics through the establishment of the Irish Free State (for the 26 Counties) and devolved government for Northern Ireland (comprising the six north-east counties), eased, although by no means eradicated, Labour's difficulties in Scotland in relation to religious sectarianism. The appeal now could be made to Protestant and Catholic workers on social and economic questions free of the burden of commitments to 'Irish self-determination' and of threats of betrayal from both sides. In fact, the Labour movement in Scotland, from the ILP through to revolutionaries like MacLean, had never shown a very sophisticated understanding of Irish problems in spite of the closeness of ties and of the problem's distinctive echo in Scotland. In The *Forward* or elsewhere there was no evidence of any real appreciation of the changing balance of class forces in the South of Ireland after the Wyndham Land Act of 1903, or of the power wielded by the Catholic Church and other such factors which would make the attainment of socialism extremely difficult in an independent Ireland. Nor was there recognition of the depth of Ulster Protestant political, cultural and economic objections to Irish nationalism and the extent to which the Protestant working class were class conscious and adamantly anti-nationalist.

Instead, there was a facile if understandable enthusiasm for Irish Home Rule as a matter of radical liberal political inheritance, and a thoughtless endorsement of the republican aspiration in 1920–21, on the basis of an abhorrence of the 'Black and Tans' and what was seen simply as 'Carsonite Tory Unionism'. There was little sign of appreciation in Scottish Labour circles of the extent to which the Irish question was a national conflict within Ireland itself. If Labour leaders in Scotland were not merely reducing it misleadingly to political terms they could grasp such as 'ruling class conspiracy', then they were, in the manner of Tom Johnston, editor of the *Forward*, despairing of a 'theological war'.[26] The history of interaction built up between Scotland and Ulster in the Labour cause ought to have yielded more considered and less politically shallow observations,[27] the legacy of which can still be discerned.

III

From the 1920s the central theme in the story of Labour's political development in Scotland is that of increasing integration into the structures of the wider British movement, both politically and industrially. As a result, as writers from disparate political standpoints have argued, much of a radical nature that was distinctively Scottish, particularly in relation to the ILP, got lost.[28] This not surprisingly led to political developments of a nationalist kind, as detailed in the previous chapter.

Labour's record in Scotland since the 1920s has not caught the imagination of historians who have tended to lament the weakening of a distinctive Scottish identity and the development of a strong bureaucratic corporatism, particularly when Labour was in office in the 1940s and 1960s, and a descent into jobbery and corruption at local municipal level.[29] The achievement of transcending Scotland's religious sectarian divide in terms of electoral success has been grudgingly acknowledged, but many have felt that Labour has paid a high price for this in pandering to just those sectarian impulses, and in some cases being implicated in sectarian practices.

This question will be taken up in relation to contemporary events in Scotland in the final chapter. It is the intention here to consider the nature of the task which faced Labour in relation to sectarianism from around 1920, and the different interpretations of how it dealt with the problem. The significance of the religious issue for Labour politics in Scotland throughout the period c. 1920–70 offers a useful counterpoint to the experience of Labour in Northern Ireland which will be examined in the next section.[30]

Popular perception of the Labour Party in Scotland in the twentieth century has tended to focus on the strength of the Party's Catholic vote in the industrial central belt of the country. The extent to which Labour became a natural home for Irish immigrants and their descendants and a means of assimilation into wider Scottish society has been stressed in the previous chapter. However, it is necessary to look at aspects of this process more closely, for they have become matters of important scholarly debate.

Tom Gallagher's arguments about Labour and assimilation constitute one, very cogent, line of interpretation about the significance of the Labour-Catholic alliance. On the other hand, Ian McLean in his book *The Legend of Red Clydeside* has offered an alternative: a negative reading of this alliance which takes the view that it is responsible for the decline in socialist idealism and the crusading radicalism of the ILP and the rise in machine-style sectional interest politics in many ways reminiscent of the 'Tammany Hall' politics of exiled Irish communities elsewhere. McLean has pointed to the Labour Party's championing of Catholic schools, its avoidance of morally controversial issues like birth control, and its alliances at local level in the inter-war period with Catholic sectarian organisations like the Ancient Order of Hibernians (AOH), as evidence of Labour's sacrifice of idealism for the assurance of a well-organised block vote.[31]

In an important article published recently, the historian John

McCaffrey has in turn taken issue with the McLean thesis.[32] Firstly, McCaffrey points out that the loss of idealism was not peculiar to Clydeside socialists, that the character of Labour politics in Britain in general from the 1920s was geared to electoralism. Secondly, McCaffrey questions assumptions about Catholic support being the result of Labour's supposed opportunism in relation to the 1918 Education Act and State provision for Catholic schools. McCaffrey suggests that wider social issues were of more importance in Labour's appeal to Catholics, that municipal electoral evidence indicates that Catholics (many of them newly franchised) were moving to Labour from 1918 onwards, and that the Catholic Church itself did not rush to secure Labour's backing — on the contrary, it was by no means obvious in 1918 and the years immediately following that Labour would turn out to be the political force it did. McCaffrey demonstrates that, ironically, it was the Glasgow Education Board Chairman and leading Orangeman, Charles Cleland, who was the Church's most useful political ally in the testing times of the 1920s. All in all, McCaffrey's revisionist work encourages us to look beyond a simple Labour-Catholic pact on education and to question long-held assumptions about Protestant perceptions of Catholic support for Labour being a result of the education issue. It also suggests that an important reason for the durability of Catholic support for Labour lies in the relative failure of rival political parties to address social and economic questions. Thus, until recently at least,[33] the SNP might be said to have been viewed negatively by most Catholics because its commitment to social issues was too vague, and eclipsed by the goal of Scottish independence (or a Scottish Parliament) which Catholics felt extremely wary of for religious reasons.

Catholic hostility or indifference to Scottish nationalist goals probably owed much to the experience of their co-religionists in Northern Ireland; the Province was certainly not viewed as a good advert for devolution. The Catholic experience in Scotland[34] (outside intellectual circles), combined with their communal attitude to politics, seemed to lead them to connect devolved government possibilities with local government practices. By the Second World War Catholics were tasting better things through the medium of local authority control, and they may have felt that such gains would be jeopardised by any Scottish devolved legislature which would be Protestant–dominated. Religion and the fear of religious discrimination was, at any rate, at the front of their political calculations. It

might thus be suggested that this largely communal way of thinking was profoundly influential in moving Labour away from
Scottish Home Rule as a political priority, something most historians simply attribute to centralisation on the part of the Party
nationally (in a British sense) and the demise of the ILP in
Scotland, especially after its disaffiliation from the Labour Party in
1932. However, like birth control, education and in some ways the
conduct of a campaign on the Spanish Civil War,[35] Scottish Home
Rule could be considered another issue on which Labour felt it had
to bend to accommodate its spinal column of Catholic support in
West-Central Scotland.

It is hard to exaggerate the role played by a 'boss' politician such
as Patrick Dollan[36] in all this; Dollan instinctively knew the political priorities and values of the community he came from and he
directed Labour operations in Glasgow with them uppermost in
mind. It was Dollan who orchestrated the Labour Party's opposition to the ILP's campaigns of the 1920s in which fellow Irish
Catholic John Wheatley was deeply embroiled.[37] The ILP, from the
mid-twenties, attacked vigorously the parliamentarianism of the
Ramsay McDonald Labour Party and moved to a Leftist position
close to the Communist Party. The taint of Communism, of course,
was anathema to the Catholic Church and the bulk of Catholic voters, and efforts to establish a fully-fledged Catholic political party
to combat it were made seriously in the 1920s and 1930s. Dollan
more than anyone was alive to the dangers of such developments
for Labour and moved to insulate the Party against communist
influence.

The agreeable irony in all this for Labour was that it hardly
harmed their image among the bulk of Protestant voters. For it is
the case that, a strong working class Protestant Unionist vote
notwithstanding, Labour attracted substantial Protestant support
around social and economic issues and reassured those Labour-
minded Protestants who shared the Catholic phobia of communism and were suspicious, for the reverse religious reasons, of
nationalism.[38] If Labour inherited much of the skilled working class
Presbyterian Liberal vote, then it could even appeal to some
Protestants of a more Orange disposition. Certainly it can be
argued that on the Protestant side of the religious fence, as well as
on the Catholic, class loyalties and religious group loyalties co-
existed. It was certainly easier for Orangemen and women to vote
Labour in Scotland when the Irish issue was taken out of British

politics, and it seems that many were induced to vote Labour because of worsening employer-worker relations in heavy industry, as discussed earlier. Over and above this, however, the British constitutionalist credentials of the Labour Party were greatly enhanced by their distance from communism and nationalism and their 'safe' parliamentary character. Continuing attempts by Orange Order leaders to depict Labour in the guise of a Bolshevik-style bogey long after the upheavals of the 1918–22 period, simply lost them credibility in the eyes of many working class Protestants.[39]

Labour, largely in the person of Tom Johnston, pursued administrative devolution as a way of responding to peculiarly Scottish needs. This approach, indeed, was epitomised by Johnston's tenure of office during 1941–45 as Scottish Secretary of State.[40] However, Johnston's retirement from politics left an ambiguous legacy to the party in Scotland; the Attlee government's missionary approach to post-war Britain left little scope for attention to Scottish sensibilities concerned about Labour's metropolitan mind-set, and distinctively Scottish boards and bodies set up by Johnston were largely ill-equipped to resist the centralising tide. The conditions were ripe for the nationalist 'Covenant' movement which duly fired the imagination of a large part of the nation in the late forties and early fifties. The imagery of the 'Covenant' suggested a certain equation of the cause with the established religion and Catholics seem in the main to have been unmoved.

This was hardly surprising if, as Keating argues, the 1950s and 1960s were to see Labour confirmed as 'the local political establishment, the path to municipal power and parliamentary careers' and attractive particularly to Catholics as a result.[41] In this context nationalism could seem more of a romantic leap into the unknown than ever before, and certainly not worth the risk.

Labour's hour was to come round again in 1964 by which time the Conservative/Unionist decline in Scotland had truly set in. Labour was to be the main beneficiary but the fall-out also had nationalist repercussions by the late 1960s as Labour toiled over the troubled Scottish economy. In terms of the religious question, however, Labour had consolidated its cross-community strength while largely stemming the flow of treacherous sectarian currents, something it would have to take care to maintain in view of the outbreak of the Northern Ireland troubles from 1968–69.

III

The Labour Party (Northern Ireland), later to become known as the Northern Ireland Labour Party (NILP), was set up in 1924. It signalled the intention of Labour to fight their corner in the new State, although it was not till the report of the Boundary Commission the following year that the survival of the State was assured for the foreseeable future. The NILP was overwhelmingly concentrated in Belfast — as it was to be throughout the history of the State — and in the 1920s, as in Scotland, it was the ILP which continued to provide the impetus for propaganda activities. In particular, the ILP branch in North Belfast brought together most of Labour's stalwarts and younger energetic figures around an impressive array of propaganda and leisure events and a newspaper, *The Labour Opposition in Northern Ireland.* The latter bore many resemblances to the *Forward* which continued to be promoted and sold in Belfast. The movement's leading lights were men like Hugh Gemmell (a Scot who had come to Ulster to avoid conscription in the Great War), Sam Kyle, Harry Midgley, Bob McLung and Alex Stewart (also a Scot) and a few women such as Margaret McCoubrey. The outlook of these people was still very much shaped by the British Labour movement. Besides the ILP, the Co-operative Society and municipal politics were areas in which energies were focused: such activists were 'reformists' who believed there was no short cut to social progress, only long hours of hard educational and propaganda work, and tireless effort spent on working people's everyday problems.

Labour, however, had to face the fact that in Northern Ireland the effort of winning people to socialism was considerably constricted by the impact of 'the National Question'. The movement, overall, still took the socialist line against partition, that it divided the working class in Ireland to the detriment of their own interests. As far as possible the National Question was prevented from causing internal divisions, and the emphasis always laid on social issues; the NILP did not declare a position one way or another on the legitimacy of the Northern Ireland State. Nevertheless, divisions within the movement were discernible and it was difficult to deal with the legacy of socialist pioneers like Connolly and Walker who had contributed so much respectively to the development of the movement, but who had taken opposed stances in relation to the National Question.[42] Equally, the fence-sitting approach to the

issue of the State's legitimacy only resulted in Labour becoming a
punch bag for both Unionists and Nationalists from their respective standpoints. In addition, in 1929, Craig's abolition of proportional representation for the Northern Ireland Parliament elections
solidified the Unionist-Nationalist polarisation of the State's politics to the detriment of 'third parties' such as the NILP.

Over and above such factors lay the basic problem of making
Labour seem *relevant* in the context of Northern Ireland politics; of
making its appeal transcend traditional loyalties on the national
question. The task was made considerably harder by the lack of a
credible target to attack politically: in short, the Unionists refused
to play the game of left-right politics which Labour was geared for.
As argued in an earlier chapter the Unionists' refusal to regard
devolution in any kind of innovative light, their willingness to leave
major decisions on social and economic questions to Westminster,
and their pursuit of a 'step-by-step' policy with the rest of the U.K.
in respect of social services, all had the effect of cutting the ground
from beneath Labour's left-of-centre social programme in
Northern Ireland. This added up to an enormous sense of frustration for Labour leaders such as Harry Midgley, elected to the
Stormont Parliament in 1933.[43]

Midgley emerged as the NILP leader in the 1930s, a decade
which saw the Party make little progress, even against a background of unemployment and economic misery for the working
class, both Protestant and Catholic. Midgley's period of leadership
is notable for the NILP's rivalry with Communists, and serious
internal disputes over partition. The latter worsened on account of
a hardening of attitudes on the part of elements in the Party of a
nationalist or republican tendency and of the circle around
Midgley who became increasingly exasperated with their efforts.
Midgley himself was moving to a small 'u' unionist Labour position
in the early 1930s, and was confirmed in this direction by his experience of attempting in the fashion of socialists everywhere at the
time to argue the anti-Franco line on the Spanish Civil War for
1936–39. Catholic hostility to him was vicious and resulted in him
losing his Stormont seat, an outcome about which certain elements
in his own party who were opposed to his 'Walkerist' line were not
unhappy. From the early 1930s Midgley's main rival for the leadership of Labour in Northern Ireland was the maverick figure of
Jack Beattie, also a Protestant and Stormont MP, who adopted the
alternative 'Connolly' approach to the national question.[44] When

the issue was so evidently divisive at leadership level, it was idle to suppose that it could be smoothed over among the rank and file.

The NILP had many Catholic members, but the strength of anti-partitionism in the Party also drew on Protestants. Besides Beattie, there were men like Victor Halley and Jack MacGougan,[45] and the largely Protestant (and middle class) literary circle around the writers John Hewitt, Sam Hanna Bell and John Boyd.[46] These Protestants felt a particular obligation to attack Unionism as the proclaimed voice of Protestant Ulster in order to maintain a tradition of *dissent*. This was a tradition subordinated or marginalised in the controversy over Home Rule, and threatened with extinction in the period of the Northern Ireland State. Many Protestant socialists espoused anti-partitionism as a way of resisting what they perhaps viewed as the Unionists' brand of communal totalitarianism, the relentless calls for Protestant unity in the cause of the survival of the Union and their community identity. On top of this, of course, the Unionists were generally right-wing and anti-socialist.

All of this was understandable, but it made the task of improving Labour's political prospects all the more difficult: the more the anti-partitionism, the easier it was for the Unionists to alarm Protestant workers. Eventually, Midgley attempted to identify the NILP with a clear commitment to the Union, and — this was 1942 — the British and Allied war effort. His reasoning was that the Protestants had to be reassured, and that any loss of Catholic support could be made up if it became evident that the NILP was capable of challenging the Unionist dominance, in contrast to the perennially ineffective and largely abstentionist Nationalist Party. But Midgley had also become by this time a lyrical advocate of a socially progressive British State and Commonwealth, and a convinced opponent of Irish nationalism. In 1941 he rhapsodised about the Scottish Labour Party's combination of British loyalty and Scottish patriotism. The scars of his Spanish Civil War tribulations were also evident in several anti-Catholic outbursts.

It soon became clear that Midgley and the bulk of the NILP were on a collision course. Those in the NILP who denounced partition possessed a motivating rationale, whether socialist, nationalist or indeed literary and cultural, which was rarely to be found among the majority not in sympathy with anti-partitionism. A willingness to accept the constitutional status quo was usually as far as most were prepared to go; to evangelise about the Union ran the risk of appearing to steal the Unionists' clothes and was difficult to square with the 'oppositional' role Labour occupied. Midgley found this out to his cost when he tried to rally the Party around support for the Union; very few were prepared to follow him that far.

Midgley thus left the NILP at the end of 1942 to seek to realise his dream through the medium of a new pro-Union Commonwealth Labour Party (CLP).[47] The NILP remained non-committal on the national question but polled strongly, along with the CLP and the Communists, in the 1945 Northern Ireland election,[48] another reflection of why the Unionists had reason to be worried about the challenge from the Left. It was a result, indeed, which goes a long way to explaining the Unionists' desire to reach a working agreement with the Attlee Labour government and to implement the Welfare State legislation.[49]

Cradden sees the events of the 1940s in the Northern Labour movement as something of a triumph for what he calls the 'democratic alternative' over the rival schools on the national question.[50] He distinguishes the NILP from Midgley on the grounds that Midgley had come to the 'Orange' point of seeing the Union as 'sacrosanct and immutable'.[51] This rather begs the question of whether or not Cradden's 'democratic alternative' in the NILP cared about the Union's preservation in some shape or form, and if so what? The Labour activists he sympathises with such as Bob Getgood were probably old-style 'Home Rulers' and Cradden is right to suggest that they were not anti-partitionist in any anti-British sense; rather, they did not want to see the border impede working class co-operation and unity. However, this glosses over the strength of anti-British feeling in Irish nationalism and republicanism both North and South and does not face up to the reality of the term 'anti-partitionist' having been hijacked beyond retrieval by nationalists, particularly in the post Second World War years of the Anti-Partition League's campaign. The old Home Rule option, arguably the only way anti-partitionism and some preservation of the Union could have been mutually achieved, was simply not a viable option by the 1940s. In terms of pragmatism at least, Midgley's argument in 1942 had the virtue of facing less daunting obstacles: he accepted the risk of losing Catholic support but knew he could play on the evident desire of many Catholics for social justice first and a united Ireland a long way after; the 'democratic alternative' had to surmount the hurdles of Protestant Unionist antipathy to Irish self-government *and* the anti-Britishness of a considerable part of Nationalist Ireland.

Such theoretical speculation was in effect cut short by the NILP's decision to commit itself to Northern Ireland's constitutional position in 1949. This led immediately to the defection of many anti-partitionists and the formation of branches of the Irish Labour Party in Northern Ireland. Some were to find that sectarian intransigence of another kind was waiting for them. In 1951, for example, the socialist republican candidate, Harry Diamond, jibed at Jack Beattie who stood against him on the Irish Labour ticket for the municipal seat of Smithfield: 'In my opinion there [is] no room for any but Catholics in the National movement'.[52]

The NILP recruited a new generation of younger activists in the 1950s, the able party secretary Sam Napier being a good example. The party's decision of 1949 was compounded by moves to strengthen the relationship with the British Labour Party. In 1948 the NILP had in fact debated whether or not to apply for affiliation to the British Labour Party as a regional council. It was decided in the negative and the indications were that the British Labour Party would have refused in any case.[53] However, the British party were interested in the Westminster seats in the Province and appointed a full-time organiser in 1948 to Northern Ireland with a view to improving the NILP's chances in these elections. During the 1950s and into the 1960s the NILP sought to interest the British Party in Northern Ireland affairs, with limited success, and boasted about fighting elections and formulating policy 'in association with the British Labour Party'.[54] The association in reality amounted to little and in 1966 the NILP raised the issue of formal affiliation. By this time the Executive Committee of the party was of the view that such a move 'could well be the end to Northern Ireland's isolation from the mainstream of British politics'. Meetings with members of the British Labour Government duly took place, but do not seem to have been encouraging from the Executive Committee's point of view.[55] Clearly, the British Labour Party had not changed its view on the desirability of steering clear of involvement in Northern Ireland politics.

The NILP had nonetheless reached the strongest position in their history by the mid-1960s. Electoral improvement began in the Stormont contest of 1958 when the Party at last reaped the dividend of their acceptance of the constitutional position in relation to Protestant working class votes and seats; they won four in 1958 and retained them on an increased vote in 1962. The total NILP vote of 77,000 in the latter year alarmed the Unionists greatly, and when

Terence O'Neill took over the Unionist leadership in 1963 he made the counter-attack on the NILP a priority.[56] In 1965 he succeeded in winning back two seats. However, both the 1964 and 1966 general elections saw the NILP poll over 100,000, and the Party's progress seemed to be vindicating the decision of 1949 and, indeed, the Midgley policy of earlier; certainly, the Party was attracting Catholics, such as Paddy Devlin, who saw it as the only credible force to fight the Unionists and push social and economic questions higher up the Northern Ireland political agenda.[57]

In retrospect the success achieved among Protestant voters caused problems for the NILP at a crucial juncture. In attempting to stave off the Unionist assault which their progress had given rise to, the NILP was not best placed to respond to the rising tide of protest from the Catholic community on the issues of local government electoral reform and discrimination in housing and employment. The NILP's political project required an easing forward on both community fronts with the focus as much as possible on shared social concerns. The party had, from the early sixties, put electoral reform into its programme, and it had always spoken out against discrimination, but the climate in the second half of the 1960s moved rapidly in the direction of protest and confrontation, a context in which the NILP's tactical priorities were buffeted and eventually rendered redundant. The world closed in from all sides: Catholic protest and the profusion of campaign groups, like the Campaign for Social Justice (CSJ) and the Campaign for Democracy in Ulster (CDU) and, in 1967, the Northern Ireland Civil Rights Association (NICRA); a revival of militant Protestant populism around the Reverend Ian Paisley, initially in response to the perceived 'appeasement' policies of O'Neillism; plus the aforementioned Unionist Party backlash led by O'Neill against the NILP.[58]

The NILP could not, of course, afford the polarisation of the civil rights issues along Protestant and Catholic lines. It sought an even-handed approach which many Catholics felt was inappropriate. The NILP's attitude is well caught in a letter from Napier to Peter Shore of the British Labour Party who in 1963 had written enquiring if the McCluskey case in Dungannon[59] was an isolated one or not. Napier replied:

> The truth of the matter is that in Northern Ireland the Nationalists allege that Unionist controlled councils house Protestants in preference

and the Unionists allege the Nationalist controlled councils house Roman Catholics in preference.

Napier added that the NILP had offered to form a branch in Dungannon but 'apparently these people prefer to carry on the old sectarian argument.'[60]

The people Napier accused of wanting to carry on 'the old sectarian argument' certainly wanted to publicise the plight of the Catholic minority and to launch a politics of protest which put the NILP into a dilemma it never really resolved. The party was always a voice in the broad civil rights chorus for change, but it never felt comfortable with the 'politics in the streets' of the NICRA and later People's Democracy (PD). It could not articulate the sense of outrage which gave the pressure-groups their justification.

By the outbreak of the Troubles the NILP was pinning its faith on the broad acceptability of a 'British rights for British citizens' appeal, but events had effectively overtaken it. Had British Labour responded to the promptings of the NILP in the 1960s it might have applied the necessary pressure on O'Neill to carry out reforms speedily. The dawn of the Troubles, however, only found the British governing party in a state of confusion and ignorance. Their neglect of Northern Ireland, which could not be excused in the manner of the Conservatives and the relationship with the Unionists, had now come to haunt them.

V

The contrasting fortunes of Labour politics in Scotland and Northern Ireland in the period 1920–70 reflect the different contexts in which the two movements operated. Both had to deal in varying degrees with sectarian conflict and with the problematic inheritance of ideological conflict over the relationship between socialism and nationalism. However, in Scotland conditions obtained to make these manageable; in Northern Ireland devolved government was in effect made a tool of ethnic politics. Labour in Scotland took refuge in the wider shelter of British political life — a viable option which yielded social democratic improvement if at the cost of the loss of a distinctively Scottish radical cutting edge. As David Howell has put it:

> In Britain, denominational prejudices could normally be contained. The construction of a Labour agenda focusing on economic and social

issues which reached its apogee between the early 1920s and the mid 1960s can be understood as part of the solution. Within this strategy, potentially divisive issues such as secular education and birth control were not incorporated into party platforms despite powerful advocacy. In Belfast, especially after Partition, this solution was not readily available since such a discourse involved the marginalisation of the central political question. The travails of the Northern Ireland Labour Party (NILP) demonstrated the power of a Labourist perspective, but also in the context of Belfast, its limitations. Labourism could advance in times of economic depression and in the radical promise of 1945, but partition was always a potentially divisive question and Unionist aggression proved generally effective.[61]

Labour politics in Northern Ireland suffered from their detachment from the mainstream of British politics; and the NILP of the 1960s strove unsuccessfully to alter this. They faced the obstacle of the British Labour Party's refusal to broaden its organisation to Northern Ireland, a matter later to be taken up by strands of left wing opinion in Northern Ireland during the present Troubles. In this the British Party could claim that it was only recognising a convention in British politics since partition; the whole point of the Northern Ireland State from a British Government viewpoint in 1921 had been to exclude it from British politics as part of the removal of the wider Irish question. However, as time progressed British Labour should have recognised that the convention was working to the exclusive advantage of the Conservatives[62] and thus invited a revision of the established view from a Labour perspective.

In Scotland, crucially, the cause of social justice could usually be kept apart from divisive issues surrounding religion and national identity. In Northern Ireland this proved impossible: the Unionists lumped all rival political forces together and labelled them constitutional enemies; when Labour strove to convince the people that it stood alone for social justice the Nationalists and Republicans would promptly assert that social justice was dependent on an end to partition. As Terry Cradden has remarked, this was 'music to the ears' of the Unionists who could cite it, illogically but effectively, as proof that demands for social justice were part of a plot against the State.[63]

If Labour in Scotland sacrificed much in the way of idealism, they succeeded in cultivating a strong and durable sense of class consciousness and class priorities; John Foster has suggested that the extent of this 'proletarianisation' was an important factor in

Glasgow not becoming another Belfast in dangerous periods such as the 1930s.[64] In Scotland there was a sharper decline of the culture of workers' deference and of paternalistic boss-employee relations. But Scottish Labour had always to be wary of sectarian conflict[65] and of the potentially problematic relationship of Protestant and Catholic workers to questions both of Irish and Scottish nationalism. The outbreak of the Northern Ireland Troubles in 1969 caused much concern in Scottish Labour circles already preoccupied with a highly-charged Scottish nationalist threat. An era was opening up in which the strength of class politics was to be put to the test. The responses of Labour in Scotland to developments in Northern Ireland will be considered in the next chapter, along with their interaction with broader issues of Scottish and British identity and constitutional change.

NOTES

1. See the observation made by Bob Purdie in 'An Ulster Labourist in Liberal Scotland: William Walker and the Leith Burghs Election of 1910', in Ian S. Wood (ed.), *Scotland and Ulster*.
2. See F. Wright, *Northern Ireland: A Comparative Perspective* pp. 77–78.
3. 'An Ulster Labourist'.
4. The most substantial treatments of Walker's politics are: A. Morgan, *Labour and Partition* (London, 1991) chpt. 4; H. Patterson, *Class Conflict and Sectarianism* (Belfast, 1980); and Purdie, 'An Ulster Labourist'.
5. Purdie, 'An Ulster Labourist'.
6. Scholarly and polemical work on Connolly is voluminous. See J. Newsinger, 'Connolly and his biographers', *Irish Political Studies* Vol. 5 (1990) pp. 1-9, for a useful guide; A. Morgan op. cit. chpt. 7, and D. Howell, *A Lost Left* (Manchester, 1987) are penetrating and incisive discussions.
7. See, for example, J. Newsinger, 'James Connolly and the Easter Rising', *Science and Society* XLVII, 2 (Summer 1983) 152–177; and A. Morgan, *James Connolly: A Political Biography* (Manchester, 1988).
8. See H. Patterson op. cit.; Morgan, *James Connolly*, chpt. 5.
9. See B. Ransom, *Connolly's Marxism* (London, 1980), especially chpt. 1, for a discussion of the importance of Connolly's Catholicism and view of Gaelic society.
10. For an illuminating discussion of MacLean's career (and that of Connolly) see Howell op. cit. Scholarly controversies surrounding

MacLean are highlighted in T. Brotherstone, 'Internationalism in the Twentieth Century: some comments on John MacLean', in T. Brotherstone (ed.), *Covenant, Charter and Party* (Aberdeen, 1989).

11. See J. McHugh and B. J. Riley, *John MacLean* (Manchester, 1989).

12. See G. Cairns, 'John MacLean, Socialism and the Scottish Question', *Scottish Labour History Review* no. 4 (Winter 1990) pp. 7–9.

13. J. D. Young, 'John MacLean, Socialism and the Easter Rising', *Saothar* 16 (1991) pp. 23–33; 'A Very English Socialism and the Celtic Fringe 1880-1991', *History Workshop* 35 (Spring 1993) pp. 136–151.

14. The Belfast ILP was affiliated to the Scottish area division of the party.

15. See M. Fry, *Patronage and Principle* (Aberdeen, 1987) chpt. 6.

16. For a panoramic view of the ILP see D. Howell's magisterial *British Workers and the ILP* (Manchester, 1983).

17. See the comments of Tom Johnston (editor) in *Forward* 3 June 1911 and 24 June 1911 regarding 'the grander moments of the old democratic theocracy'.

18. J. Melling, *Rent Strike!* (Edinburgh, 1983).

19. The historiography of the 'Red Clydeside' phenomenon is well summarised in T. Brotherstone, 'Does Red Clydeside Really Matter Any More?', in R. Duncan and A. McIvor (eds.), *Militant Workers* (Edinburgh, 1992); see especially I. McLean, *The Legend of Red Clydeside* (Edinburgh, 1983); and B. Morris and A. McKinlay (eds.), *The ILP on Clydeside* (Manchester, 1991).

20. See discussion of this in G. Walker, *Thomas Johnston* pp. 49–58; also see Tom Johnston's comments re IRA activity in Scotland, *Forward* 14 May 1921.

21. Morgan, *Labour and Partition* p. 250.

22. Ibid. pp. 262–4.

23. See H McShane, *No Mean Fighter* (London, 1978) p. 132.

24. For UULA, see chpt. 3.

25. Morgan, *Labour and Partition* p. 326.

26. *Forward* 25 March 1922.

27. In common with the English Left they were arguably dazzled, and muddled, by Connolly — see G. Walker, 'Gaelic Communist', *London Review of Books* Vol. 11, no. 19 (12 Oct 1989).

28. See Morris and McKinley op. cit.; and Fry op. cit. The ILP disaffiliated from the Labour Party in 1932 and this necessitated the virtually wholesale re-organisation of the Labour Party in Scotland.

29. See T. C. Smout's critique in *A Century of the Scottish People* (Glasgow, 1986) chpt. 11; and I. Dunnachie et al. (eds.) *Forward! Labour Politics in Scotland 1888-1988* (Edinburgh, 1989).

30. For a further discussion of this topic see G. Walker, 'Labour in Scotland and Northern Ireland in the Inter-War Years', in R. Mitchison and P. Roebuck (eds.), *Economy and Society in Scotland and Ireland 1500–1939* (Edinburgh, 1988).

31. See I. McLean op. cit. chpt. 14.

32. J. McCaffrey, 'Irish issues in the 19th and 20th Century: Radicalism in a Scottish Context', in T. M. Devine (ed.), *Irish Immigrants and Scottish Society.*

33. See next chapter.

34. For influence of Catholic intellectuals on the Scottish nationalist movement see R. J. Finlay, 'Nationalism, Race, Religion and the Irish Question in Inter-War Scotland', *The Innes Review* XLII, 1 (Spring 1991), 46–67. See also chapter 4.

35. See T. Gallagher, 'Scottish Catholics and the British Left 1918–1939', *The Innes Review* XXXIV, 1 (Spring 1983), 17–42.

36. For Dollan see T. Gallagher, *Glasgow* chpts. 5 and 6; and Edward Boyd, 'The Spectre of Tammany Hall', *Edinburgh Review* no. 76 (February 1987) pp. 99–104.

37. The best treatment of Wheatley's career is Ian S. Wood, *John Wheatley* (Manchester, 1990).

38. See G. Walker, 'The Orange Order in Scotland between the Wars', and discussion in chapter 3.

39. Ibid.

40. See G. Walker, *Thomas Johnston*, chpt. 6.

41. M. Keating, 'The Labour Party in Scotland, 1951–1964', in I. Dunnachie et al. op. cit.

42. See G. Walker, 'The Northern Ireland Labour Party in the 1920s', *Saothar* 10 (1984) pp. 19–29.

43. See G. Walker, *The Politics of Frustration: Harry Midgley and the Failure of Labour in Northern Ireland* (Manchester, 1985) chpts. 5–7; and G. Walker, 'Labour in Scotland and N. Ireland in the Inter-War Years'.

44. Beattie enjoyed a tempestuous relationship with the NILP: he was expelled in 1934, readmitted in 1942, and expelled again in 1944.

45. See 'Letting Labour Lead: Jack MacGougan and the Pursuit of Unity, 1913–1958', *Saothar* 14 (1989) pp. 13–123.

46. See E. Longley, 'Progressive Bookmen: politics and Northern Protestant writers since the 1930s', *The Irish Review* no. 1 (1980) pp. 50–59.

47. Midgley finally ended up in the Unionist Party in 1947 and became a Cabinet Minister two years later. He was Minister of Education from 1950 till his death in 1957.

48. For a detailed analysis of the 1945 Northern Ireland election and in particular the left-wing vote see T. Cradden, *Trade Unionism,*

Socialism and Partition (Belfast, 1993), pp. 41–47.

49. See B. Barton, 'Relations between Stormont and the Attlee Labour Government', *Irish Political Studies* 7 (1992) pp. 1–20.

50. Cradden op. cit. pp. 6–10.

51. Ibid. p. 137.

52. Jack Beattie Papers PRONI D2784/22/3/1.

53. Sam Napier Papers PRONI D3702/C/10.

54. See pamphlet 'Where Ulster Labour Stands' (1953), Napier Papers op. cit.

55. See document on 'British Labour Party Affiliation' and on 'Ulster/Westminster liaison', Napier Papers op. cit.

56. See David Gordon, *The O'Neill Years* especially chpts. 4 and 5.

57. See P. Devlin, *Straight Left* (Belfast, 1993).

58. For a good discussion of the NILP's plight see B. Purdie, *Politics in the Streets* especially pp. 67–73.

59. This concerned the allegations of a discriminatory housing policy on the part of Dungannon Urban District Council by a group of Catholics led by Conn and Patricia McCluskey, founders of the Campaign for Social Justice.

60. Letter from Napier to Shore 31 October 1963, Napier Papers op. cit.

61. D. Howell, 'Irish Labour — An Exceptional Case?', *Saothar* 18 (1993) pp. 63–74.

62. The Ulster Unionist MPs at Westminster took the Conservative Party whip.

63. Cradden op. cit. pp. 220-221.

64. See J. Foster, 'A Proletarian Nation? Occupation and Class since 1914', in A. Dickson and J. H. Treble (eds.), *People and Society in Scotland.*

65. See Michael Keating's comments on the Airdrie and Coatbridge contest in 1959 for an example of religion impinging clearly on political choice — Keating, 'The Labour Party in Scotland'.

6

The Northern Ireland Troubles, Scottish Reactions and Echoes, and the Contemporary Constitutional Debate in the UK c. 1970–95

I

Since the 1970s there has been a significant revival of political controversy surrounding constitutional questions in the UK state. In 1972 the only part of the UK to have hitherto received a devolved system of government — Northern Ireland — had it taken away by the central (Conservative) government. 'Direct Rule' was then imposed from Westminster and remains in place with all its democratic deficits and administrative peculiarities. In 1978 Parliament enacted the then Labour Government Bills proposing devolved assemblies for both Scotland and Wales pending the result of referendums in which the consent of at least 40 per cent of the electorate was required. This condition was not fulfilled although a majority in Scotland did vote in favour.

The constitutional debate faltered then revived in Scotland in the 1980s by which time regionalist ideas largely inspired by developments in the European Union (EU), and a revived debate around federalism both in the UK and EU contexts, had entered the picture. In addition, support for Scottish independence, if mainly in the form of 'Independence in Europe', took firmer root. Pressure groups and Conventions, specifically Scottish and UK-wide, were established to promote the cause of constitutional reform; all had in common at the very least a desire to decentralise and break with the doctrine of Westminster parliamentary sovereignty. In Northern Ireland, from the time of the imposition of Direct Rule to the present, there have been repeated attempts to

build a solution to the Province's problems around another devolved
government scheme, only this time with power-sharing mechanisms
and/or a role for the Irish Republic to play. In stark contrast to the
Conservative governments' approach since 1979 to the constitutional debate around Scotland, Northern Ireland has been treated
as something of a constitutional 'laboratory', and many questions
concerning the nature of the UK State and 'Britishness', the concepts of parliamentary sovereignty, of legitimacy and of account-
ability, and the future constitutional shape of the British Isles have
been raised in the course of these processes.

This final chapter seeks to illuminate many of these constitutional issues — which have relevance for the UK as a whole and,
increasingly, the EU — by focusing on the interactions between
Scotland and Northern Ireland in this area of constitutional debate
dating from the 1970s. First, the extent to which the Northern
Ireland experience of devolution entered the debate on Scottish
(and Welsh) devolution in the 1970s, will be examined. Then there
will be discussion of the way the Scottish debate fed back into that
of Northern Ireland in the late 1970s, not least in terms of the
reactions of groups in Scotland concerned with the Northern
Ireland conflict. The effects of the intensification of the constitutional controversy in Scotland in the 1980s and 1990s on Northern
Ireland will be examined, and consideration given to the ways in
which the debates in both places might be said to have converged
around concepts of identity and evolving interpretations of
'Britishness'. The extent to which Orange-Green sectarian tensions
of Northern Ireland vintage still influence Scottish politics and
culture will also be assessed.

II

Devolution returned to the British political agenda at the end of the
1960s in response to the political rise of Nationalism in Scotland
and to a lesser extent Wales. The Royal Commission on the
Constitution, headed by Lord Kilbrandon, which was set up by the
Labour Government in 1969 produced a searching report in 1973
which intensified the debate with its majority recommendation for
legislative, devolved assemblies to be set up in Scotland and Wales;
a minority favoured 'executive devolution' throughout the UK. The
Kilbrandon Report,[1] as it became known, is an important landmark
in British constitutional history. Its proposals were not adopted by

the Labour or Conservative parties,[2] and the SNP recorded its 'twin peaks' of electoral success in the two 1974 general elections, winning 11 seats and some 30% of the Scottish vote in the latter.

The Labour Government produced a White Paper 'Our Changing Democracy' in 1975, but the devolutionary scheme for Scotland contained in it fell short of Kilbrandon in terms of powers and safeguards. Nationalist-minded Labour MPs in Scotland, such as Jim Sillars, left the party as a consequence.[3] The era of bitter Labour-Nationalist political rivalry in Scotland was now well underway, and the debate on devolution within the Labour Party in Scotland largely centred on whether or not it would 'dish' the Nationalists or instead strengthen them and intensify the political threat they posed. Labour in Scotland trailed significantly behind its London headquarters in enthusiasm for devolution *per se*. The way was cleared for a constitutional showdown with the Devolution Bills of 1978 and a referendum in which pro and anti-devolutionists (of all the British parties) put their cases.

In significant ways the Northern Ireland experience of devolution was drawn upon to give support to the opposing arguments. The Kilbrandon Report, indeed, carried many references to the way the experiment had operated in Northern Ireland.[4] The issue became a fertile one for scholars, mainly political scientists, to mine. In this respect it is revealing to consider in particular two scholarly articles published around the time of the debate on Scottish and Welsh devolution which take very different lessons from the Northern Ireland experience.

The first is by Paul Arthur, a 'cautionary tale' to use his words, and a warning regarding the possible drawbacks of devolution if the Northern Ireland example was taken as a guide.[5] Here, Arthur quite rightly stresses from the start that the 1920 Government of Ireland Act which conferred devolution on the six northern counties envisaged a very different set of circumstances than those which eventually arose. This factor weighed especially heavily on the financial terms on which Northern Ireland was meant to operate; the denial of significant revenue-raising powers in effect rapidly forced Northern Ireland into a state of financial dependency *vis-à-vis* the British Treasury. What was at first in theory an example of a revenue-based financial system of devolution became in practice an 'expenditure-based' one which relied on grants and subventions. The reasons for this lay in the British Government's wish to retain control of substantial taxes until both Northern and Southern Irish parliaments were set up and functioning in a co-operative manner through the Council of Ireland. Of course, only the Northern parliament came into being, and the financial issue is a prime example of the stillborn vision behind the Government of Ireland Act resulting in defective devolutionary arrangements for the Northern Ireland State. Clearly, there was a lesson in this about ensuring the soundness of the financial basis to any devolved system.[6]

Arthur, also with good reason, points to the reluctance of the Unionists in Northern Ireland to use their devolved powers innovatively and imaginatively. He comments on the sterile political situation which the Unionists' perpetual dominance gave rise to, and underlines the dangers of a complacent hegemonic governing party and a weak opposition if such a situation was to arise in Scotland under a similar system of devolution. Indeed, the scenario of a Strathclyde-based Labour Party dominating the whole of Scotland through the medium of devolution was one which was played upon by some opponents of the measure in the referendum campaign in Scotland and reputedly had its effect in areas like Grampian which recorded a negative verdict.[7] The Labour Party in Scotland seemed sensitive on this issue. In 1974 the authors of a discussion paper on devolution referred to the suggestion that proportional representation be established for a Scottish Assembly. The paper said:

> Let us be clear that proportional representation had to be introduced in Ulster because the Unionist majority abused power. Scotland is not Ulster, and the Scottish Labour movement bears no resemblance whatever to the Ulster Unionists.[8]

However, Scots may have been even more influenced by thoughts about potential *one-issue* dominance in a devolved parliament, something again which invites a parallel with Northern Ireland. Whereas in Northern Ireland the issue was the one of loyalty to the State, in Scotland's case it may have been that of independence. The great fear of some outside the ranks of the Nationalists was that devolution would fuel the demand for separation rather than satisfy people's aspirations, and that the SNP, in a devolved set-up, would press the issue to the point where it dominated all others. This point is made strongly by the political scientist Vernon Bogdanor whose book *Devolution* appeared at the time of the referendum.[9]

Arthur makes the point that there was great confusion in the public mind in Northern Ireland about what Stormont and Westminster were respectively responsible for, a point also made at this time by the constitutional lawyer Harry Calvert.[10] Indeed, Northern Ireland politicians themselves seemed confused. Stormont tended to be blamed by the public for things it actually had no control over, particularly financial matters. And, in the passing, Arthur highlights the anomalies devolution gave rise to in Northern Ireland, for example the question of the Province's MPs at Westminster voting on non-Northern Ireland issues in that parliament, while at the same time a convention operated by which Westminster did not discuss or interfere with purely Northern Ireland business. This was an anomaly which caused much debate at the time of the Scotland and Wales Bills of 1978 when it was dubbed 'The West Lothian Question' after the constituency of Tam Dalyell, the anti-devolution Labour MP who made such an issue of it. And, of course, it was a question which had been around a long time, from the very first stirrings of the devolution issue in British politics in the 1880s as previously noted in chapter two.

Arthur's pessimistic conclusions in this 1977 article rested rather heavily on the particular nature of political conflict in Northern Ireland and the extent to which the Unionists' approach to devolved government and its potentialities was always strictly harnessed to their overriding priorities of securing their State and the Union and not losing their grip on power. In Scotland where a very different political situation obtained, it seems likely that any elected assembly which might have been set up had the referendum result been conclusive enough, would have regarded its role in a more dynamic fashion than did Stormont. Nonetheless, Arthur drew attention to some of the ways in which a Scottish experience of devolution could be similarly troubled to that of Northern Ireland, and even if the two political situations were very different it was at least questionable if a Scottish assembly could meet Calvert's basic conditions for making such a settlement work: that is, that it satisfied the aspirations of some, and enjoyed at least the acquiescence of virtually all the rest.[11] In any potential Scottish case the existence of a sizeable number of Nationalists who could not accept it as anything but a temporary measure, and a similar number of non-Nationalists who considered it an expensive and unnecessary addition to the State's bureaucracy, would provide a test for these conditions. One Nationalist commentator much later, in 1990, doubted the prospects of any devolved measure for Scotland, but stressed that if one was to have a chance of working, at the very least lessons had to be learned from the Northern Ireland example and independent revenue-raising powers and constitutionally entrenched autonomy vested in a Scottish parliament.[12]

The interpretation of W. D. Birrell in a 1978 article[13] of the Northern Ireland experience and its relevance for Scotland and Wales is a lot more positive, although he too points to possible pitfalls. To an extent he shares the views of one of Stormont's stoutest academic defenders, former civil servant John Oliver,[14] in that he is impressed by the body of legislation unique to Northern Ireland which Stormont did introduce. Examples of this can be found in agricultural policy, special care for the mentally handicapped, the fight against tuberculosis and policies to attract new industries in the 1960s.[15] Birrell, unlike Oliver, is not concerned to defend the overall record of the Stormont Parliament; rather he wants to make the point that even in the special troubled circumstances of Northern Ireland and given the financial difficulties, there is plenty of evidence which suggests the advantages of regional government. In this Birrell echoes the conclusion of the Kilbrandon Commission:

> ... despite the great difference between the theory of home rule and its practical application, and despite the special difficulties inherent in the Northern Ireland situation, in many fields, notably those which were unaffected, or at least were not dominated, by the community problem — the home rule experiment had considerable success.[16]

However, Birrell argues that the Kilbrandon report was wrong, on the basis of the Northern Ireland experience, to propose that a Scottish assembly be financed by a system of block grants and feels that Kilbrandon unduly shaped the form the 1978 Bills took in this respect.[17] He is in favour of at least some tax-raising powers. What Birrell may have overlooked is that there were hidden taxation powers in the 1978 Bill: a Scottish Parliament could, for instance, have retained funds intended for local government thus giving itself more spending power and forcing local government to increase its rates.[18] Birrell is also impressed with the way Northern Ireland governments in the 1960s became involved in economic planning, and argues that Scotland and Wales should be allowed the means and the scope to do the same.

All in all, Birrell is concerned to emphasise the increase in Stormont's powers over the fifty years of devolution *in spite of* the political conservatism of the Unionists; he believes that in

Scotland, where there would be a *political* demand for a progressive extension of powers, this would reinforce the internal dynamic of the devolved government system towards such an extension anyway. Birrell is thus optimistic about the possibilities of devolved government for Scotland and Wales, and he does not believe that the Northern Ireland experience should be seen as a cause for pessimism. His argument is an interesting counterpoint to Arthur's but it rather glosses over the financial problems encountered by Stormont, the continual wrangling between it and the British Treasury, the extent to which the Northern Ireland legislation on social and economic issues until the 1960s had a 'step by step' purpose and spirit, and the very real confusion which existed in people's minds about the division of power and responsibility. Neither did the Northern Ireland example bode well in terms of relations between different tiers of government. Perhaps it would be true to say that much of Northern Ireland's trouble was the result of the central government turning a blind eye to Stormont which turned a blind eye to the local authorities. In a Scottish devolved system the trouble might be the reverse: that central government would interfere with a Scottish Parliament which would interfere with local authorities; it should be remembered that much inconclusive debate in Scotland in 1978–79 surrounded the potentially problematic relationship between a tier of devolved government and the then recently established upper tiers of local government, one of which (Strathclyde) contained about half of the Scottish population.

III

The imposition of Direct Rule in Northern Ireland in 1972 by the Conservative government led by Edward Heath was a humiliation for Unionists. It also signalled to many Unionists and those in sympathy with them that IRA violence had achieved its proclaimed goal of destroying the Northern Ireland State. In the short term it produced an angry reaction and the growth of the Vanguard Party of William Craig which stood for an Independent 'British Ulster', in effect a fresh assertion of Protestant exclusivism although this time in outright defiance of Westminster. This mood of defiance was exemplified during the general strike called and co-ordinated by the Ulster Workers' Council (UWC) in May 1974 against the power-sharing Executive led by Brian Faulkner.[19] The Executive

had been the product of the Sunningdale agreement at the end of
1973 by which power would be shared between Unionists and
Nationalists in the form of the Faulkner Unionists and the SDLP,
and a Council of Ireland would be set up to provide an all-Ireland
dimension. The great majority of Unionist representatives, as
returned for the Assembly elections in June 1973 and the British
General Election of February 1974, repudiated the scheme. Without
the support of the bulk of the majority community the Executive's
future was always in doubt, although its actual fall in the event of
the UWC strike elicited from its members accusations of betrayal
against the new Labour government, and declarations of faith in
the long term viability of the initiative if only it had received the
requisite backing from Westminster.

One effect of these political events in Ulster in 1972–74 was the
severe straining of relations between the Conservative Party in
Scotland (since the mid–60s no longer called the Unionists) and
the Orange Order. Indeed, during the period of Labour government from 1974–79, the Orange Order in Scotland attempted with
some success to set up channels of communication and dialogue
with Labour over the issue of devolution and wider constitutional
reform in the UK. The Order's constitutional outlook embraced a
possible 'federal devolution' scheme for the whole of the UK along
with a Bill of Rights.[20] This outlook, which was starkly at variance
with the Tories' steady retreat to undiluted Unionism under
Margaret Thatcher after 1975, was primarily the result of the desire
to see devolved government restored to Northern Ireland, and not
in the form of the 1974 Executive. The Order's reasoning seems to
have been that securing Northern Ireland's position in the Union
could be achieved more effectively through the medium of the
constitutional debate occasioned by Scottish, and to a lesser extent
Welsh, devolution demands. It was an attempt to exploit the situation largely created by a revived Scottish claim to self-government
in order to restore devolution to Northern Ireland on the same
terms: the return, in other words, of Unionist political domination.
It was an approach to be used later, in the late 1980s and early
1990s, by Ulster Unionist politicians when, again, Scotland had
provided a catalyst to speculation about comprehensive constitutional re-structuring.

In 1975 the Orange Order condemned the Labour White Paper
proposals as not going nearly far enough in the devolutionary
direction, and holding out 'the possible development of an Ulster

type situation in our own land'. This was on account of what it perceived as 'the colonial style of concentration of authority in the hands of a Secretary of State and his power of veto' which paralleled all too closely the role of the Northern Ireland Secretary of State under the conditions of Direct Rule.[21]

The Grand Master of the Order in Scotland, Thomas Orr, stated in December 1977 that Direct Rule had reduced Northern Ireland to a 'Coconut Colony' and that the system was 'an offence to our nostrils'.[22] The Order thus wanted no mild devolutionary proposals which would not tackle the perceived iniquities of Direct Rule; it desired an end to this system and power returned to the representatives of the majority. There is no reason to doubt that the Order was also sincere in its belief that devolution would also be beneficial for Scotland and the other parts of Britain; in the Referendum Campaign of 1979 it sought a 'Yes' vote in opposition to the Conservatives.[23] However, in the 1980s it has to be noted that the organisation's enthusiasm for devolution, and constitutional reform of any significance, seemed to wane. The issue of Ulster and of making gains for the Unionists out of the given political situation was the primary objective.

The Order attempted to discuss devolution with the Labour ministers responsible for it, who included Michael Foot, in 1977. They made representations through Hugh Brown, a pro-devolutionist Labour MP for Glasgow Provan whose contacts with the Order from this time on were close and cordial, notwithstanding Brown's anti-Unionist position on the Irish question and membership of the Northern Ireland Committee of the Parliamentary Labour Party which functioned in effect as a Nationalist pressure group.[24] Brown was one of the few Scottish Labour figures who attempted to get the measure of his constituents' feelings about the Northern Ireland troubles,[25] and who was inclined to remind his colleagues of the strength of sectarian feeling on both sides in Scotland and of 'the Orange vote' in particular.[26]

The Order's top level consultations were in the event stymied, not it appears by any section of the Labour Party, but by the Scottish Office which feared the effects that publicity of such a meeting might have on Catholics in Scotland.[27]

Orange enthusiasm for devolution may indeed have confirmed some Catholics in their opposition to it in the Referendum in 1979. Gallagher has noted how the spectre of sectarianism was invoked in the campaign with reference to the Northern Ireland experience of devolution, and cites Hugh Brown's impression that more Catholics than Protestants were apprehensive about the proposal.[28] Possibly too, significant sections of opinion in the Labour movement which played a crucial campaigning role against devolution in 1979, were happy to encourage this negative perception among Catholics for fear of the potential disruption of local government fiefdoms in a devolved Scottish system. Wariness among Catholics regarding even the intentions of the Church of Scotland and the role it could play, or seek to play, in a self-governing Scotland, may have been occasioned by the Church's lively involvement in the debate, overwhelmingly on the side of devolution if at the cost of public rows between ministers.[29]

The Conservative government of Margaret Thatcher after 1979 suffered further loss of support from the Orange constituency much of which had once been a prop of her party, a fact to which Mrs Thatcher's memoirs make reference.[30] As Tom Gallagher has suggested it is possible that a majority of Orange members were voting Labour or SNP by the 1983 general election.[31] Certainly by 1990 an official Orange publication could state:

> The politics of the average Scottish Orangeman is all embracing, with Labour, Tory, Scottish Nationalist and SDP members in the ranks. Indeed, because of the working class roots of the Scottish Order Labour has a broad appeal to many brethren.[32]

That appeal may also have been strengthened by Labour's record in office regarding Northern Ireland 1974–79, and in particular the Secretaryship of Roy Mason, notwithstanding the Party's pro-Irish unity policy statements in theory.

Given this Tory-Orange estrangement it is not surprising that the Orange Order in Scotland attempted to make the Tories suffer for the signing of the 'Anglo-Irish Agreement' in November 1985. While Unionist fury erupted in Ulster, the Orange Order in Scotland brought into being a new political party, the Scottish Unionist Party (SUP), with the express intention of fighting Conservative-held seats in Scotland at the following election. When the election eventually took place in June 1987 the SUP did not stand candidates but used the considerable publicity it received to advise voters opposed to the Anglo-Irish Agreement to vote against the government. In his analysis of this episode, Gallagher concludes that the SUP's intervention might have helped significantly to oust the incumbent Tories in key West of Scotland seats like Renfrew

West and Inverclyde and Cunninghame North.[33] It was an inconclusive foray on the part of the Order into Scottish politics, but a
demonstration of its influence and by extension concern about
Ulster nonetheless. It may also have suggested that in the absence
of a Northern Ireland policy seen to be sufficiently pro-Unionist in
the eyes of the Orange movement, the Conservatives had no apparent winning card to play in its quest to broaden the social base of
its Scottish support; other working class opinion in Scotland, and
most middle class, were culturally at odds with the theory and
practice of 'Thatcherism' and its perceived attack on Scottish values
and sensitivities.[34]

The other political parties in Scotland endorsed the Anglo-Irish
Agreement, an indication of the way that the Northern Ireland
issue was avoided in Scottish politics than of serious cross-party
commitment to solving the Province's problems. By the 1980s it
was clear that the reluctance of Scottish political parties to involve
themselves in debate about Northern Ireland, an understandable
and perhaps prudent response to the initial outbreak of the
Troubles and the threat they seemed to pose to Scottish society,
had ossified into a general lack of ideas about the issue and in many
cases of interest. The very term 'Anglo-Irish Agreement' suggested
a London-Dublin framework in which a Scottish perspective was
lacking, and the term was readily accepted and used by Scots.

No Scot held a significant position in the Northern Ireland Office
under both Tory and Labour governments from 1972 until the
appointment of Michael Ancram in 1992. There was more robust
English Conservative support for the organisation of the Tory Party
in Northern Ireland than Scottish, and there was no noticeable
Scottish Labour support for the demand that the Labour Party
organise until Calum MacDonald and George Foulkes backed the
demand in the 1990s. The trend of constituency branch opinion on
Northern Ireland in the Labour Party was Nationalist, as in
England, but this lobby too, although numerically strong, was kept
largely in check by a cagey leadership beyond the Party's formal
commitment to a united Ireland as a long term goal. The SNP if
anything avoided debate on the issue even more scrupulously than
the Labour or Tory parties;[35] the issue's potential to exacerbate
sectarian divisions ensured that the party fought shy, although
morally it might be said that the SNP had the greatest obligation to
address the question openly and to tackle head-on, rather than
wish away, the religious friction which may have ensued. A future

independent Scotland in which such divisions festered unacknowl-
edged would be the antithesis of the party's proclaimed vision.[36] It
might even be said that the SNP have fallen back on the Irish
nationalist tendency simply to blame the Union and the British
government for all such problems; that independence would of itself
resolve them. It was only in the 1990s that a recent SNP convert,
Bob Purdie, deliberated with careful insight on how Scotland might
help the situation in Northern Ireland,[37] while party spokesman
Paul Scott urged, with little insight or care, that Scottish Nationalists should take inspiration from Irish nationalism.[38] Another
SNP convert, Professor Chris Harvie, ruminated in 1994 of how
the Northern Ireland troubles had inhibited Scots in relation to
their own struggles for constitutional change,[39] which at least was
an indication that the Scottish disposition to avoid the matter, or
simply to fall in uncritically with whatever the London and Dublin
governments were attempting to do, was being questioned.

To return to the Anglo-Irish Agreement, it is appropriate to conclude this section with an extract from the contribution of Hugh
Brown to the debate on the measure at Westminster in which a
serious dereliction of duty is implied and admitted to. Brown, in his
first contribution to a debate on Northern Ireland in twenty-one
years (by his own calculations) stated:

> I think that there should be a voice from Scotland. I am not presum-
> ing to speak for Scotland. In fact, that is one of the disadvantages. Even
> in the parliamentary Labour party and the Northern Ireland group, of
> which I have been a member for many years, there are only a few
> members from Scotland who even take part in discussions on Ireland.
> One of the things that we have to offer is that in Glasgow and the West
> of Scotland we understand what a Billy and Dan situation is . . .
>
> My contribution has some significance because in Glasgow and the
> West of Scotland, even the media — I make no complaint about
> that — accept that we have been muted in all the previous delibe-
> rations on the subject.[40]

IV

In the late 1980s and early 1990s it was Scotland which was viewed
as something of a catalyst to fertile constitutional debate and
reform. However, this only crystallised after a period of reaction to
the devolution referendum; in the public eye the cause of devolution

and constitutional reform generally had been discredited in the tortuous and tawdry parliamentary wrangles preceding the referendum when the Labour government was clinging to power with its threadbare majority. There seemed to be a widespread turning away from the issue as the Thatcher Conservative government, returned at the general election of May 1979, set about its radical agenda. Labour moved back into its more comfortable adversarial role in the great two-party-class-politics syndrome, while the SNP (reduced to two MPs in 1979) split acrimoniously into factions over what to do next.[41]

The constitutional debate re-emerged in a new form during the 1980s, influenced to some extent by the spirit of decentralisation around the European Community. In the process of this the distinctiveness of Scotland's political identity within the UK was further enhanced. On top of the distinct administrative system by which Scottish governmental business was conducted,[42] the impetus to constitutional reform and the stubborn resistance to the Thatcher Conservative prospectus, combined to produce a Scottish popular mood which imposed the most severe strains on the Union to date. Questions of legitimacy became staples of political debate in Scotland as never before; what were viewed as abuses of power by central government — in the Scottish case the foisting of a political agenda on a country which had clearly rejected it at the polls — raised demands for constitutional changes which would decentralise power, give sovereignty to the people, and promote local democracy. The Tories' electoral weakness in Scotland throughout the Thatcher era made the issue of legitimacy a powerful one for the opposition to exploit, although in doing so a party like Labour was forced to follow an essentially Nationalist agenda. This will be considered below.

As Mrs Thatcher's government strengthened its identification with the constitutional status quo, and with the doctrine of the supreme and undivided sovereignty of parliament, so more and more Scots began to think again about how adequately such constitutional conservatism served their needs. The debate intensified to the point where radical change, and certainly a high SNP vote, was anticipated in the 1992 election. The result of that election, in which the SNP's progress was slight and was matched by that of the Conservatives', again produced an anti-climax. However, it should not be forgotten that some 75 per cent of those Scots who voted did so for parties advocating constitutional change.

The idea of Scotland as a catalyst to change was well-aired in the late 1980s and early 1990s by political commentators as well as those actively pushing for change. Robin Cook, a Scottish Labour front bench spokesman and opponent of devolution in the 1970s, had this to say in 1987:

> If Scotland's demand [for a devolved assembly] is successfully pressed, it could prove the battering ram that releases parallel claims for decentralisation, regional autonomy and local democracy throughout Britain.[43]

Similarly, the political scientist David Marquand took the view just before the 1992 election that pressure for Scottish Home Rule would lead to radical constitutional change.[44] Pressure groups for constitutional reform such as 'Charter 88' and the Institute for Public Policy Research also made much of Scotland as the prime mover of change, and of the idea that the rest of the UK could not remain unreformed if Scotland was given what it demanded.

In March 1989 the Scottish Constitutional Convention was set up as a cross-party and cross-community body with the objective of producing a blueprint for Scottish self-government. Its founding document — 'A Claim of Right for Scotland' — advanced the essentially Nationalist view that sovereignty lay with the Scottish people, and it castigated the British Constitution's concentration of power in the hands of the Executive.[45] The SNP and the Conservatives boycotted the Convention for respective Nationalist and Unionist reasons, and in the belief that it was a vehicle constructed to the advantage of the Convention's largest participating group, the Labour Party. However, if anything the Convention demonstrated just how far Labour had travelled by this time down the Nationalist road.

In a sense Mrs Thatcher's brand of politics made this hard to avoid. There was the question of legitimacy for Labour to stress in order to highlight the Tories' lamentable progress in Scotland. There was also the danger of any kind of identification with a centralised concept of government when the Tories had become, under Thatcher, synonymous with it. Most of all there was the extent to which the anti-government mood in Scotland was also a nationalistic one. Thatcherism was widely seen as an attack on distinctive Scottish institutions and values, and an attack on the idea of the Union as a two-way street. In order to face a renewed SNP challenge which was infused with the developing importance of Europe and the anticipated changes in the balance between nation states and autonomous regional units, Labour adopted much of the Nationalist political language. They harped on the legitimacy theme and endorsed the idea that Scotland possessed a concept of political sovereignty which vested it in the people rather than Parliament. They were convinced by the argument that a Scottish Parliament would have prevented the Thatcherite project being implemented in Scotland. They emphasised, rather incongruously for a party which still, ultimately, set its sights on power at Westminster, the negative consequences of the system of government as it stood. They now stood for a Scottish Assembly with tax-raising powers, unlike the 1970s. All of this was welcome to the many party activists who espoused a 'Nationalist Left' approach and who were convinced that political upsets such as Jim Sillars's by-election victory for the SNP at Govan in 1988 took the political battle into a new Nationalist framework. They saw Labour casting off its staid and often corrupt image and connecting with the new cultural nationalism of the 1980s which was manifesting itself in the arts, popular music, literature and drama.[46]

On the other hand there were still doubters within the movement. Two such, Geekie and Levy, set out the case against the pursuit of the Nationalist agenda in a scholarly article published in 1989.[47] In it they foresaw the possible secession of the Labour Party in Scotland from the British party, and a whittling down of the party's strength and power base in Scotland and in Britain generally under the conditions of a PR elected devolved assembly, with reduced Labour representation at Westminster. After 1992 this more traditionalist strand of labour thinking began again to make itself heard to effect.

The Constitutional Convention was widely viewed as signalling a new type of politics in Scotland — more consensual and with more recognition given to different identities. It was a sign of what David McCrone has identified as a form of nationalist movement fundamentally in tune with post-nationalist times, primed to exploit a new pluralism and a new politics of identity.[48] The Convention reported at the end of 1990[49] and advocated a 'maximalist' form of devolution leaving little to Westminster except defence, foreign affairs and macro-economic policy. It called for stronger financial powers than had been proposed back in the 1970s. Overall, it fell somewhere between devolution and federalism, and was guided by a future vision of 'Europe of the Regions' in which a Scottish Parliament would play a significant part.

The relation of this wide-ranging and intense Scottish debate to Northern Ireland was and is manifested in several ways, both directly and indirectly. The importance of devolution to the debate on Northern Ireland's constitutional position has remained as great over the period since 1972 when the Province lost its devolved status, as it was when she actually possessed it. It has, quite clearly, been the preferred option for successive British governments in their attempts to bring stability to the Province. All the initiatives launched since 1972, as Harvey Cox points out,[50] have pursued essentially the same solution: the re-establishment of devolved government with power-sharing and with some all-Ireland and British-Irish dimension. As Cox also argues, the devolved government-power-sharing Irish dimension option offers most from a British point of view: it keeps Northern Ireland at a distance, it involves the Republic as a co-guarantor, it involves cross community participation, and it honours constitutional guarantees.

Devolved government is regarded much more ambivalently by the major political parties in Northern Ireland. Simple majority style devolution — as in the 1921–72 period — is firmly opposed by even the most moderate of Nationalists who equate it with Unionist domination and see in it no scope for the expression of an Irish nationalist identity. The preferred British option of power-sharing with some kind of Irish dimension has been rejected by Unionists with Dublin involvement the main sticking point. And there has emerged a strand of Unionist opinion which is against any form of devolution because this would render Northern Ireland anomalous in the context of the UK, and help sustain the belief that Northern Ireland is a 'place apart'. The arguments of these integrationist Unionists, around the demand for 'Equal Citizenship' have gained influence since the signing of the Anglo-Irish Agreement. They have called for Northern Ireland to be governed in the same way as the rest of the UK.[51]

But there is a difficulty here. The UK, while it is a unitary state, is not governed or administered in a uniform manner. There is the example of the distinctive way Scotland is governed and the distinctiveness of Scottish political culture, which has been highlighted. Northern Ireland too is distinctive, not least on account of civil strife. It is also politically set apart by its local party divisions which have to a great extent persisted since the Stormont era, and by the refusal or reluctance of the major British parties to organise there. The latter issue has been one of the central preoccupations of the 'Equal Citizenship' Unionists in their quest for equality of treatment with the rest of the UK, and the question has caused particular controversy within the British Labour Party whose refusal to organise is expressly linked to its 'Unity by Consent' policy. Those urging Labour to organise in Northern Ireland have made much of the Party's relative success in *Scotland* in prevailing over sectarian divisions, and have accused Labour of shunning its duty to the cause of working class co-operation and unity.[52]

In political terms Northern Ireland is undoubtedly more anomalous than any other part of the UK, and the argument rages over whether this is brought about mainly by successive British Governments' desire to keep it at a political distance, or by the wishes and behaviour of the Northern Ireland people, both Unionists and Nationalists themselves. In giving Northern Ireland devolved government in the first place, and in attempting such initiatives as Sunningdale and the Anglo-Irish Agreement during the present troubles, it is clear that British Governments have not applied the sovereignty of Parliament doctrine to Northern Ireland as they have to Britain. The fact that Northern Ireland is not included in the term 'Britain', only in 'the United Kingdom', underlines the same point.

The idea of Northern Ireland as a constitutional anomaly is a vital one to consider because it underlies a lot of the political and strategic thinking of the main political players in contemporary times. Certainly, it was uppermost in the minds of Official Unionist politicians at the time of the 1992 election when Scotland's constitutional debate encouraged them to look at Northern Ireland's future in the same context. Three prominent Unionists at this time — James Molyneaux, David Trimble and Chris McGimpsey — all intervened to make the point that if Scotland was to be granted devolution in any constitutional shake-up, then Northern Ireland should also receive it.

Molyneaux indeed made contact with the Scottish Constitutional Convention, and the Chairman of the Convention, Canon Kenyon Wright, expressed delight that the debate was spreading from Scotland to other parts of the UK in this way. Molyneaux recognised that any Northern Ireland assembly would not be likely to be a replica of a Scottish Assembly, but that, to use his words, 'the same basic pattern could be followed with arrangements made for Northern Ireland's special features.' The Unionist newspaper in which this was reported, the *Belfast Newsletter*, welcomed Molyneaux's statements and commented:

> Scotland has strong historic and cultural links with Northern Ireland and Unionist politicians therefore are on solid ground in pursuing avenues that will further cement these relationships.[53]

Chris McGimpsey, speaking just after the general election, expressed the view that Scotland was justified in seeking full legislative devolution and that Northern Ireland should get the same if Scotland succeeded. He went on to say that he foresaw a 'coalition' government in Northern Ireland under such a set-up, although it is not clear whether or not he was contemplating power-sharing.[54]

Finally, David Trimble in recent years has put much emphasis on the Scottish connection in his brand of Unionism; the sense of identity he has articulated on numerous occasions seems inspired by Ulster-Scottish links past and present. For some time he pressed for reform of the way Northern Ireland was governed under Direct Rule by urging imitation of Scottish practices. He called, for example, for a Northern Ireland Select Committee to be organised on the same lines as the Scottish Select Committee in the House of Commons.[55] The Unionists succeeded in wringing the concession of a Select Committee from the Major Conservative Government in 1993. Overall, like Molyneaux and McGimpsey, Trimble has also stressed the point about Northern Ireland being part of a 'system' of decentralisation throughout the UK; it is an approach which seeks to make Northern Ireland compatible with the rest of the UK.[56]

This Unionist strategy of striving to remove the 'anomalous' character of Northern Ireland within the UK had the attraction of meeting traditional Unionist objectives about securing Northern Ireland firmly within the UK while appearing to be amenable to reform and constitutional renewal. It was a position which allowed them, unusually, to turn the tables on the major Nationalist constitutionalist Party, the Social Democratic and the Labour Party (SDLP), and accuse them of being negative and obstructive. For the SDLP certainly do not favour the Northern Ireland problem being tackled in this UK context. Under the leadership of John Hume the SDLP has stressed the need for an Irish dimension to any solution and the pertinence of the wider context of Europe. They do not believe that Northern Ireland resembles Scotland or any other part of the UK in terms of political management. Just as Irish Nationalist politicians like John Redmond in the early twentieth century resisted the idea that Ireland's case should be treated in the context of 'Home Rule All Round', so Hume and the SDLP have resisted its absorption into a similar quasi-federalist context of constitutional thinking today.

This is an obstacle not really faced up to by most of those who have in recent years pursued such federal or quasi-federal approaches to constitutional matters. Scottish Labour MPs such as George Foulkes and Tony Worthington have come up with 'across-the-board' decentralisation schemes which have included Northern Ireland,[57] and a leading Scottish political thinker, Isobel Lindsay — who left the SNP over its refusal to take part in the Constitutional Convention — wrote in the Northern Ireland current affairs journal *Fortnight* about the virtue of Northern Ireland being brought into the whole process of reform and not treated as a constitutional anomaly.[58] These were, however, rare examples of Scots attempting to extend schemes of constitutional reform with Northern Ireland in mind, and none of them really addressed the hard question of how Northern Ireland's involvement would remove the obstacles which presently prevent consensus being reached about political change.

Another proponent of federal-type ideas, the political scientist Bernard Crick, probes such questions more rigorously.[59] He starts out with the premise that Northern Ireland must accommodate the reality that it faces both ways: both to Britain and to the Irish Republic. Crick usefully reminds us that the UK, although it has pretended to be a sovereign, centralised State, in practice has had to permit a kind of informal federalism. Crick writes:

> . . . there might be something to be said for examining how federal a state the United Kingdom really is and whether 'de jure' institutionalisation of 'de facto' practices might not be advantageous.[60]

He contends that there must be flexibility about constitutional arrangements, that there can be no one model of devolution throughout the UK. 'I argue that power should be federalised', he writes, 'not that we necessarily need a formal federal system.'[61] Crick considers it more important to change presuppositions about parliamentary sovereignty and the nature of power.

People like Crick thus see Northern Ireland as part of a constitutional reform package — as do the Unionists quoted above —
but Crick also wants to accommodate the Irish dimension (the
Unionist bugbear) and to see radical changes to ideas of *sovereignty*;
he attacks the sovereignty of parliament doctrine as the means by
which *English* domination is secured, and he considers it a static,
debilitating notion, holding up the process of the distribution of
power.

V

As the constitutional debate has taken its course in the 1980s and
1990s, it has also brought into focus the need to re-examine and
revise and re-define ideas of 'Britishness'. This concept, recently a
much-debated and controversial one but for so long uninterrogated,
is at the nub of the contemporary debate, and the two places on
which it has borne down with the greatest relevance have been
Scotland and Northern Ireland. As with schemes of devolution
and other constitutional reforms, the way Scotland and Northern
Ireland have related to this debate on 'Britishness' is of central
importance.

First, it might be appropriate to pick up the theme from the
previous section and consider how possible Scottish developments
might alter perceptions of 'Britishness' and the structure of allegiances in Northern Ireland. Although the question has been
damped down since the 1992 election, much speculation has
surrounded the consequences of Scottish independence. 'In a disunited Kingdom,' Simon Lee has written, 'what price Ulster
Unionism?'[62] Certainly it is an intriguing question as to whether or
not the idea of 'Britishness' and concepts of loyalty in Northern
Ireland would be able to adapt to a Britain which no longer contained Scotland. It has been speculated that such a development
would make an independent Northern Ireland a more likely
political choice for many erstwhile Unionists.[63] Paradoxically, it
also seems that Scottish independence is regarded favourably by
many Unionists, which may indicate that their Unionism is more a
reflection of ethnic identity and the assertion of cultural difference
in the context of the conflict in Ireland, than of a devout faith in
British political institutions and political doctrines such as the
sovereignty of parliament.

There is also no doubt that some observers take the view that

Scotland striking out on its own might prompt Unionists to consider the contribution they might make to re-defining Irishness, and, as Kevin Boyle argues,[64] fashioning their own inclusion in such a redefinition. Then, on the question of political violence, some observers like Simon Lee believe that if change occurs in Scotland peaceably, then this may strengthen the anti-violence forces in Northern Ireland.[65]

The Scottish journalist Joyce McMillan has written thoughtfully about Scotland's role in challenging the British Constitution and myths of Britishness so that other groups of people like the Ulster Unionists will have to re-define their position. McMillan sees the Scots as creating movement, as causing a loosening of constitutional and governmental, and indeed cultural, rigidities. She hopes that this will create a more fluid political context in which people can devise structures to accommodate difference, and to get away from the kind of politics which is stuck fast to traditional allegiances and shibboleths. Both she and Kevin Boyle among others consider traditional Ulster Unionism and Irish Nationalism to be obsolete.[66]

Developments in Scotland since the 1980s have certainly altered perceptions of 'Britishness' to the point where consideration of the implications this might have is justified. The Scots, as chronicled in earlier chapters, saw the Union as beneficial in the past in that great opportunities were opened up in the context of the Empire. Scots took on a global role with relish and it is perhaps no accident that the SNP's 'Independence in Europe' policy seemed to strike strong chords among Scots: here was the idea of Europe replacing the Empire in providing that bigger stage, the international context in which Scots can exert influence. In the light of this the British State's strained relationship with Europe could be said to have contributed to a weakening of many Scots' sense of British identity. Europe has become part of a British problem in that postures struck by the British Government (and its predecessors) in relation to Europe have compounded already strained relationships between central government and Scotland. Many Scots in this respect have come to view the British Government as backward-looking, jealously guarding the outworn idea of parliamentary sovereignty, and refusing to adopt the spirit of the EC and devolve power. The perception of an insular Britain, over-centralised and out of step with international developments has blunted the appeal of Britishness for many Scots.

In Northern Ireland ideas of Britishness are bound up with the conflict over national identity and allegiance and have deeper layers of meaning. On the part of Unionists ideas of Britishness are re-affirmed in terms of a guarantee of liberty and of security and are constructed against perceptions of the Irish nationalist adversary. British symbolism, particularly the monarchy, is central to a sense of community identity which constantly has to justify its opposition to Irish unity by asserting difference in terms of visible allegiance. Nevertheless, many Unionists and Loyalists have questioned the British link and declared themselves willing to break it on account of their perception of British Government 'betrayal' of their cause. There has always been a significant, if politically weak, tradition of Ulster independence. And, in 1990, in the *Scotsman* newspaper, Rhonda Paisley, daughter of Ian, declared: 'I don't think my gener-ation has the same overt loyalty to Britain that my Dad's generation had. We are more willing to move away from the big link.'[67]

A significant difference between Scotland and Northern Ireland regarding a sense of British identity is now the greater tendency on the part of most Scots who are not separatists to identify with the British State rather than the idea of a British nation. The small 'u' unionism of Labour and Liberal Democratic parties in Scotland, for example, is of this nature: it is a Britishness which sees political, social and economic advantages in a British State structure and is not necessarily underpinned by a belief in — or enthusiasm for — the British nation idea. There is, indeed, a scepticism about all 'nationalisms' and a belief, perhaps, that the wider context of the British State serves to inhibit chauvinism and xenophobia in its constituent parts. In many ways while there is a dual sense of iden-tity still held by most Scots, it might be said that the British part of it is now regarded far more pragmatically and less emotionally. As Bernard Crick has pointed out, acceptance of a 'British' label is a recognition of what is held in common with the rest of the UK.[68] In a survey undertaken in 1992, 32% of Scots said they saw themselves as Scottish and not British, while a further 29% said they were more Scottish than British. Only 9% gave priority to being British.[69]

In contemporary Northern Ireland it seems that the concept of a British *nation* has a stronger hold on imaginations and emotions, although this is not to suggest that the relationship of Unionism to the British State and the demand for equality of treatment on the part of some Unionists is not a political priority.[70] In a survey concerned with attitudes to national identity conducted in the early 1980s, Eddie Moxon-Browne found that among Northern Ireland Protestants a British sense of national identity had grown stronger in comparison to findings taken in the early stages of the Troubles. A later survey confirmed this trend.[71]

Today, perhaps as a result of a hardening of attitudes and of a defensive state of mind over the course of the Troubles, many Protestants seem to see virtue in casting off ambiguities concerning their national identity and embracing in an unequivocal way, Britishness: this might be regarded as a way of more clearly polarising the terms of the conflict. However, ambiguities still remain, and many Protestants are too aware of British Government impatience with the Unionist stance, and too suspicious of the British public's lack of identity with them, to embrace a British national identity so enthusiastically. Hence the persistence of variations of Ulster nationalism or of Protestant communal or ethnic identity. And it is important not to forget the significant if short-lived episodes in which such attitudes have manifested themselves politically: the example of William Craig's Vanguard movement in the early 1970s stands out clearly.

Many commentators have drawn attention to what they have perceived as the *conditional* nature of the Protestants' sense of British loyalty — that their loyalty is conditional on the British government supporting their demand not to be forced into a united Ireland. This type of 'contractarian' loyalty, as discussed in David Miller's seminal study considered in chapter two, is not as anomalous as some have suggested — indeed, the rise of nationalist feeling in Scotland may in a sense be the result of what many Scots feel is the breaking of a contract by the Government about the need for the British polity to reflect and accommodate the interests and distinct national characteristics of Scotland as well as England. In both cases — the Northern Ireland and the Scottish — there are important questions raised about what Britishness means politically, questions which indicate that the British State, although a unitary one, is underpinned by different, and perhaps conflicting, interpretations of how it should work. One of the most important of these interpretations is that distinctive national or ethnic identities have to be recognised and given political satisfaction: in this sense Britain and Britishness take on the nature of something negotiated, bargained for, covenanted, or contracted. In the light of this genuine British national feeling is a somewhat elusive, or at any rate deeply ambiguous, concept.

The point can be further developed. In an interesting article published in 1991,[72] the Scottish academic Lindsay Patterson stresses that Scotland never lost its national identity and never really lacked some form of national autonomy: it chose simply to exercise this autonomy within a British framework. Patterson is sceptical about the rhetoric of Scottish nationalism around notions of 'reawakenings' and a new national consciousness. He prefers to consider the emergence of the political mood in the late 1980s, early 1990s as a result of a desire among Scots to protect and strengthen the distinct identity and relative autonomy which Scotland has never ceased to have, but which did seem under attack in the Thatcher years. Patterson argues that Scottish civil society asserted itself against what was seen as the Thatcherite threat to Scottish institutions, Scottish values, and Scottish culture. Under Thatcher it seemed that the Union was working only for the benefit of the South of England, that the concept of the Union as something negotiated and something which should work for Scotland as well was being forgotten or discarded.

Conditional loyalty to the Union is, therefore, something which can be said to apply to Scotland as well as the Ulster Loyalists. Basic to the latter's conditional loyalty is the notion of security: the desire for protection from the perceived threat of Irish nationalist domination. Ulster Unionists negotiated their position within the Union on that basis in the nineteenth century, and the Unionist relationship to the British State is still discussed by Unionists in these terms.

In Scotland the process takes a very different course. It is connected there not with security or with an external threat to its identity; rather it is concerned with preserving Scottish national distinctiveness and preserving relative autonomy, and preventing the kind of English nationalist trampling over Scottish institutions and sensitivities which was held to have occurred in the Thatcher years. This heightened the anomaly of a government ruling Scotland with so little actual support in Scotland, and linked the idea of legitimacy to a perception of the Union as something which involved recognition of distinctive identity and something not to be travestied by an idea of sovereignty which was at odds with many Scots' view of what sovereignty should mean.

All this has led to a large majority in Scotland in favour of some kind of constitutional change in a 'renegotiation of the Union' in Patterson's phrase — and this may in the future even lead to the break-up of the Union. But the point to stress is that the concept of negotiation and bargaining is central to the relationship between Scotland and the British State, and Northern Ireland and the British State. Questions of legitimacy of course also characterise Northern Ireland with, respectively, substantial Nationalist opposition to British rule in any form, and Unionist opposition to certain features of the system of government applied to Northern Ireland since 1972.

There have been, and remain, 'push and pull' pressures exerted in this context. Scotland could again exert great pressure for constitutional change which may create a crisis in the British State regarding its identity and governance. Such a crisis would have repercussions for Northern Ireland if the nature of the State underwent significant alteration.

There are other comparative points which might be made around this theme of 'Britishness'. The great majority of Catholics in Northern Ireland, most surveys show,[73] identify themselves unequivocally as 'Irish', although it should be said that there has been a reverse trend to that of the Protestants since the start of the Troubles: in 1969 more Catholics were willing to accept the label 'British'. In recent years this percentage has fallen sharply, although it is important to note that a steady 25–30 per cent of Catholics in opinion polls show a preference for remaining in the Union. Among these Northern Ireland Catholics willing to subscribe to a degree of Britishness, it is a pragmatic identification with the State and not a celebration of the British nation idea — in other words their attitude is comparable to that of most Scots today and probably similar to that of the bulk of Catholics in Scotland during the century.

However, even a pragmatic identification with 'Britishness' causes problems for Nationalists, both Irish and Scottish. In Northern Ireland the standard Irish nationalist critique of the concept of a dual sense of identity — that is, Irish/British or Ulster/British — is that this is an identity crisis, that a divided sense of identity in any sense is a *problem*. Some Unionists on the other hand have argued the case for viewing it as a strength, as evidence of a healthy balance of influences, although the Unionists have never really made the most of the way this approach to national identity is now far more in tune with the new language of pluralism and of the new Europe which sees the nation state as having had its day.

In Scotland, over the last decade especially, the dual sense of Scottish-British national identity which had long been the comfortable norm for most Scots, came increasingly under attack as being, as in Northern Ireland, something problematic. Over the last decade Scottish Nationalists have depicted such a dual identity as something belonging in the past, something which is now holding up progress. Scottish Nationalists — like Irish Nationalists for a lot longer — are demanding that Scots make a *choice*, that they clarify this vital question of identity and leave no ambiguities. In his influential book, *The Divided Kingdom*, John Osmond (a non-Scot) perceives the issue of Scottish/British identity as one which the Scots will 'resolve', presumably in his view at the expense of any notion of Britishness.[74] In the contemporary political climate in Scotland impatience is often expressed with divided loyalties and similarly pejorative terms used by Irish Nationalists in Northern Ireland, such as the term 'confused' as applied to the Unionists, are increasingly heard in Scotland where Unionists (both large and small 'u') have been put on the defensive. While the vast majority of Scots seem secure in their Scottishness, it may be the case that some only feel it so securely when they are confident about a sense of Britishness as well. Any threat to the latter, therefore, might in turn make problematic the meaning of Scottishness.

There is a certain irony here in that what is being attacked by Nationalists is very much in the spirit of post-nationalist thinking particularly around the European Community/Union. While commentators like David McCrone have argued that Scotland, with its regional and cultural diversity and a plurality of identities, is well placed to take advantage of this mood, much of the language employed by Scottish Nationalists of late seems more in tune with older concepts of the nation state and ideas of nations and states as co-terminous. A similar point might be made about the discrepancy between SDLP leader John Hume's use of the language of post-Nationalist Europe and his pursuit of the traditional Nationalist goal of persuading Unionists that their future lies in some kind of all-Irish (and non-British) framework.[75]

A final comparative point around this theme concerns the way ambiguities and inconsistencies about the idea of a British nation and 'Britishness' are reflected in the Conservative governments' (both Thatcher's and Major's) policies towards Scotland and Northern Ireland. Their approach to Northern Ireland has been characterised by a willingness to adopt constitutional experiments and consider a dilution of sovereignty or a devolution of power from the centre. In relation to Scotland there has been no such flexibility; the message here is that there is a single British nation and that there should not be any weakening of parliamentary sovereignty. On the one hand the Tory governments have given guarantees about Northern Ireland remaining British for as long as a majority there desire it; on the other its policies have been in marked contrast to the unequivocally British perspective adopted in relation to Scotland.

In the wake of one of the latest developments concerning Northern Ireland's future — 'The Downing Street Declaration' of December 1993 — some Scottish commentators highlighted this inconsistency in order to give a fillip to Scottish constitutional demands.[76] In February 1994 the Scottish Liberal Democrat MP Russell Johnston called for Scotland to be given the same rights to 'self-determination' as the Northern Irish, pointing out that the different administrative history and structure of Northern Ireland was no reason to treat it differently from Scotland since Scotland's history and structure was also different from the rest of the UK.[77] Scots reformers have thus in turn viewed events in Northern Ireland as a possible catalyst in the widest constitutional sense.

VI

Resilient as traditional nationalist thinking is in both Scotland and Northern Ireland, it can still be said that the current concern with identities and the political accommodation of them in Europe and beyond makes Northern Ireland and Scotland good examples of contemporary political debate. In relation to an agenda which stresses questions of ethnic nationalism, cultural identity, and regional distinctiveness, both places are eminently germane.

The Northern Ireland conflict can perhaps most plausibly be interpreted as one between ethnic nationalisms which is expressed to a great extent through religious sectarianism.[78] Irish nationalism is often held up as an inclusive ideology, but Unionists perceive it adamantly as an ethnic, Catholic nationalism and a repudiation of their British identity. This British identity, as instanced at several junctures in this book, is an ambiguous phenomenon. It can be expressed in ringing symbolical terms and in a 'Queen and Country' idiom, but is arguably more substantively shaped by the interpretation of a shared history and the experience of interaction with Britain, and in particular Scotland. And there might also be said to have been a consistent theme central to it in modern times: the perception of the British connection as security against being subsumed by a restless, insatiable and culturally antagonistic Catholic nationalism. There is a strand of Unionism which disavows ethnic nationalist designs and formulates its British identity in terms of membership of a State which in contemporary times is culturally pluralist and thus inclusive. However, most Unionists combine, and, they believe, complement their British identity with an 'Ulster' one, and during the present troubles this form of cultural identity has been popularised to a greater extent than before. Finlayson has argued cogently that the relative weakness of the political movement for Ulster independence should not be taken as evidence of the weakness of an Ulster ethnic nationalism.[79] The importance of this form of identification as a political 'fall back' position has seemingly grown in accordance with perceptions of British government betrayals, especially among Loyalist paramilitary groups in the 1980s and 1990s. An historical basis for an 'Ulster' ethnic identity has been supplied by writers such as Ian Adamson, as discussed in the first chapter.

The exclusive equation of 'Ulster' with 'Protestant' or 'Loyalist' was contested by some in the past like John Hewitt. In more recent years the idea of Ulster as a region commanding cross-community loyalties has been given new life, largely through the development of the regionalist political thinking which has accompanied the development of the European Community/Union. New regional political structures have been envisaged as superseding outdated ones centred on nation states. The more idealistic have predicted a new Europe in which the stateless nation will become the norm.

As a stateless nation already, Scotland has been viewed as well placed to benefit from this trend.[80] Some Scottish commentators, frustrated with the current constitutional arrangements but wary of traditional Scottish nationalism, turned to these ideas with some eagerness in the early 1990s. Regional thinking held out the prospect of a flourishing regional and cultural diversity within Scotland, and a melting down of the Scottish-English basis of chauvinistic and xenophobic nationalism as the sovereignty of the London centre dissolved. Joyce McMillan urged her fellow Scots to 'remain open to new, flexible and "softer" structures in Europe', including the emergence of a 'Europe of the regions', rather than to 'encourage the idea that only full nation-state status is worth tuppence in the European virility stakes, and everybody who hasn't got it — or doesn't want it — is a cissy'.[81] In another article, she argued in addition that 'regional' consciousness had the virtue of facing the fact of difference and diversity.[82]

Much of this idealism rested on notions of Scottish national identity as a healthy, progressive force in tune with the new Europe, a nationalism which was 'civic' and pluralist and not 'ethnic' or exclusive. Yet other developments in Scotland in the early nineties, such as the appearance of the small organisations 'Scottish Watch' and 'Settler Watch', served as a warning that an ethnic nationalism and exclusivist forces were still part of the cultural fabric. These groups took as their goal the driving out of those English 'incomers' whom they deemed to have exploited Scots or trampled over Scottish cultural values.[83] Although repudiated by the SNP, such groups raised the spectre of anti-Englishness in an unequivocal way and prompted a re-examination of the question of whether Scottish nationalism was at its core ethnic in this sense. Certainly, the civic nationalism promoted by the SNP in their enthusiasm for the new Europe could not entirely erase suspicion that it was a nationalism with some sense of ethnic grievance.

To return to the case of Northern Ireland, it is worth considering in more detail arguments put forward for a regionalist approach to the problem there. The Scottish journalist Neal Ascherson, for example, held out the hope that a common Northern Ireland identity could be developed at the expense of the respective community allegiances to London and Dublin. He argued in favour of the breaking down of Dublin centralism as well as that of London; it is indeed salutary to remember that both the British State and that of the Republic of Ireland are the two most centralised in the European Community. Ascherson identified as the core of the Northern Ireland question the rigidity of *allegiance*, both Unionist and Nationalist, to their respective sovereign states, and called for more identity and less allegiance'.[84]

Another statement in favour of a regionalist approach came in 1989 from the Ulster literary critic John William Foster in an article entitled 'Radical Regionalism'.[85] In common with Scots like Joyce McMillan and Neal Ascherson, Foster condemned the centralisation of the British and Irish states, and argued that the remote and bureaucratic nature of Northern Ireland's governance only exacerbated problems of identity conflict. Foster too was influenced by the 'Europe of the Regions' thinking, and saw in the case of Scotland's constitutional struggle a possible phenomenon to which both sides in Northern Ireland might respond. Foster's objective, like that of literary figures such as Hewitt before him, was the cultivation of a basis for an Ulster regionalist identity, and a Scottish dimension was clearly part of the project. However, as with Hewitt and his regionalist ideas of the 1940s, Foster was criticised in turn for adopting regionalism as a way of avoiding hard issues such as sectarianism and the competing definitions of what should constitute 'Ulster' in the first place.[86]

However, the European regionalist perspective could not be easily dismissed, and another blueprint for a new Northern Ireland influenced heavily by it appeared through the medium of the Citizen's Inquiry launched in the Province in 1992.[87] Authored by the journalist Robin Wilson and the academic Richard Kearney, this argued for Northern Ireland's future as a European region, freed from the constitutional conservatism of the British State.[88] This scheme drew on concepts, such as *citizenship*, and priorities, such as minority rights, which the authors identify with Europe: it added up to a power-sharing scheme between the ethnic groups involved based on citizenship rights. Its call for new democratic structures for Northern Ireland included an assembly elected by Proportional Representation which would have a high degree of autonomy enshrined in powers similar to those sought for Scotland by the Scottish Constitutional Convention.[89]

In another article, for the journal *Scottish Affairs*,[90] Wilson urged the separation of the concepts of 'people' 'nation' and 'state', the strengthening of the concept of 'citizens', the legal recognition of Irish nationalism in Northern Ireland, and the right of people in the new European region of Northern Ireland to participate in the political life of the Irish Republic. The right to participate on more satisfactory terms in the political life of the British State (perhaps through the main British political parties) is not mentioned; perhaps it is implicitly assumed. However, the lack of clarity on this point is significant: the thrust of such reformist schemes as Wilson and Kearney's is in the direction of the accommodation of the clearly expressed Irish Nationalist identity of a large part of the Northern Ireland people; there is less concern with the more tortuous concept of how the majority's identity can best find expression. It is a good example of how much in the way of new political thinking and initiatives concerning Northern Ireland is vague on the question of how Unionists can fit into new structures while being positive about their identity. Part of the problem in Northern Ireland, it might be said, is that the Unionists have only been offered a positive role by those they distrust and fear, and in the context of an all-Ireland framework which they perceive it a 'surrender' to comply with. The latest constitutional initiative at the time of writing — the joint 'Framework Document' presented by the British and Irish governments in February 1995 — serves to underline this point; in it there is a distinct absence of mechanisms and suggestions for strengthening the links between Northern Ireland and the rest of the UK.

VII

Shortly before the general election in 1992, *The Herald* newspaper carried an editorial entitled 'Election a secular affair'.[91] This short piece was a concise and sure-footed guide to the religious factor in Scottish political history and its conclusions about the weakening of the correlation between political parties and religious affiliations drew strength from the judicious nature of its overall analysis. The thrust of the scholarly arguments of investigators of religion's role in Scottish society was emphatically towards the conclusion that religious friction had become anomalous and confined to avenues of leisure like football: 'Just a Boy's Game' in fact.[92] In a thought-provoking critique of the cultural re-casting of Glasgow in the 1980s, Ian Spring depicted religious sectarianism as an exercise in nostalgia which led only into itself.[93] While the communal troubles continued to convulse Northern Ireland, Scotland could appear able to congratulate itself on having remained calm without any further hesitation.

Not long after the 1992 election the sense of sanguine certainty surrounding the threat of religious discord, particularly in relation to politics, was challenged by certain developments. The first related to the election result itself in which the Conservatives, widely expected to be reduced to an ignominious single-figure total of Scottish seats, actually steadied their decline and gained one. Economic factors might have adequately explained this, but some currency was given to the possibility of a Unionist backlash having occurred on the constitutional question.[94] The latter, of course, had grabbed the pre-election headlines in a manner reminiscent of the 1970s with opinion polls at one stage claiming that over half of Scots favoured independence.

This notion of a revival in popular support for the Union was taken up and developed by the novelist and political commentator (and Unionist) Alan Massie. Later in 1992 he called for the Tories to re-adopt the name 'Unionist' and gear its appeal once again to those who had deserted it: 'The name 'Unionist' could bring back the Rangers vote in Glasgow, the respectable white collar Labour vote in the suburbs, the Liberal vote in the counties'.[95]

Massie was immediately denounced for reintroducing sectarianism into politics, and influential Scottish Tories moved quickly to disown him; one such, Gerald Warner, wrote in response: 'the old bowler-hand-and-watch-chain bigotry is not susceptible to political resuscitation'.[96] Such expressions of distaste for any kind of sectarian dabbling were no doubt genuine, although they may also have been based on the calculation of the limited political benefits to be gained from 'ghettoising' the party religiously in such a way in the very heterogeneous and indeed secular social and cultural climate of the 1990s.

The second development was of greater substance. It concerned the emergence of the political scandal which became known as 'Monklandsgate': the alleged corruption and malpractices of the Labour-controlled Monklands District Council. Among the charges brought against this local authority was that of religious sectarianism: that Catholic Labour councillors had favoured their co-religionists (and indeed relatives) in matters of employment and patronage, and that more generally sectarian bias had resulted in the heavily Catholic–populated areas of the district receiving grants and investment at the expense of others. In the over-simplified terms employed by the media this was boiled down to 'Catholic Coatbridge' being indulged at the expense of 'Protestant Airdrie'.

The issue was first investigated and publicised by the local newspaper, *The Airdrie and Coatbridge Advertiser* but it soon received detailed treatment in the mainstream Scottish press. During 1993 interest in the affair was heightened outside Scotland largely on account of the local authority area being part of the constituency of the Labour Party leader John Smith, and Smith was widely criticised for maintaining a pregnant silence on the matter. An internal Labour Party investigation into the affair ignored the allegations of sectarianism, financial mismanagement and nepotism, and fuelled demands for a full independent inquiry.[98] John Smith's tragic death, on 12 May 1994, then necessitated a by-election in the area and an opportunity for passions and prejudices to be expressed around the allegations against the 'Monklands Mafia'.

The Monklands East by-election of 30 June 1994 occasioned second thoughts in many who had fondly imagined sectarianism to be a dead issue in Scotland. It was certainly one of the roughest by-elections in Scottish political history and one of the closest fought: in the event a seat with a 16,000 Labour majority was held by just 1,640 votes from the SNP.

The Nationalists had quite clearly been the beneficiaries of a massive protest vote on the part of those, particularly in the Airdrie area, who felt discriminated against. Moreover, one of the grounds of this discrimination was perceived to be religion. A poll[99] taken just before election day revealed that more than half of the voters sampled believed that religious background made a difference in relation to the way they were treated by the Council. The same poll, which predicted the outcome correctly, found that 80% of Catholics voted Labour and 65% of Protestants voted SNP.

The election campaign was conducted in an atmosphere rife with allegations of sectarian practices and of exploitation of the issue for party political ends. The parties accused each other of pandering to prejudice. On the day after the election *The Herald* leader singled out the SNP for criticism in this respect,[100] a charge which brought an angry response from the SNP party leader Alex Salmond and an apology from the newspaper the following day. Among Salmond's comments were accusations that the Tory candidate had played the 'Orange Card' quite openly, while Labour canvassers had told Catholic voters that the SNP would close Catholic schools and 'create a Northern Ireland'.[101] The victorious Labour candidate, Helen Liddell, while equally biting in her comments about the SNP campaign, admitted that the evidence on council spending suggested that Coatbridge had indeed been given priority over Airdrie.[102]

The fall-out from the contest was far-reaching, and shocked commentators and pundits wrung their hands for months afterwards. 'Clearly,' wrote *The Scotsman's* Peter Jones, 'those, including this writer, who thought that real sectarianism in Scotland today had been locked into the cul-de-sac of ceremonial marching bands and distasteful football songs, are wrong.'[103]

Along with other observers, Jones was forced to admit the

lingering potency of bitter folk memories and historical injustices. After all, as was made clear to other journalists, were Catholics not simply paying back in kind the discrimination they had experienced in earlier decades?[104]

The impact of Monklands was thus to lead many people to re-assess the significance of religious divisions in Scottish society. More media attention was devoted to the phenomenon and the spotlight inevitably fell on the perennially controversial question of Catholic schools, an issue which had in the past been coupled by the media with that of Rangers football club and the signing of Catholic players. The arrival of footballer Maurice Johnston at Ibrox in July 1989 took much of the steam out of the latter matter, although the activities of the Orange Order in Scotland continued periodically to attract negative media comment on alleged Protestant sectarianism.[105] Education, however, remained the issue of greatest moment: in October 1994 the *Scotland on Sunday* newspaper revealed opinion poll findings which suggested that an overwhelming majority were in favour of integrated schools. In its editorial, the paper argued that if the Catholic community was entitled to separate state-funded schools, then so too were other communities like the Muslims.[106]

Catholic schools had also been the subject of party political jousting between Labour and the SNP in the Govan constituency in the 1992 election.[107] This was an example of the SNP's efforts to win Catholic votes from Labour by giving assurances about Catholic schools; significantly, Catholic support for the SNP in the 1992 election registered some 16% which, while some way short of the figure needed for a nationalist breakthrough, was roughly double the proportion for the 1970s. It remains to be seen if the Monklands episode has stalled this apparent trend among (mostly younger) Catholics towards the Nationalists.[108]

The central issue Monklands gave rise to — that of discrimination on religious grounds at local government level — was not a new one. Since the 1960s the perception among many Protestants in certain areas has been one of local Catholic politicians looking after their own community. To a long history of Catholic grievances were added those of some Protestants who felt marginalised in a rapidly-changing society in which the Catholic community profile enlarged. In terms of identity, the Catholics could appear to have maintained a coherence and a vigour in the midst of social, economic and demographic changes which had weakened to a large extent the Protestant self-image, particularly among the working class.[109] Secularisation clearly affected Protestant denominations more adversely in terms of a decline in adherents, and there was, relatively, a less keen sense of Protestant 'mission' among those who felt socially demoralised or economically impoverished. Resentments over loss of identity, or feelings of insecurity about identity in the context of a perception of a powerful Catholic presence,[110] could draw some towards the militant Protestantism of Loyalist flute bands and paramilitary style groups (discountenanced by the Official Orange Order) which took their inspiration from Northern Ireland. In some ways this was also the case on the Catholic side where Republican bands and 'Connolly Societies'[111] attempted to bring about a closer identification among Scottish Catholics with the Nationalist minority in Northern Ireland.

The occurrence of Loyalist/Republican street marches and disturbances and the persistence of the 'Old Firm' football rivalry with its culture of Irish republican and Loyalist imagery, songs and chants, is evidence enough of the vitality of sectarianism in a popular cultural sense at least. However, Monklands also seemed to suggest that there might be increased expression of this through formal politics, and that the rather faint political echo of religious divisions of recent times had been somewhat deceptive. With issues like Catholic schooling still topical, might Scotland thus be entering a future political era in which religion, if only in terms of a badge of identity, will loom larger? Does Monklands suggest that Scotland possesses the ingredients of the Northern Ireland conflict?

It is right to acknowledge the salutary nature of the Monklands affair in terms of waking many Scots up to the continuing prevalence of religious tensions and the possibility that without proper attention and open debate, they could get worse. There is also the remote, but still conceivable, possibility that a severe downturn in the situation in Northern Ireland could lead to problems in Scotland concerning refugees and population movements.

On the other hand, we should also be cautious about reading too much into Monklands. For all the acrimony of the campaign, there was no serious violence. Protestants and Catholics do not lead the rigidly segregated lives which are a feature of the Ulster situation, even in Lanarkshire. It should be remembered too that Lanarkshire is the historical cock-pit of sectarian friction in Scotland, and is in no way typical of large parts of the country. Scottish civil society remains relatively healthy, and its political culture now largely inimical to sectarianism at least at national level. Notwithstanding Massie's speculations, the Conservatives are unlikely to try to tap religious loyalties and would probably fail to revive their overall fortunes if they did. Scotland is a much less isolated society than Northern Ireland and its level of interaction with the rest of Britain forms a counterweight to any local sectarian squabbling.

What should be of concern is that there are people who feel marginalised and unrepresented and who cannot make their frustrations heard. As Scottish society changes and hard-bitten myths are debunked, there are those who feel alienated and who must in some way be brought back into the mainstream of debate and made to feel that both their regrets and sense of loss, and their hopes for the future, really matter.

VIII

'Alienation' has become a key concept in analyses of the Northern Ireland situation. Before the 1990s it was often loosely used, along with other terms, to describe the feelings of the Catholic Nationalist minority about the Northern Ireland State and British rule. Since then it has been used most commonly in relation to the Protestant working class and the Loyalist paramilitaries.

This development is grounded in a number of factors which have contributed to social and economic, as well as political, disaffection on the part primarily of poorer Protestant communities in Belfast. In terms of urban re-development and inward investment the conclusion has been reached by these communities, particularly in North and West Belfast, that they have been left to deteriorate as a matter of government policy. They have seen employment vanish, houses knocked down and population scattered. For example, in the past twenty years some 30,000 people have left the Greater Shankill area. In certain parts of this area the unemployment rate was 60% or above at the time of the 1994 IRA and Loyalist cease-fires.[112] Statistics pertaining to the entire Protestant and Catholic communities of Northern Ireland conceal in particular these chronic levels of social and economic misery among sections of the Protestant working class; in many cases it is precisely these sections who have been most affected by, and most actively involved in, paramilitary violence.

The despair felt by such communities was also fuelled by a perception of Catholics improving their position and Irish nationalism making political gains. Much was made of the 1991 census figures which revealed that the Catholic proportion of the Northern Ireland population had risen to around 43%.[113] Protestants claimed that they had been 'forced out' of areas previously considered part of their 'territory' by the growth of Catholic numbers and intimidation.[114] They also viewed with a grim 'zero sum' logic reports of Catholics moving into employment in larger numbers than Protestants and earning larger salaries.[115] They expressed incredulity when Catholics pointed to disadvantages suffered by their community, and the dogged persistence of the unemployment statistics which indicated that Catholics were still twice as likely to be unemployed.[116] Measures to tackle disadvantage and discrimination, such as fair employment legislation, were looked upon by many Protestants as designed exclusively to help the Catholic community.[117] As Marianne Elliott has put it, many Protestants characterise Catholic culture as one of 'complaint'.[118]

The Catholic community clearly has come a long way from its depressed condition within the Northern Ireland State. Direct Rule has brought benefits, particularly in the realm of public sector employment. On the other hand, employment opportunities have not opened up for working class areas such as Ballymurphy and Turf Lodge in Belfast and in such areas deprivation still goes hand in glove with political extremism. The republican axiom regarding the necessity of a United Ireland as a means of ending social injustice is deeply embedded; politically, the perspectives which hardened in the critical period 1969–72 in the context of Ulster Unionist rule and British military intervention, have not been transcended. Fionnuala O'Connor's study of Northern Ireland Catholics reveals the increasing tensions between the rising middle class and these impoverished communities.[118]

It is difficult, in the light particularly of the way resentments have accumulated in the respective poorer communities, to be optimistic about hard political compromises as opposed to an opening up of dialogue. Perhaps the latter, which in many ways has begun, will bring about the former. Certainly, on the Protestant side, new voices have been heard: men like David Ervine, from a paramilitary background, have spoken the language of badly-off Protestant communities who have so often in the past been inadequately represented by Unionist political figures.[120] This language, moreover, has sounded a great deal more flexible and forward-looking than much conventional Unionist political argument.

Ervine and the other new Loyalist spokesmen are, nevertheless, still firmly Unionist. They want to see the British link strengthened and not weakened; and the readiness of Nationalists and Republicans to treat with this is at the very best open to doubt. For all the debate and re-assessments, the Nationalist analysis of Unionism remains essentially the traditional one: that Unionism is something artificially shaped by the British presence and that when that presence is gone Unionists will take their place in the Irish nation.

Irish Nationalists of all shades have a vested interest in depicting Unionists as bigoted supremacists clinging to privileges. Over twenty years since the Unionists lost their source of political power and the Unionist working class any marginal economic advantage it may have possessed the line remains the same. The inference is that Loyalists are Loyalists because they are privileged, rather than that they are privileged because they are Loyalists. Thus, amidst the language of 'healing' and 'reconciliation' he is adept at employing, the SDLP leader John Hume has likened the Unionists to the 'Afrikaaners' in South Africa,[121] a parallel intended for consumption in liberal circles outside Northern Ireland. In the guise of statesmanlike and conciliatory utterances, Hume carefully consigns Unionists to the 'pariah' category of contemporary political discourse, as people who have to be dragged out of their laagers.

It is also quite clear that the only direction Hume and of course republicans like Gerry Adams want them to be dragged is that of Irish unity. In the wake of the joint declaration of the British and Irish governments in December 1993, Adams stated:

> The British hold the power to keep the Unionists locked in a negative mindset for ever or abandon them to their fate, or persuade them, to help them along the road to an agreement with the rest of the people of Ireland.[122]

In the course of the political row over the leaks, in January 1995, from the 'framework document', he commented:

> The logic of all progress . . . has been to move more and more in an all-Ireland context. It has not been to strengthen the ties with London; it has not been to strengthen the London-Belfast axis. It has been in the opposite direction — in Belfast-Dublin or North-South'.[123]

Many Unionists fear Adams is right when he says that the Union has been weakened and that the logic of the 'peace process' is in an all-Ireland direction. This remains to be proved. The 'framework document', published in February 1995, provides for a Northern

Ireland devolved assembly and a North-South all-Ireland body with executive powers. At the time of writing it remains to be seen if what is envisaged will become reality, but the reaction of Hume, Adams, and nationalists and republicans generally has been significantly positive. However, the assumption that Unionists can be 'persuaded' into a united Ireland by the British government, and the utter refusal to take seriously the Unionism of the Unionists, bodes ill for an eventual harmonious settlement. Nationalists have certainly enjoyed a lot of success in depicting Unionists as intransigent to outside observers, but they have signally failed to engage in any kind of meaningful dialogue with Unionists about how they actually perceive themselves and what they in fact feel, as opposed to telling them how well they would be treated by Nationalists in the all-Ireland context to which the Unionists remain implacably hostile. There has been no effort made to appreciate what the *Unionists'* conception of the Union and Britishness might mean; rather there has persisted the time-worn assumption that the British government hold the key. 'Progress' is defined by Nationalists as the weakening (and eventual breaking) of the British link; Unionists, of course, would have to cease to be Unionists to fall into line with this definition.

Yet it is in reality the Unionists who are most under pressure. Nationalists are, perhaps, being forced to justify their ideology more strictly in accordance with the shifting concerns of a 'post nationalist' age: the influence of regionalist ideas, the questioning of established notions of sovereignty and nation-states, and the recent conflicts of ethnic nationalism in the former Soviet bloc, have all posed challenges. Nevertheless, in the Northern Ireland context, it is the Unionists who have most ground to make up in overturning the negative stereotypes widely entertained about them and in presenting an ideological vision which is positive, pluralist and inclusive. In relation to the new ideological and intellectual trends away from traditional nationalist concepts, Ulster Unionists have of course been laid open to critical interrogation as much as Irish nationalists.

In attempting to fashion a positive vision the Unionists will have to prove themselves to the rest of the UK to be reformers, and the most obvious way of doing that would seem to be to support the movement for wider UK constitutional renewal. It is to that this chapter will finally turn.

IX

In the 1990s debates on constitutional change in Scotland and in Northern Ireland have increasingly implied a wider debate on the constitutional reform of the UK as a whole. The movement for Scottish independence has gathered pace, notwithstanding the poor electoral performance of the SNP in 1992. However, it still seems the case that a radical reform of the Union rather than its break-up, would satisfy most Scots. In Northern Ireland there remains a clear majority for the Union in some form. Pressure groups for constitutional reform based largely in England, such as Charter 88, have energetically promoted federal and 'Euro-friendly' constitutional packages, although the apparently low level of English public interest is a formidable obstacle to be overcome. Nevertheless, those who would defend to the hilt the constitutional status quo and the concept of undivided and undiluted Westminster parliamentary sovereignty, are now fighting a rearguard action. Constitutional issues may, at the time of writing, play a bigger part in the next general election than at any other since 1911.

The aftermath of the ceasefires in Northern Ireland witnessed a greater level of open debate across traditional divides. On one television discussion a Presbyterian minister (and former Moderator), the Reverend John Dunlop, attempted to impress upon Sinn Fein representative Mitchel McLaughlin that the Union for him meant the Scottish connection above all else. He made it clear that he feared the breaking of the Union for the survival of such cultural affinities.[124] Dunlop's point was at once a rare example of a positive defence of the Unionist position and a rebuke to the Irish republican tendency to equate the Union with Englishness, and with English misrule.

In order to challenge notions of the 'inevitability' of Irish unity, which are prevalent in Britain, Unionists have to define more positively what the British link means to them, and how they might participate constructively in the development of the Union. To continue simply to appear obstinate in the face of Irish nationalist demands is not, and has never been, enough; similarly, it would not be wise for Ulster Unionists to throw in their lot with those who set their face against constitutional change of a kind which diminishes parliamentary sovereignty. The present Conservative Government have shown that they are prepared to entertain constitutional adjustments that bolster the Irish nationalist agenda and render

Northern Ireland yet more 'anomalous'. The best means Unionists have at their disposal of containing Irish nationalism is to support the movement for all-inclusive, 'all round', UK constitutional reform. In so doing they will also have to accept that the price of the Union is the loss of outworn and exclusivist ideas of Britishness with which they, as Protestants, were prone to identify.[125] Indeed, a UK federal republic may well be the terminus of the reform movement, and in such a form the Union could well make a greater appeal to the Northern Catholic minority. Arguably, it would certainly be better able to accommodate their sense of Irish nationalist identity, than any all-Irish arrangement could accommodate the Unionist identity, especially if a meaningful all-Ireland dimension was to be incorporated into the Northern Ireland part of the reform package.

As the present Labour opposition in Britain struggles to make its devolution plans for Scotland convincing, the attractions of a federated UK, building on existing differences and in no way directed at achieving uniformity across the State, stand out in bolder relief. Scottish political commentators have noted the opportunity which the Northern Ireland and Scottish questions together pose for wider re-structuring.[126] The two issues converge around this constitutional reform question as well as around debates on identity, on the meaning of Britishness past, present and future, on pluralism, and on matching political opportunities with cultural diversity. In Scotland's case interacting with Northern Ireland about the constitutional future of both places might be the most effective way of addressing the issue of its religious divisions and the way they have shaped so much of Scottish culture, and of ensuring that a culturally pluralist environment can be created for the other ethnic groups in Scotland whose profile has increased significantly.

Scotland and Northern Ireland, if there is sufficient will in both places for the task, could help each other to steer the contemporary constitutional debate in the UK in a mutually beneficial direction and to ensure that the Union truly reflects national, cultural, and regional diversity. As this book has attempted to show, the two places have a striking historical intimacy; their future can be no less close and potentially rich in social, cultural and political interaction.

NOTES

1. The Royal Commission on the Constitution 1969–73, Report, Cmnd. 5460 (1973). Hereafter referred to as 'Kilbrandon Report'.
2. It should be noted that the Conservatives under Edward Heath were committed to the principle of a Scottish Assembly.
3. Sillars formed the short-lived Scottish Labour Party, then later joined the SNP.
4. See Kilbrandon Report, part X, and p. 396.
5. P. Arthur, 'Devolution as Administrative Convenience: A Case Study of Northern Ireland', *Parliamentary Affairs* Vol.30 (1977) pp. 97–106.
6. Kilbrandon Report p.54, and pp. 166–69.
7. The most comprehensive guide to the referendum is J. Bochel, D. Denvir and A. McCartney (eds.), *The Referendum Experience* (Aberdeen, 1981).
8. A. Eadie, H. Ewing, J. Sillars and J. Robertson, 'Scottish Labour and Devolution — a discussion paper'. Copy in J. M. Craigen Papers NLS Acc. 10476.
9. V. Bogdanor, *Devolution* (Oxford, 1978) pp. 219–220.
10. H. Calvert (ed.), *Devolution*, Chpt. 1.
11. Ibid.
12. See B. Purdie, 'Lessons of Ireland', in Gallagher, *Nationalism in the Nineties.*
13. W. D. Birrell, 'The Mechanics of Devolution: Northern Ireland Experience and the Scotland and Wales Bill', *Political Quarterly* Vol. 49 (1978) pp. 304–321.
14. See J. Oliver, 'The Stormont Administration', in B. Barton and P. Roche (eds.), *The Northern Ireland Question* (Aldershot, 1991).
15. See also Bogdanor, op. cit. pp. 62–67.
16. Kilbrandon Report p. 54. See also p. 380 regarding the perceived advantages of devolution in Northern Ireland such as greater accessibility to government, and the tailoring of legislation to meet local needs.
17. See Kilbrandon Report p. 396. The Report also concluded that 'enforced parity with the rest of the UK, service by service, and direct influence on the expenditure plan by the UK Government are inconsistent with the role of an independent legislature' (p. 396). This, the authors of the Report believed, was the main lesson of the Northern Ireland experience.
18. See B. Miller, 'The Tax Factor and Devolution', *Glasgow Herald* 28 December 1991.
19. Two journalists have written accounts of the strike: R. Fisk, *The Point of No Return* (London, 1975); and D. Anderson, *14 May Days* (Dublin, 1994).

20. See document, 'Devolved Government and the Future of Ulster' (November 1977), in Hugh Brown Papers, SRA TD 1252 Box 5; and *The Scotsman* 4 July 1977.

21. See press release of Thomas Orr speech 6 December 1975, in Brown papers op. cit. Box 5.

22. Copy of speech by Orr 3 December 1977, in Brown Papers Box 5.

23. Although the Conservatives were split on the principle: indeed, Sir Alec Douglas Home hinted during the campaign that the Tories would produce a better devolution scheme when back in office.

24. Reports of meetings of this Committee are contained in Brown Papers op. cit. Box 4.

25. See remarks in House of Commons Debates 26 November 1985, Column 797; also T. Gallagher, *Glasgow* p. 298.

26. Minutes of the Northern Ireland Committee of the Parliamentary Labour Party 13 May 1981, Brown Papers Box 4.

27. See letter from Lord President's Office to Prime Minister's Private Secretary 5 December 1977, in Brown Papers Box 5.

28. See Gallagher, *Glasgow* p. 327.

29. See J. H. Proctor, 'The Church of Scotland and the struggle for a Scottish Assembly', *Journal of Church and State* Vol. 25, no. 3 (1983) pp. 523–543.

30. M. Thatcher, *The Downing Street Years* (London, 1993) pp. 618–624.

31. T. Gallagher, 'Scotland and the Anglo-Irish Agreement: The Reaction of the Orange Order', *Irish Political Studies* Vol. 3 (1988) pp. 19–31.

32. *The Orange Institution: A Celebration 1690–1990* (1990).

33. Gallagher 'Scotland and the Anglo-Irish Agreement'.

34. A. Dickson, 'The Scots: National Culture and Political Action', *Political Quarterly* Vol. 59, no. 3 (July–Sept 1988) pp. 358–368.

35. Gallagher, *Glasgow* p. 328; and M. Dyer, 'Does Northern Ireland make a difference?', *Parliamentary Brief*, November 1994.

36. See criticism of SNP in T. Gallagher, 'The SNP faces the 90s', in Gallagher, *Nationalism in the Nineties*; see discussion of Monklands episode below.

37. Purdie, 'Lessons of Ireland'.

38. P. H. Scott, 'Time to forge a new alliance with Ireland', *Scotland on Sunday* 8 September 1991.

39. See *Scotland on Sunday* 17 April 1994.

40. House of Commons Debates 26 November 1985 Columns 794–5; See Tam Dalyell's contribution also, columns 940-42.

41. For a fascinating account of the whole devolution episode and its aftermath in Scotland see A. Kemp, *The Hollow Drum* (Edinburgh, 1993) Part 3.

42. On whether this amounts to a 'Scottish Political System' as such see J. Kellas, *The Scottish Political System* (Cambridge, 1973) who believes it does, and A. Midwinter et al, *Politics and Public Policy in Scotland* (London, 1991) who take a different view.
43. See article in *Glasgow Herald* 3 September 1987.
44. See article in *The Observer* 26 January 1992.
45. See O. D. Edwards (ed.) *A Claim of Right for Scotland* (Edinburgh, 1989).
46. See S. Deacon 'Labour's Response to the National Question', in *Scottish Government Yearbook* (1990); also C. Craig, 'Scotland, Nationalism and Socialism', *Irish Review* no. 8 (Spring 1990).
47. See J. Geekie and R. Levy, 'Devolution and the Tartanisation of the Labour Party', *Parliamentary Affairs* Vol. 42 (1989).
48. McCrone, *Understanding Scotland* Chpt. 8.
49. The Report is contained in *The Scottish Government Yearbook* (1990); see also J. Kellas, 'The Scottish Constitutional Convention', in *Scottish Government Yearbook* (1992).
50. Harvey Cox, 'Constitution-making for Northern Ireland', *Parliamentary Affairs* Vol. 44 (October 1991).
51. The arguments are cogently advanced in A. Aughey, *Under Siege*; see also C. Coulter, 'The Character of Unionism', *Irish Political Studies* Vol. 9 (1994) pp. 1–24, for a discussion of the integrationist case in the wider context of Unionist politics.
52. For an academic treatment of this argument see H. Roberts, 'Sound Stupidity: The British Party System and the Northern Ireland Question', *Government and Opposition* Vol. 22, no. 3, (Summer 1987) pp. 315–35.
53. *Belfast Newsletter* 25 May 1992.
54. Reported in *Sunday Tribune* 26 April 1992.
55. See article by Trimble in *Orange Standard* August 1992.
56. In 1994 it was reported by Frank Millar of the *Irish Times* that Molyneaux was seeking a legislative assembly for Northern Ireland which was 'akin to the Strathclyde Regional Council', *Irish Times* 2 February 1994.
57. For Foulkes see article in *Glasgow Herald* 16 April 1992; for Worthington see *Scotland on Sunday* 31 May 1992.
58. I. Lindsay, 'At the Leading Edge', *Fortnight* no. 301, December 1991.
59. See B. Crick, 'If Scotland fights might Ulster be righted?', *Fortnight* no. 282, March 1990; also 'The Sovereignty of Parliament and the Irish Question', in D. Rea (ed.), *Political Co-operation in Divided Societies* (Dublin, 1982).
60. B. Crick 'The Sovereignty of Parliament and the Irish Question'.

61. B. Crick, 'On Devolution, Decentralism and the Constitution', in B. Crick, *Political Thoughts and Polemics* (Edinburgh, 1990).
62. Simon Lee, 'A New Pattern of Islands', *The Guardian* 26 March 1992.
63. See relevant articles in *The Times* 24 February 1992.
64. K. Boyle, 'Northern Ireland: Allegiances and Identities', in B. Crick (ed.), *National Identities* (Oxford, 1991).
65. Simon Lee op. cit.
66. See J. McMillan, 'The Scottish factor in an Irish solution', *Scotland on Sunday* 21 September 1989; and Boyle op. cit.
67. *Scotsman* 20 April 1990.
68. B. Crick, 'The English and the British', in Crick (ed.), *National Identities*.
69. See section on Opinion Polls regarding 'National Identity' in *Scottish Affairs* No. 4. (Summer 1993).
70. Aughey op. cit.
71. E. Moxon-Browne, 'National Identity in Northern Ireland', in P. Stringer and G. Robinson (eds.), *Social Attitudes in Northern Ireland* (Belfast, 1991).
72. L. Patterson, 'Ane End of Ane Auld Sang: Sovereignty and the Re-Negotiation of the Union', *Scottish Government Yearbook* (1991).
73. See Moxon-Browne op. cit.
74. J. Osmond, *The Disunited Kingdom* (London, 1988) p. 77.
75. On this point see articles by Edna Longley and Paddy Roche in *Irish Review* No. 15 (Spring 1994).
76. See, for example, Ian Bell in *The Herald* 17 December 1993, and, after the 'Framework Document' of Feb. 1995, *The Herald* editorial 24 February 1995 and Robbie Dinwoodie in *The Herald* 24 February 1995.
77. *Scotsman* 18 February 1994.
78. See S. Bruce, *At the Edge of the Union* (Oxford, 1994) chpt. 5.
79. A. Finlayson, 'Nationalism as Ideological Interpolation: the case of Ulster Loyalism', *Ethnic and Racial Studies* (forthcoming, 1995).
80. McCrone, *Understanding Scotland* chpt. 8.
81. J. McMillan column *Scotland on Sunday* 23 February 1992.
82. J. McMillan column *Scotland on Sunday* 2 August 1992.
83. See comments of Neal Ascherson on 'Settler Watch' in *Independent on Sunday* 21 April 1993.
84. N. Ascherson, 'Europe of the Regions', in M. Crozier (ed.) *Cultural Traditions in Northern Ireland; All European Now?* (Belfast, 1991).
85. J. W. Foster, 'Radical Regionalism'; *Irish Review* no. 7 (Autumn 1989).
86. B. O'Seaghdha, 'Ulster Regionalism: the unpleasant facts', *Irish Review* no. 8 (Spring 1990).

87. See A. Pollock (ed.), *A Citizens' Inquiry: The Opsahl Report on Northern Ireland* (Dublin, 1993) pp. 206–9.

88. A similar view of Scotland in relation to 'Europe of the Regions' is argued by Chris Harvie in *Scottish Affairs* No. 1. (Autumn 1992) pp. 78–87.

89. See Pollock (ed.) op. cit; also R. Wilson and R. Kearney, 'Northern Ireland's Future as a European Region' in *Irish Review* No. 15 (Spring 1994).

90. R. Wilson, 'Northern Ireland: Peoples, Nations, States and Sovereignty', *Scottish Affairs* No. 8 (Summer 1994).

91. *The Herald* 23 March 1992.

92. See Steve Bruce's review of Gallagher's *Glasgow* in *Times Higher Education Supplement* 1 January 1988.

93. I. Spring, *Phantom Village* (Edinburgh, 1990) p. 90.

94. See A. Massie, 'A vote that rails against home rule', *Scotland on Sunday* 12 April 1992.

95. A. Massie, 'In Union there is strength', *Scotland on Sunday* 27 September 1992. 'The Rangers vote' is shorthand for the Protestant working class/orange support for the Conservatives in the past.

96. *Sunday Times* (Scotland) 11 October 1992.

97. See Arnold Kemp (then editor of *The Herald*), tribute to *The Airdrie and Coatbridge Advertiser* in *The Herald* 6 March 1993.

98. See various articles in *The Scotsman* 5 March 1993.

99. For poll findings see *The Scotsman* 28 June 1994.

100. *The Herald* 1 July 1994.

101. *The Herald* 2 July 1994.

102. See *The Herald* Leader 2 July 1994.

103. *The Scotsman* 5 August 1994.

104. See piece by William McIllvaney in *Scotland on Sunday* 26 June 1994.

105. See piece by Euan Ferguson, *Scotland on Sunday* 20 July 1994.

106. *Scotland on Sunday* 23 October 1994.

107. See *The Herald* 26 March 1992.

108. Statistical evidence in James Mitchell, 'Religion and Politics in Scotland' (Paper presented to Seminar on Religion and Scottish Politics, University of Edinburgh, 4 December 1992).

109. See the important article by Joan McAlpine in *The Scotsman* 11 July 1992 regarding working class Orangemen and women who return to the Bridgeton area of Glasgow each 12th July to keep alive a communal sense of identity around Orangeism.

110. Mitchell op. cit. found significantly greater Catholic support in Scotland for a United Ireland than Protestant support for the Ulster Unionist position.

111. The Connolly Society interpret the legacy of James Connolly (see chapter five) in a straightforwardly Irish republican fashion. Their public demonstrations have led to outbreaks of disorder and clashes between their supporters and loyalists. See, for example, the controversy over a march in 1993 as reported in *The Herald* 19 May 1993.
112. *Irish Times* 9 September 1994.
113. See *The Independent* 1 November 1992, and 14 April 1993.
114. See, for example, *Belfast Telegraph* 22 March 1993, and *Irish News* (Special Investigation) 25–29 January 1993.
115. *Irish News* 30 November 1994, and 1 December 1994.
116. For a discussion of this question see letter from Graham Gudgin in *Irish News* 1 December 1994.
117. See *Belfast Newsletter* 23 September 1993 regarding comments of Gregory Campbell (DUP).
118. Report of lecture in *Irish Times* 28 July 1993.
119. See O'Connor, *In Search of a State*; also E. Longley 'A Northern 'Turn'' in *Irish Review* No. 15 (Spring 1994).
120. See *Guardian* 8 December 1994 for one of many profiles since the ceasefire; also contributions in *Beyond the Fife and Drum* (Island Pamphlets, Newtownabbey, 1994).
121. See, for example, *Sunday Independent* 18 September 1994, *The Guardian* 9 October 1993.
122. *Independent on Sunday* 19 December 1993.
123. *Irish Times* 6 February 1995.
124. 'Spotlight' (BBC Northern Ireland), broadcast 6 October 1994.
125. See Will Hutton, 'The State we're in', *Fortnight* No. 333 (November 1994).
126. See Iain McWhirter, *Scotland on Sunday* 11 September 1994, and 25 September 1994.

Index

Abercorn, Duke of, 33
Adams, Gerry, 186–7
Adamson, Ian, 2, 4, 176
Allison, Francis, 5
American Revolution, 5
Ancient Order of Hibernians (AOH), 26, 37, 40, 44–45, 46, 72, 107, 108, 113, 133
Ancram, Michael, 159
Andrews, John Miller, 84, 85
'Anglo-Irish Agreement' (1985), 158–160, 164, 165
Anti-Partition League, 84, 140
Armour, Rev. J. B., 37
Arthur, Paul, 151–4
Ascherson, Neal, 177
Aspinwall, Bernard, 22
Asquith, H. H., 52, 54

Bairds of Gartsherrie, 9
Balfour, Arthur, 28, 51
Beattie, Jack, 138–141
'Belfast News Letter', 30, 87, 166
'Belfast Weekly News', 36, 42, 43
Birrell, W. D., 154–155
Boer War, 23
Bogdanor, Vernon, 152
Boyce, George, 25, 100
Boyle, Kevin, 169
British Empire, 13, 17–29, 31, 34–35, 39, 40, 45, 48, 86, 89, 99–102, 104–105, 127, 129
    and Protestantism, 19–23, 28–29, 47
    and Scottish Identity, 20–23, 26–29, 34–35, 47, 90–93
British national identity, 7, 12–13, 17–29, 43, 45–47, 54, 86–93, 99–102, 104–105, 168–175, 175–176, 189
Brooke, Sir Basil, 71, 73, 77, 85, 88
Brown, Hugh, 157–158, 160
Brown, Stewart J., 67, 68, 70
Bruce, Steve, 76, 77, 82, 92
Bryce, James, 49
Buchan, John, 20–21, 23
Burns, Robert, 7, 89

Calvert, Harry, 120, 153
Campbell-Bannerman, Henry, 32, 49
Carson, Edward, 37, 54, 64, 83, 132
Catholics in Ireland, 4, 6–7, 11–13, 26–27, in Northern Ireland, 54, 61, 72–74, 99, 106–119, 173, 184–185
    See also 'Roman Catholic Church'
Catholics in Scotland, 74–78, 89, 106–119, 173, 180–184
    See also 'Roman Catholic Church'
Charlemont, Lord, 73, 81, 82
'Charter 88', 162, 188
Church of Ireland (Anglican), 1, 5, 10, 31, 45
Church of Scotland (Presbyterian), 9–10, 12, 21, 32, 41, 62, 67–68, 69–70, 158
Civil Rights Movement (Northern Ireland), 118–119, 142–143
Clark, G. B., 49
Cleland, Sir Charles, 69, 76, 134
Colley, Linda, 7, 17–21, 25, 27, 99
Communist Party in Scotland, 79, 135
Communist Party in Northern Ireland, 83, 140
Connolly, James, 127–129, 137, 145, 183, 195
Conservative Party in Ireland, 10–11, 31
Conservative (and Unionist) Party in Scotland, 9, 11, 22–23, 32–33, 41, 61, 62, 66–68, 74–78, 88–93, 136, 156, 158–160, 161, 179–180, 184
Constitutional debate in the UK (1980s and 90s), 149, 160–175, 188–189
Cook, Robin, 162
Cooke, Rev. Henry, 10
Cormack, John, 68, 75–77
Covenanters, 3, 6, 13, 22, 89
Cox, Harvey, 164
Cradden, Terry, 140, 144
Craig, James, 52, 64, 70, 73, 84, 85, 138
Craig, William, 155, 171
Crick, Bernard, 17–18, 19, 167–168, 170

Dalriada, Kingdom of, 4

Dalyell, Tam, 50, 153
de Valera, Eamon, 87, 108
Devlin, Joseph, 46, 109
Devlin, Paddy, 142
Devolution (re Scotland in the 1970s), 149, 150–155, 156–158
See also 'Irish Home Rule' and 'Scottish Home Rule'
Diamond, Harry, 141
Dicey, A. V., 29, 51
Dickson, William Steel, 6
Dillon, John, 46
'Direct Rule' (re Northern Ireland from 1972), 149, 155, 157, 166, 185
Discrimination,
  in Northern Ireland, 63, 109–110, 116–120
  in Scotland, 110–112, 115–116, 182–183
Dollan, Patrick, 135
Dominion Status,
  Irish Free State, 53, 105
  Northern Ireland, 88, 89
Dorrian, Frank, 70, 79
'Downing Street Declaration' (1993), 175, 186
Dunlop, Rev. John, 188

Edinburgh University, 5
Education controversies, 64, 69–72, 109–110, 116, 133–134, 182
Elliott, Marianne, 37, 185
Erskine of Mar, 103, 105
Ervine, David, 185, 186
European Union (EU), 149, 150, 161, 167, 169, 174, 175–179
Evangelicalism, 10, 16, 43–44

Faulkner, Brian, 155
Ferguson, John, 107
Fianna Fail, 87
Finlay, Richard, 65, 105
Foot, Michael, 157
Football (in Glasgow), 75, 182, 183
Foster, John, 144–145
Foster, John William, 177–178
'Framework Document' (1995), 179, 186–187
Free Church of Scotland, 10, 12, 16, 20, 32, 35
Freemasonry, 6, 68, 80, 124
French Revolution, 6, 7

Gallagher, Tom, 8, 65, 107, 112, 113, 133, 157, 158
Getgood, Bob, 140
Gibb, Andrew Dewar, 105
Gibbon, Peter, 23–24
Gilley, Sheridan, 107, 112
Gilmour, Sir John, 67, 76

Gladstone, W. E., 10–13, 17, 18, 31, 32, 33, 49–52, 54
'*Glasgow Herald*', 38, 41, 179
Glasgow University, 5–6
Glass, Jack, 92
Government of Ireland Act 1920, 17, 53–54, 61, 151, 152
Grainger, J. H., 18
'Great Disruption' (1843), 9–10, 16, 35
Griffith, Arthur, 45
Guthrie, Rev. W. A., 70

Handley, J. E., 8
Hanna, Rev. Hugh, 12
Hardie, Keir, 127
Harvie, Chris, 160
Heath, Edward, 155
Hempton, David, 43–44
Henderson, James, 30
Hewitt, John, 120, 139, 176, 178
Hill, Myrtle, 43–44
Hogg, Douglas, 42
'Home Rule All Round' ('federal devolution'), 18–19, 28–29, 47–55
See also 'Irish Home Rule'
Houston, T. G., 42, 44
Howell, David, 143–144
Hume, John, 166–167, 174, 186–187
Hutcheson, Francis, 5–6

Immigration controversies, see 'Migration from Ireland to Scotland'
Independent Labour Party (ILP), 49, 79, 126–127, 129–137
Irish Home Rule, 2, 3, 11–13, 17, 24–29, 30–43, 44–47, 47–55
Irish Nationalism, 10, 11, 24–29, 33–35, 46, 47, 62, 63, 71, 87, 102–104, 118–119, 120, 128–129, 132, 140, 169, 174, 175, 178, 184, 186–187, 188–189
Irish Nationalist Party, 11, 37, 42, 44, 51, 53, 107, 109, 117
'*Irish News*', 111, 117
Irish Republican Army (IRA), 53, 63, 65, 73, 107, 108, 131

Jackson, Alvin, 23–25, 27, 37
Jacobitism, 19, 27, 47, 104
Jeffrey, Sir John, 66
Johnston, Russell, 175
Johnston, Tom, 106, 132, 136
Johnstone, Rev. T. M., 13

Kearney, Hugh, 100
Kelvin, Lord, 30
Kendle, John, 50
Kennedy, Denis, 73
Kilbrandon Report, 150–151, 154
Knights of St. Columba, 108, 113

Labour Party in Scotland, 8, 55, 67, 78–81, 102, 107, 112–113, 115, 116, 127, 132–136, 150–155, 156–160, 160–164, 165, 170, 180–184
Lanarkshire, 9, 180–184
Law, Andrew Bonar, 28
Lee, Joseph, 43
Lee, Simon, 168, 169
Liberal Party in Ireland, 10–11
Liberal Party in Scotland, 8, 18, 30, 32–33, 49, 55, 107, 127
Liberal Unionists in Scotland, 9, 11, 30, 32–33, 41
Liberal Unionists in Ulster, 11–13, 30, 32–33, 36–43, 84
Liddell, Helen, 181
Lindsay, Isobel, 167
Livingstone, David, 20, 21, 89
Lloyd George, David, 53
Logan, Rev. Victor, 36
Loughlin, James, 23, 24–26

MacAfee, W. A., 3
McBride, Ian, 5
McCaffrey, John, 134
MacCormick, John, 106
McCrone, David, 102, 106, 163, 174
MacDiarmid, Hugh, 103
MacDonald, Ramsay, 135
McFarland, Elaine, 6, 8
McGimpsey, Chris, 165–166
McInnes Shaw, Archibald, 67, 76, 77, 79, 80
McKenzie, John, 18, 20
McLean, Ian, 133
MacLean, John, 128–129, 130, 132
McMillan, Joyce, 169, 176–177
MacRory, Cardinal Joseph, 71, 118
Major, John, 175
Marquand, David, 162
Marr, Andrew, 55
Massie, Alan, 180, 184
Midgley, Harry, 137, 138–40, 142, 147
Migration from Ireland to Scotland, 7–10, 22, 47, 65–68, 74–75, 105, 107–108, 110–112
Miller, David, 23–26, 171
Milner, Lord, 20, 28
Mitchell, James, 62
Molyneaux, James, 165–166
Monklands controversy and by-election, 180–184
Morley, John, 34
Morrison, Herbert, 83–84
Munro Ferguson, Ronald, 30

Nairn, Tom, 100–101, 104
Napier, Sam, 141–143
Naylor, Adam, 18, 29

Northern Ireland Government (Unionist), 2, 61–64, 70–75, 76–78, 81–85, 86–88, 139, 151–155
Northern Ireland Labour Party (NILP), 81, 84, 85, 137–145
Northern Ireland State, 17, 53–55, 61–64, 99–100, 109, 116–121, 131, 144, 149
'*Northern Whig*', 10

O'Connell, Daniel, 10
Oliver, Frederick Scott, 19
Oliver, John, 8, 51, 154
O'Neill, Terence, 85, 88, 91, 92, 120–121, 142, 143
Orange Order (Ireland), 7, 9, 11, 27, 31, 32, 37, 43–45, 59, 62
  in Northern Ireland, 64, 72–73, 82–83
Orange Order (Scotland), 9, 32–33, 41, 45, 57, 62, 65–68, 69–70, 74–78, 78–81, 89, 135–136, 156–159, 181–184
Osmond, John, 174

Paisley, Rev. Ian, 79, 92, 142, 170
Parnell, Charles Stewart, 11, 46, 103
Patterson, Lyndsay, 172, 173
Pearse, Patrick, 47, 103
'*People's Journal*', 22, 33
Pittock, Murray, 104
Plantations (17th century Scottish settlers in Ulster), 1, 3–4
Presbyterian Church in Ireland, 2, 4–6, 9–10, 13, 16, 35, 38, 43, 57, 62
Presbyterians in Scotland (all Churches), 9–10, 12, 32, 35–36, 40–41, 45, 46, 104
Presbyterians in Ulster (all Churches), 4–8, 10–13, 36–43, 45, 46–47
  Anti-Home Rule Convention 1912, 36–43
  '*The Witness*', 37, 38
Protestant Action (P.A.), 68, 75–77, 96
Purdie, Bob, 103, 127, 160

Ratcliffe, Alexander, 68, 75–77, 79
Redmond, John, 37, 38, 46, 52, 167
Regionalism, 120–121, 149, 162–164, 175–179, 187
'Rhyming weavers', 15
Robbins, Keith, 102
Roman Catholic Church in Ireland, 4, 10, 11, 34–35, 38–40, 72–74, 106–119, 132
  and AOH, 44–45, 113
  and mixed marriages, 39, 114, 116
  and education, 38, 39, 69–72, 109, 116
Roman Catholic Church in Scotland, 8, 21–22, 66–68, 106, 119
  and education, 69–72, 110, 133–134, 182
Rose, Richard, 118, 119
Rosebery, Lord, 18–19, 30, 32, 33, 36, 48, 49

Ross, William McGregor, 21
Russell, T. W., 31

Salmond, Alex., 181
Samuels, A. W., 29, 44
'*The Scotsman*', 170, 181
Scott, Alexander McCallum, 19
Scott, Paul H., 160
Scottish Constitutional Convention,
  162–164, 165, 178
Scottish Enlightenment, 5, 6, 104
Scottish Home Rule, 22–23, 48–49,
  54–55, 89–90, 102–106, 127, 130,
  135
Scottish national identity, 17–23, 26–29,
  34–35, 55, 88–93, 102–106, 168–175
Scottish National League (SNL), 105
Scottish National Party (SNP), 91,
  105–106, 134, 158–160, 161–164, 169,
  177, 180–184, 188
Scottish Nationalism, 18, 55, 102–106,
  153–154, 172, 173
Scottish Office, 48, 110–111, 157
Scottish Protestant League (SPL), 68,
  75–77, 79, 96
'*Scottish Watch*', 177
Sectarian divisions in Ireland, 6–8, 43–45
  in Northern Ireland, 61–64, 72–74,
  143–145
Sectarian divisions in Scotland, 8–10, 62,
  74–78, 132, 136, 143–145, 179–184,
  189
Shearman, Hugh, 82
Sillars, Jim, 151, 163
Sinclair, Thomas, 32, 33–35, 39–40, 84
Sinn Fein, 45, 53, 107, 109, 188
Slessor, Mary, 20
Smith, John, 180–181
Smyllie, Bob, 127
Social Democratic and Labour Party
  (SDLP), 156, 166–167, 174
Spender, Sir Wilfrid, 81, 82
Stewart, A. T. Q., 1, 5
Stewart, Dugald, 5, 6
Sunningdale Agreement (resulting in

power-sharing Executive for Northern
  Ireland), 155–156, 165

Taylor, John, 85
Thatcher, Margaret, 156, 158, 161, 162,
  172, 175
Thomson, George Malcolm, 105
Todd, Jennifer, 43, 87, 119
Topping, Col. W., 87, 90
Trades Unionism, 80, 126–127, 130–131
Trimble, David, 165–166
Trinity College Dublin, 5

Ulster Covenant (1912), 42
Ulster Defence Association (UDA), 14
Ulster identity, 12–13, 23–29, 45–47,
  86–88, 90–93, 99–100, 118, 120–121,
  168–175, 175–179
Ulster nationalism, 23–29, 120–121, 171,
  176
Ulster Protestant League (UPL), 72–73, 82
'Ulster-Scots' (also known as 'Scotch-
  Irish'), 2, 28, 29–32
Ulster Society, 2
Ulster Unionist Labour Association
  (UULA), 80, 83, 84, 131
Ulster Volunteer Force (UVF), 52
Ulster Workers' Council (UWC), 155–156
Unionism in Ulster 10–13, 23–47, 49–55,
  61–64, 86–88, 90–93, 99–100, 168–175,
  175–176, 178–179, 186–187, 188–189
  Official Unionist Party, 165–166
United Free Church of Scotland, 41, 67–68
United Irishmen, 4, 5, 6–7, 10, 37
Upper Clyde Shipbuilders (UCS), 80

Walker, William, 127–128, 137
'West Lothian Question', 50, 153
Westminster Confession of Faith, 5
Wheatley, John, 135
White, John, 68
Whitelaw, William, 40
Whiteley, Rev. R. F., 74–75
Wilson, Robin, 178–179
Wright, Frank, 119
Wyndham Land Act (1903), 132